GENERATIONS

And the Challenge of Justice

Daniel E. Lee

University Press of America, Inc.
Lanham • New York • London

Copyright © 1996 by
University Press of America,® Inc.
4720 Boston Way
Lanham, Maryland 20706

3 Henrietta Street
London, WC2E 8LU England

Library of Congress Cataloging-in-Publication Data

Lee, Daniel E.
Generations : and the challenge of justice / Daniel E. Lee.
p.   cm.
Includes bibliographical references and index.
1. Justice. 2. Intergenerational relations--United States. I. Title.
JC578.L44   1996   320'.01'1--dc20   96-10434 CIP

ISBN 0-7618-0302-5 (cloth: alk. ppr.)
ISBN 0-7618-0303-3 (pbk: alk. ppr.)

The paper used in this publication meets the minimum requirements of
American National Standard for information Sciences—Permanence
of Paper for Printed Library Materials,
ANSI Z39.48—1984

For my daughter,
whose joining us caused me to think about things
I had never thought about before,

for my parents,
from whom I have learned much
(often far more than I realized at the time),

and in memory of my grandparents,
who first made me aware of how enriching
intergenerational experiences can be

Contents

Preface

While working on intergenerational issues related to programs such as Medicare and Social Security, I came to the conclusion that there is no way that we as a society can constructively deal with these issues if we don't break down the age-segregation so typical of our society and do a better job of understanding and relating to those of different age-groups. The result, as I started writing this volume, was the inclusion of portraits of the various generations which currently comprise the population of the United States, portraits which are intended to help the reader understand and relate to the humanity of other generations.

As I began working on the generational portraits, it became apparent to me that simply reading historical accounts and sociological analyses wasn't enough. The best way to gain an understanding of the perspectives of other people is to talk with them and listen to what they have to say. Such being the case, I decided to interview members of various generations to gain a better sense of how things look from their perspectives. Spending time listening to people whose experiences extend beyond the range of our own experiences does more to expand our horizons than anything else we can do.

I chose not to interview celebrities or those in positions of prominence. It seemed to me that more was to be gained from listening to "just plain folks"--those we see at work or at the local supermarket, at church or at school, or wherever else we might be. In some cases, those I interviewed are people I have known for years--or at least thought I had known for years. I discovered, however, that I really didn't know them all that well because I had never taken the time to listen in depth to what they have to say and what they have experienced. In other cases, the interviews were facilitated by acquaintances. In still other cases, I simply introduced myself to various individuals while traveling or "surfing" the Internet, told them a bit about the project and asked if they were willing to be interviewed. With two exceptions, everyone I asked was willing.

Sitting down and listening to the life stories of other people and gaining an awareness of how they see things has been one of the most interesting and enjoyable experiences I have ever had. There is a certain warmth of humanity which emerges when others share their experiences and concerns. One discovers deeply insightful observations made by people who don't consider themselves to be particularly well-educated, stories about acts of great courage by people who don't view themselves as heroic, and moving stories of triumph and failure which tug at the most basic human emotions.

In terms of my own thinking, this volume represents a fairly significant watershed. Prior to working on intergenerational issues, I had for years been inclined to agree with Reinhold Niebuhr's assertion that if a greater measure of social justice is to be realized, power must be challenged by power (a view discussed in greater detail in the first chapter of this volume). When it comes to intergenerational issues, however, attempting to achieve social justice by some sort of a balance of power doesn't work since the youngest members of society are inherently powerless (as are the oldest members, in many situations). Such being the case, we must either resign ourselves to injustice or seek some other approach. The latter is clearly preferable. Identifying a workable approach to addressing and dealing with intergenerational issues forms a major portion of the agenda of this volume.

I am indebted to Augustana College in Rock Island, Illinois, where I have been a member of the faculty since 1974 teaching courses in ethics, for providing sabbatical support during fall term of the 1994-95 academic year while I was working on the book. I am also appreciative of the college's library and computer resources, which are so essential to doing the research for and writing a book of this sort. Appreciation must also be expressed for funding received from the Augustana Faculty Research Committee to help cover expenses related to research and preparation of the manuscript.

Portions of the manuscript appeared in the weekly column I write for *The Dispatch*, published in Moline, Illinois. I am indebted to the Moline Dispatch Publishing Company for permission to use this material in the book.

I am also indebted to the following individuals, who read various portions of the manuscript and offered numerous useful suggestions: Richard Ballman, Peter Beckman, Conrad Bergendoff, Myron Fogde, Peter Kivisto, Paul Ohman, Ralph Radloff, Jennifer Rodriguez, Heidi Storl and J. Thomas Tredway. Any errors which persist, of course, remain solely my responsibility. Special words of gratitude to Joan Robinson and Beth Peluso are also in order; they proofread the manuscript and made a number of helpful editorial suggestions. I am especially appreciative of my wife, Ruth, who has been encouraging and supportive of the project throughout the three years I have spent working on it.

Introduction

We stand at the brink of a chasm of frightening proportions--
the chasm of a war between generations. We don't know how
deep this chasm is. We don't know what lies in its depths. We
don't know if there is any escape from it, should we fall into it.
But this we do know--the chasm can be bridged if we have the
foresight and strength of character necessary to get the job done.
If we all pull together, if we affirm the humanity of all of our
fellow human beings, if we are sensitive and responsive to the
needs and concerns of those of all ages, we can construct a
bridge sturdy enough to carry all of us over this chasm.

On the other hand, if denial continues to be the order of the
day, if Americans of various ages persist in pursuing their own
agendas and maintaining the narrowest focus possible, if events
continue to move forward without anyone giving serious
consideration to where we are going, we will find ourself torn
apart by turmoil as we plunge into the chasm.

There have been other gaps between generations. During the
1960s, a turbulent decade in which many younger Americans
viewed with skepticism all types of authority as they took sharp
issue with the government's decision to involve the country in an
unpopular war in Vietnam, a widely-repeated mantra among
student activists held that "you can't trust anyone over the age of
thirty." A generation gap of even greater proportions occurred
during the 1920s, when many younger Americans thumbed their

noses at the Victorian values of their elders as they danced the decade away in an era of frivolity and bootleg gin.

Like other generation gaps, the gap we are facing today is, in part, cultural. Tastes in music, styles of dress, sexual values, and views about work and recreation differ greatly among those of different ages. Alienation is rampant in our age-segregated society. Sensitivity to the needs and concerns of those in other age-groups is rare. Harsh words of criticism spill forth in profusion as the fault lines between generations deepen.

Unlike many previous generation gaps, the conflict which stares us in the face isn't simply the result of cultural differences. The underlying problems pushing us toward a war between generations are, in substantial measure, economic. This struggle between generations involves competition for resources as decisions must be made about how resources (and costs) are allocated among generations--issues being pushed to the forefront as budget battles over Medicare and other programs heat up. It is about jobs and opportunities, about retirement benefits and health care, about short-term economic gains versus long-term environmental costs. And with a never-ending series of crises ranging from the impending collapse of the hospital insurance part of Medicare to serious questions about the long-range viability of Social Security coming down the tracks at us like a train out of control, these times of difficulty stretch ahead of us as far as the eye can see.

We will be strained to the breaking point if we cannot articulate a shared sense of justice based on inclusiveness and the affirmation of the dignity and significance of those of all ages. We will be torn apart if we are not responsive to the concerns and well-being of young and old alike. The years to come will be disastrous if we plunge headlong into the chasm of a war between generations.

It is very easy to think only about the present and our own narrowly-defined agendas. It is very easy to be preoccupied with ourselves to the detriment of those in other age-groups and those yet to be born. Yet the intergenerational issues facing us are of such tremendous significance and of such pressing urgency that to fail to address them is in all probability to opt for injustice and, by so doing, to rush headlong into the chasm. That is why we must wrestle with the unwieldy issues of justice among generations as best we can.

In *A Theory of Justice*, Harvard philosopher John Rawls observes that the question of justice among generations "subjects any ethical theory to severe if not impossible tests."[1] He is right about that. Identifying criteria to be used in addressing issues of intergenerational justice is no easy task. Determining what is fair when it comes to allocating costs and benefits across generational lines is no simple matter. Yet it is something which must be done if we are to ensure a greater measure of intergenerational justice and avoid a war between generations.

Gaining a sense of what justice entails is not enough. If intergenerational justice is to be a reality, a deeply-ingrained sense of justice must inform the decisions we make in our personal lives, at work and in the voting booth. If justice is to mean anything, it cannot be just a theoretical exercise; it must be put into practice.

The conclusion reached in this volume can be very simply summarized: inequities between generations are likely to get worse if we don't do a better job of recognizing and responding to the humanity of those in other age-groups. War between generations is inevitable if we fail to articulate and adhere to plausible standards of intergenerational justice.

The first part of the volume notes the futility of intergenerational conflict and proposes a theory of intergenerational justice based on the notion that everyone is our neighbor. This view of justice challenges us to keep things in balance as we establish priorities with respect to our own well-being and the well-being of others and as we participate in the democratic processes which shape public policy decisions.

Since a greater measure of justice among generations is not likely to become a reality if we don't do a better job of recognizing and responding to the humanity of those in other age-groups, the second part of the volume is devoted to portraits of the different generations which currently comprise the population of the United States. The portraits, which include profiles of individuals from various generations, serve to remind us that justice among generations involves real people--people with hopes and fears, moments of joy and moments of sorrow, times of success and times of failure. Recognizing this basic fact of life is the first and most crucial step toward building bridges across the chasms which divide generations. The portraits of generations, which are intended to underscore the humanity of older generations and younger generations alike, set the stage for the discussion in the third part of the volume of difficult issues such as federal budget deficits, Medicare and Social Security.

Issues of intergenerational significance, of course, extend far beyond those discussed in this volume. For example, many environmental issues such as depletion of the ozone layer and groundwater contamination involve delayed costs imposed disproportionately on future generations. And intergenerational justice involves personal decisions, as well as public policy decisions. Many of the decisions we make as individuals significantly affect our children and grandchildren and, in some cases, our parents and grandparents as well. Exploring all of these issues in all of their complexity, however, is beyond the range of any single volume. All that can be accomplished is to focus attention on certain key issues as examples of the way intergenerational issues might be addressed.

The volume concludes on a note of optimism by noting some ways to move from conflict to a greater sense of community. Times of difficulty are also times of opportunity. By breaking down the walls of age-segregation, by rediscovering what it is to be a neighbor and by gaining greater awareness of the humanity of those with whom our lives intersect, we will all experience greater quality of life. We will bridge the chasms separating generations, averting a war between generations as we work together to find constructive solutions to the problems facing us.

When addressing intergenerational issues, it is convenient to make reference to the various generations which comprise a particular population. When mapping out someone's family tree, identifying the generations is easy enough. There are the sons and daughters, the parents, the grandparents and the great-grandparents. But when talking about an entire population, identifying generations is far more complicated since the generations of the families which comprise any given population do not neatly coincide. As historian Julián Marías observes, "Generations do not come and go in single file, but are overlapped, joined, and interlaced."[2]

It is possible to define population groups which are characterized by a dominant experience or set of experiences--post-war baby boomers, for example. However, even groupings of this sort are somewhat artificial. Leading-edge baby boomers (those born in the years immediately after World War II) often have more in common with those born during the last year or two of World War II than with trailing-edge baby boomers (those born as the baby boom reached its conclusion in the mid-1960s). Moreover, even among those born in a particular year, there are individuals with vastly different experiences. Someone born in 1963 in a single-parent family in a deteriorating urban area undoubtedly has had a significantly different range of experiences than someone born the same year in an upwardly-mobile two-career family living in a rapidly-developing suburb. Similarly, those raised on farms or in small towns often have significantly different ranges of experiences than those of the same age raised in an urban environment--differences often reflected in the views they express. And those who have experienced serious illness or other personal tragedies might have more in common with those in other age-groups who have experienced similar tragedies than with those in their own age-group who have not experienced tragedy. In short, any effort to categorize population groups by age results in lines being drawn that are somewhat artificial.

Nevertheless, for reasons of convenience it is useful to do so, while fully recognizing that no way of categorizing generations is completely satisfactory. To facilitate the discussion of intergenerational issues in this volume, the current U.S. population is divided into six generations as follows:[3]

Generation	Year of Birth
World War I Generation	1886-1905
World War II Generation	1906-1925
Silent Generation	1926-1945
Baby-Boom Generation	1946-1965
Generation X	1966-1985
Twenty-First Century Generation	born after 1985

There is room for debate as to whether this is exactly where the lines should be drawn. And, as will be noted in subsequent chapters, there is considerable debate as to what some of the generations should be called--the generation which follows baby boomers, for example. The purpose of the present volume, however, is not to develop an elaborate population theory subject to endless debate. Rather, this volume is directed toward encouraging thought about issues of justice pertaining to different

Figure I-1:   Composition of U.S. Population

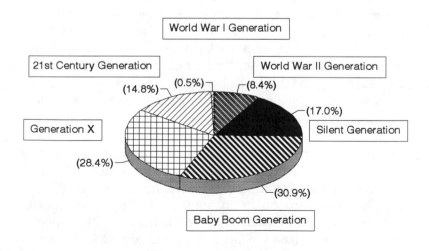

Based on U.S. Bureau of Census Data, 1994

age-groups. The six generations listed above provide useful reference points for this discussion.

Historical events, it might be added, often have different meaning to those of different ages. The events which comprise history are always deeply personal to those who experience them, with the significance of these events varying according to the age and circumstances of those experiencing them. Some personal recollections illustrate the point. Those in my age-group know exactly when the Cuban missile crisis pushed the world to the brink of nuclear holocaust. I was a senior in high school at the time. The evening the news about the Soviet missiles in Cuba dominated television news programs and front pages of newspapers, I joined several of my classmates in our high school library to work on our school yearbook. We didn't

Figure I-2: The Progression of Generations

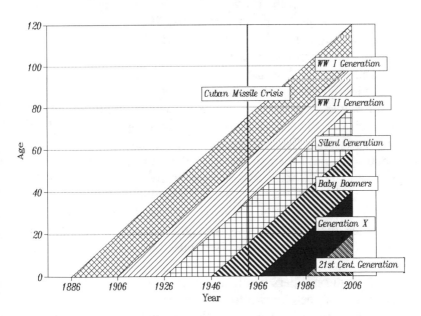

The line denoting the Cuban missile crisis illustrates the way historical events intersect the lives of those who experience them at various stages of their lives.

get much work on the yearbook done that evening. Instead, the conversation returned repeatedly to the events of the day, interspersed with grim one-liners such as "You'll look great in olive drab." Prior to the Cuban missile crisis, wars were something that involved our fathers and grandfathers, our uncles and great-uncles. But suddenly, here we were, about to turn eighteen, with the clouds of war hovering ominously on the horizon. It was painfully apparent to all of us that this one could involve us.

Fortunately, the Cuban missile crisis did not result in war. But in another part of the world, war did trap the United States in a costly quagmire. Many from my high school class, myself included, ended up in uniform.

I was in my first year of graduate school when my local draft board informed me that my student deferment would not be continued beyond that year. A short time later, I happened to read the section on the protection of life in Karl Barth's *Church Dogmatics* in which he observes that "being killed is a very personal experience."[4] A statement which might have seemed trite in other circumstances was suddenly very profound.

The Vietnam War had a far different meaning for those of us of draft age than for those in the middle years of life, some of whom were sitting in comfortable offices in Washington making the decisions to send young men in my age-group to die in the jungles and rice fields of Vietnam. Even though a quarter of a century has passed since those terrible times, many in my age-group still have a deep-seated anger directed toward the president and Pentagon officials who were quite willing to sacrifice our lives to accomplish their policy objectives, whatever they were. (Whether one generation has the right to make commitments on behalf of other generations is a question of intergenerational justice which will be discussed later.)

Enough on a personal level about a time period my teenage daughter has been known to refer to as "the olden days." The underlying point, however, is that everything that happens is deeply personal to someone. Understanding other people is possible only if one has at least some awareness of what they have experienced. That is why a substantial portion of this volume is devoted to an overview of the historical experiences which have been formative for various generations and portraits of individuals who have experienced them.

There is a related point to be made here as well. Public policy decisions, be they decisions about war or funding decisions pertaining to programs such as Medicare and Social Security, profoundly affect people. Even though such decisions might be made in the abstract, they are intensely personal in their impact.

Whether making decisions as individuals or participating in the formulation of public policy, we are more likely to act in an ethical manner if we are in tune with the humanity of our fellow human beings. It is for precisely this reason that in this volume, intergenerational issues such as the federal budget deficit and the financing of Social Security and Medicare are discussed against the backdrop of portraits of generations intended to put a human face on those who comprise the U.S. population. In short, Part III of this volume is not possible without Part II.

Part I

Of Generations and Justice

Chapter 1

Conflict, Power and Justice

The battle lines are already forming. As newspaper and television news reports tell of efforts to slow down the growth of spending for Medicare and Medicaid, anxiety levels increase among older Americans who depend heavily on these programs. The indifference with which older Americans are often treated in our age-segregated, youth-oriented society contributes to this growing insecurity. The American Association of Retired Persons (AARP) and other senior-citizen lobbying groups are fighting hard to preserve funding for programs benefiting older Americans.

At the same time, anger is growing among the younger generations who are asked to pay for these programs. In a letter to the editor published in *The Chicago Sun-Times*, Generation X member Scott Schmidt states:

> I don't foresee a Social Security system intact when I reach retirement. Medicare and Medicaid will be bankrupt long before. I can't afford to buy a house on my income because of rising costs . . . . I can't get a loan because my generation is still paying [for] all the bank failures during the so-called

glory years of the Reagan-Bush [presidencies] . . . . Let this be a wake-up call to Congress. The Generation X population is very large and very angry."[1]

The years ahead of us are likely to be very difficult ones.

Self-Interest, Flawed Vision and Conflict

The influential American theologian Reinhold Niebuhr, whose career spanned the middle part of this century, asserts that because of pervasive flaws of character which afflict every human being, achieving perfect justice is beyond the realm of the possible. The best we can do is opt for relative justice--the greatest measure of justice attainable under the circumstances. He suggests that "the validity of the principle of equality on the one hand and the impossibility of realizing it fully on the other, illustrates the relation of absolute norms of justice to the relativities of history."[2]

But even if perfect justice is beyond the realm of the possible, must we conclude that no measure of justice can be achieved? Is attempting to assure at least a modicum of justice among generations an exercise in futility? Though not commenting specifically on matters related to intergenerational justice, Niebuhr cautions, "Since reason is always, to some degree, the servant of interest in a social situation, social injustice cannot be resolved by moral and rational suasion alone, as the educator and social scientist usually believes. Conflict is inevitable, and in this conflict power must be challenged by power."[3]

Niebuhr suggests that since we all are always motivated, at least to some extent, by self-interest, justice cannot be achieved by moral persuasion alone.[4] Concentrated power is inherently dangerous since even the best people have flawed vision. If unchallenged concentrations of power inevitably result in injustice, an increased measure of justice can be realized only if balance of power can be maintained among the various interest groups constituting society. It is for this reason, for example, that Niebuhr strongly supported the union movement, believing that labor had to be organized in order to offset the power concentrated in the hands of management.[5] Whether Niebuhr is excessively cynical about human nature is debatable. He is right, however, in suggesting that when there is competition for scarce resources, power relationships play an important role in distribution patterns. For example, older Americans vote in greater numbers than members of younger generations (70.1 percent of those 65 or older voted in the 1992 presidential election, compared to 38.5 percent of those 18-20[6]) and have powerful, highly-effective groups such as the AARP lobbying on their behalf. Such being the case, it is not surprising that older Americans have been treated favorably when the federal government has made funding decisions in recent years. Younger Americans who believe they are being short-changed would be well advised to register to vote and become politically active.

It is theoretically possible that voting-age members of younger generations could organize and offset the political power of older generations. The numbers are potentially there to do so and will become even more favorable to those currently comprising younger generations as the march of time continues to thin the ranks of older generations. But even if the power of AARP were offset by baby boomer and Generation X lobbying groups of skill and sophistication equal to that of AARP, justice among generations would still not be realized because those too young to vote or otherwise participate in the political process would still be left out.

For this reason alone, it is inconceivable that intergenerational justice can be achieved simply by challenging power with power. The young and the very old are inherently powerless. Justice resulting from balance of power is an impossibility when some have no power with which to challenge those who are using their power to further their own self-interest. Niebuhr's analysis might be useful when addressing issues of justice in areas such as international relations. But the theory that the path to a greater measure of justice is to be found in challenging power with power breaks down when it comes to intergenerational justice because of the powerlessness of the young and the very old.

The Vector-Sum Theory of Politics

The widely-held vector-sum theory of politics suggests that the body politic ought to move in whatever direction the sum of the political forces comprising it moves it. It is as if all members of the body politic were surrounding a huge ball, trying to push it in whatever way each individual would like to see it move as dictated by self-interest. As they all push hard, grunting and groaning as they draw upon every ounce of strength they possess, the ball rolls in whatever direction the combined vectors of all of the forces applied to it mandate.

As in the case of Niebuhr's theory of social justice, this theory isn't particularly helpful when it comes to justice among generations because the youngest of those currently living, as well as those yet to be born, have no vote. Lacking political muscle, they aren't in a position to do any pushing. Yet what happens in relation to matters such as Social Security and the environment is of tremendous significance to them. What is done in the next few years will substantially define the political, social and economic landscape for all of the next century. Very few of those who will comprise the U.S. population in the year 2063, when the bicentennial of Lincoln's Gettysburg address and the centennial of Martin Luther King, Jr.'s speech "I Have a Dream" will be celebrated, have any voice in the decisions that will so profoundly affect them in the years to come.

The huge ball that members of the body politic are trying to push in different directions often rolls over those who are overpowered by the stronger forces pushing on the other side of the ball. As the ball rolls over those who are weaker, it crushes their hopes and sometimes even extinguishes their lives. Since the youngest members of the body politic are powerless, they are the ones who will be crushed if we simply allow a collision of special interest groups to determine what happens with respect to matters of significance for future generations. The simple fact of the matter is that there is no way that war between generations can lead to justice among generations. Intergenerational conflict is invariably costly to those who are powerless. Human decency demands that we try to find solutions to the problems facing us which will minimize intergenerational conflict and avert plunging over the precipice and into the chasm of a war between generations.

An Unsettling Question

The realization that the conflict model and the vector-sum theory of politics are inadequate when it comes to intergenerational justice leaves us with an unsettling question: is justice among generations possible? It is fine to talk about among among generations. But when push comes to shove, can we as individuals and as a society rise above self-interest and concern for the immediate and do what is necessary to ensure at least some measure of intergenerational equity?

A greater measure of justice among generations is possible only if we do a better job of recognizing and relating to the humanity of those in other age-groups. Unfortunately, we live in an age-segregated society in which relatively few spend any significant amount of time with members of other generations. We live in a fast-paced world in which it is easy to think only about the immediate--only about that next meeting or the next assignment without pausing to think about the future or about how what we do affects other people.

The challenge before us is breaking this cycle by recognizing and reaching out to members of other generations--those who are members of our own families as well as others whose lives intersect with ours, those who live in distant cities as well as those who live down the street from us, those whose lifestyles differ from our own as well as those who hold values similar to those we affirm. Breaking down age-segregation and overcoming the disconnectedness which is so typical of contemporary American society is essential if a greater measure of justice among generations is to become a reality.

The bottom line is that conflict between generations is an exercise in futility which causes all sorts of problems while accomplishing nothing. People of all ages have legitimate interests and concerns which ought to be recognized. An ethic of inclusiveness which affirms the dignity and is committed to the well-being of all persons of all generations is the only hope for averting a catastrophic war between generations.

Chapter 2

A Matter of Balance

In a Biblical story familiar to many, a lawyer asks Jesus, "Teacher, which is the great commandment in the law?" Quoting Deuteronomy 6.5 and Leviticus 19.18 from the Hebrew Bible, Jesus answers, "You shall love the Lord your God with all your heart, and with all your soul, and with all your mind. This is the great and first commandment. And a second is like it, You shall love your neighbor as yourself."[1]

Then, as now, lawyers found irresistible the urge to ask follow-up questions. In the version of the story found in Luke, the lawyer, hoping to trip up Jesus, continues, "And who is my neighbor?" Jesus responds with the parable of the Good Samaritan, which tells of a man who, while traveling from Jerusalem to Jericho, was robbed, severely beaten and left lying nearly dead by the side of the road. A priest who happened to be traveling along that road saw the injured man but passed by on the other side of the road. So also did a Levite (a member of the tribe of Levi chosen to assist the priests of that day). Who stopped to help the battered victim? A stranger from Samaria, a neighboring country to the north. When the Samaritan saw the injured man lying by the side of the road, "he had compassion, and went to him and bound up his wounds, pouring on oil and wine; then he set him on his own beast and brought him to an inn, and took care of him." The Samaritan, before continuing his journey, left money with the innkeeper to cover the costs of caring for the injured man, adding that if the costs exceeded the amount he had left, he would reimburse the innkeeper on the return trip.[2] Jesus then asks the lawyer which of the three--the priest, the Levite or the Samaritan--"proved neighbor to the man who fell among the robbers?" The lawyer concedes, "The one who showed mercy on him."[3]

The story has a double edge to it. One is to puncture the vanity of the religious types who imagine themselves to be righteous. The hero of the story is not someone pompously parading around, flaunting self-proclaimed piety and claiming to be a person of great virtue while viewing others in a condescending manner. Those who fancied themselves to be virtuous passed by on the other side of the road. The hero is a stranger from a neighboring country--a stranger who, given the rivalry and ill-will between Judea and Samaria at that time, was not highly regarded by those living in Jerusalem and surrounding areas. A stranger who, without thinking of himself as heroic in any way, did what needed to be done.

The story also suggests that our neighbors are not limited to those who live down the street from us. Rather, everyone is our neighbor. The Danish theologian and philosopher Søren Kierkegaard put it this way: "The category *neighbor* is just like the category human being."[4] The love commandment is a reminder that we do not live in isolation. Our lives are intertwined with those of others, those who live in distant areas as well as those who live near us. As Karl Barth puts it in *Church Dogmatics*, we have distant neighbors, as well as near neighbors.[5] What we do--or fail to do--is of significance not only for our immediate families and for those who live down the street from us but for countless others as well. We are all part of a broader community. That community is all humanity. Moreover, everyone counts. We cannot in good conscience walk by anyone, ignoring their humanity and failing to respond to them as human beings. Social Security, Medicare and budget deficits weren't matters of particular concern during Jesus' time. Yet the love commandment is of profound significance for any discussion of justice among generations today. The love commandment won't let us get away with pursuing narrowly defined agendas, concerned only about ourselves, our careers and our own ambitions. It demands that we take the humanity of all our fellow human beings seriously, regardless of who they are, where they come from or what generation they belong to. It requires that we ask of ourselves how what we are doing will affect other people, including neighbors we have never met and whose names we do not know. One cannot live only for oneself or only for the present if one is to take the notion of love for one's neighbors seriously.[6]

Others as Well as Ourselves
And Ourselves as Well as Others

Contrary to what is often assumed to be the case, the love commandment does not suggest that we should be concerned about others to the exclusion of ourselves or that we should be completely self-sacrificing. Rather, it is an affirmation of the humanity of all people--others as well as ourselves and ourselves as well as others. It demands of us that we be aware of and responsive to the humanity of others, as well as give recognition to our own humanity. It challenges us to love others, as well as ourselves, and ourselves, as well as others.

Taking the love commandment seriously involves doing things in the right proportion. It asks us to keep things in balance. A nineteenth-century commentator, addressing the question of how one should view his or her neighbor, suggested, "The law of charity does not require me to have a greater regard for him than for myself. But, on the other hand, the same law requires that I should not have a less[er regard]."[7]

Granted, it is not always easy to determine how our own interests and well-being sort out in relation to those of others or what priorities we should establish when deciding how to spend our time, our money and the other resources under our control. It is much easier to think only about ourselves. For that matter, it is sometimes even easier to practice complete self-denial than to adhere to a multi-faceted ethic which says that we ought to be concerned about others as well as ourselves and ourselves as well as others. But what is easy isn't always what is right. By being unconditionally inclusive, the love commandment demands of us that we address questions of priority and of appropriate balance.[8]

Future Generations

If all human beings are to be viewed as our neighbors, that includes generations yet to be born, as well as those with whom we share life on planet earth. There is, it should be noted, some debate as to whether it makes sense to talk about "rights of future generations" since, by definition, future generations have not yet been born and, accordingly, do not presently exist.[9] Whether the language of rights, which typifies so many discussions of moral issues today, can plausibly be used with respect to future generations is a matter likely to still be debated long after future generations have arrived on the scene.

Fortunately, addressing issues related to justice among generations, including those not yet born, is not contingent on resolving questions related to the appropriate use of the language of rights. If one takes the position that we ought to refrain from doing things harmful to others, it is inappropriate to contaminate the environment with cancer-causing chemicals regardless of whether those who get cancer from the toxic chemicals are currently living or not yet born. If one argues that we ought to do what we can to help create conditions which contribute to well-being, it makes just as much sense to talk about the well-being of future generations as that of present generations. If we contend that at least some sort of balance ought to be maintained with respect to various generations, there is nothing implausible about including future generations in the balance.

Quality of Life and Interpersonal Relations

There is another point which is worth noting here. While the language of rights is useful in many discussions, the strong emphasis which has been placed on various notions of rights in recent years has tended to transform discussions of ethical issues into a series of claims and demands, instead of focusing attention on modes of relating to others--for example, being caring, compassionate and understanding of others. The name of the game has been to declare that someone is a victim and then argue that compensation is due--a claim pursued, if need be, in a court of law by high-priced attorneys hired to manipulate the system in every way possible so as to produce the most favorable outcome for the client.

In a provocative essay, *Newsweek* columnist George F. Will observes, "Can there be too many rights? Yes, when every social problem is presented as a clash of rights, and all advocacy is couched in the language of rights."[10] Morality, or at least the way we go about trying to sort out moral issues, has become atomistic and confrontational, fueled by a widespread belief that we are somehow being shortchanged. We have become so preoccupied with our cut of the take that we pay little attention to other people. As a result, the quality of interpersonal relations suffers greatly. Brokenness and disconnectedness disrupt our lives.

Robert D. Putnam, the director of the Center for International Affairs at Harvard University, notes that in this country, participation in voluntary organizations ranging from fraternal groups and women's organizations to bowling leagues and parent-teacher associations has dropped dramatically in recent years.[11] We are becoming a nation of loners.

If we are to be realistic about what contributes to quality of life, the quality of the interpersonal relations we experience is just as important as, if not more important than, what we have in our pockets (though far more difficult to quantify). Faithfulness, loyalty, compassion and understanding are all factors which add quality to life, a basic fact often overlooked by those who engage in detached, clinically-sterile discussions of rights and by special interest groups preoccupied with promoting narrowly-defined agendas.

When talking about justice among generations, it isn't simply a question of which generation might or might not be getting shortchanged, though there are serious matters of imbalance which ought not be ignored. Justice among generations, a phrase being used in the present discussion as a metaphor for the full range of ethical considerations pertaining to relations among generations, also involves keeping faith with others, being caring and compassionate, and being open to others. Justice among generations involves basic questions of lifestyle, as well as considerations related to the allocation of resources.

A Matter of Proportion

In *The Nichomachean Ethics*, Aristotle states that justice in the distribution of things "can be stated as a proportion, and the unjust in this sense is a violation of proportion." He observes, "What is unjust, therefore, is what is either too much or too little. One sees this happen. When some good is at stake the man who acts unjustly is the man who takes too much; the man who suffers the injustice gets too little."[12] If whatever is being allocated is something that is not desirable (taxes, for example), the person who suffers injustice is the one who gets stuck with more than his or her fair share. Aristotle notes, "The position is reversed when the matter at stake is evil. In that case the lesser evil is reckoned as a good in comparison with the greater,

because of two evils the lesser is more desirable than the greater
. . . . "13

Aristotle, it should be added, does not suggest that everyone should get exactly the same amount of whatever is being distributed. Those who are more deserving, he argues, should get greater shares "of honour or money or such other possessions of the community as can be divided among its members." Justice in distribution, he believes, will be maintained as long as the same criteria are used in each case in the distribution of things: "The ratio will be the same in the one case as in the other, because, if the persons are not equal, their shares will not be equal. As a matter of fact when quarrels and complaints arise, it is when people who are equal have not got equal shares, or *vice versa*."14

Should Some Generations Be Allocated More than Other Generations?

In contemporary American society, merit criteria are commonly used for some forms of distribution such as determining the relative size of year-end bonuses. But should merit criteria be used to determine the appropriate distribution of goods and services (or costs) among generations? Can anyone plausibly argue that one generation is more deserving than others? That one generation is in some significant way superior to others?

There are, of course, differences among generations, both with respect to their historical experiences and with respect to their contributions to society. The World War II Generation sacrificed greatly to preserve democracy in western Europe and end the military domination of the Pacific by the Empire of Japan. When the war was over, they worked hard to help make America what it is today. Other generations, however, have also made their contributions. The ingenuity of baby boomers has revolutionized the world of computers, setting the stage for the information superhighway and making increased productivity a possibility. Many members of the World War I Generation contributed to an earlier technological revolution which made the automobile, the telephone, radio and television common features of the American landscape. Many members of the Silent Generation strongly emphasized parenting skills and devoted a good deal of time to their families. Who is to say that one generation's contributions are more significant than those of others?

Appealing to merit criteria, of course, is not the only way of attempting to argue that some ought to receive more than others. Those who take a utilitarian approach to distributive justice contend that those more likely to benefit society should receive a greater measure of whatever is being distributed. When applied to the matter of justice among generations, an unqualified utilitarian approach would suggest that health care for the elderly ought to be curtailed to enable spending more on education since those who are younger are more likely to benefit society in the years to come than are the elderly, who have already made their contributions. While there is room for debate as to whether the right balance is being maintained between funding programs for the elderly and programs such as education which primarily benefit those who are younger, to cut off the elderly and give absolute priority to those who are younger runs afoul of the notion that everyone counts and that we ought to care about all of our fellow human beings. Indeed, to fail to respond to the needs and concerns of the elderly would be unconscionable.

"The Luck of the Draw"

What about trying to offset "the luck of the draw"? Some age-groups are more fortunate than others. Those born in the late 1930s were too young for World War II and Korea and too old to be drafted during the war in Vietnam. They also had the good fortune to enter the job market when the economy was booming and jobs were readily available. Those born in other years have been less fortunate. Should the allocation of resources among generations take these disparities into account? The "luck of the draw," of course, involves far more than the year in which one was born. Children born to affluent two-parent families are in a far more advantageous situation than children born to unwed teenage mothers on public aid. Programs such as Head Start attempt to even out some of these disparities by giving extra help to those who are disadvantaged. However, characterizing an entire generation as disadvantaged and hence in need of extra help is highly questionable. As a result of historical circumstances, there might be a higher percentage of disadvantaged individuals in some generations than in others. In the course of the years, programs such as Head Start and Medicaid might end up serving a greater number of individuals in some generations than in others. This is in no way problematic insofar as any reasonable standard of justice is concerned. But to say that everyone in a particular age-group is disadvantaged is misleading and risks giving preferential treatment to the fortunate in that age-group, as well as to the less fortunate.

Apart from persuasive arguments indicating that some generations deserve preferential treatment, every generation ought to be treated equally. This does not mean, of course, everyone ought to be treated exactly the same way, regardless of age--that those who are older and have greater health needs should receive no more health care than those who are younger or that Social Security checks should be sent to those who are younger as well as to those over the age of sixty-five. But it does mean that those who are younger should reasonably be able to expect that when they are older, they will receive Social Security checks and a level of health care commensurate with what older generations are currently receiving. In a thoughtful book entitled *Am I My Parents' Keeper?* Tufts University philosopher Norman Daniels notes:

> If we treat the young one way and the old another, then

over time, each person is treated both ways. The advantages (or disadvantages) of *consistent* differential treatment by age will equalize over time. An institution that treats the young and the old differently will, over time, still treat people equally.[15]

Maintaining Balance

While the merit criteria Aristotle utilizes aren't particularly helpful in discussions of intergenerational justice, the notion that appropriate proportions ought to be maintained is useful. There are, to be sure, no precise mathematical formulas which tell us exactly what this balance between generations should be. Nor are there finely calibrated measuring scales to tell us when things are in balance. Justice among generations is, at best, an inexact science. Some would say it is more an art than a science. But difficult though it might be to draw precise lines or determine exactly when balance with respect to various generations is achieved, it is possible to sense when things are out of balance. Justice among generations has not been achieved when:

• those currently retired receive far more generous Social Security benefits than those currently working (who pay the taxes financing the benefits for current retirees) can expect when they retire;

• those currently working are taxed to finance publicly-funded health care benefits for older Americans which far exceed what they are likely to receive when they reach retirement age;

• the reluctance of current generations to make do with fewer publicly-funded benefits or pay more taxes results in a mushrooming national debt which will severely limit options for future generations;

- groundwater contamination caused by inappropriate pesticide use places the health of future generations at risk;

- careless farming practices result in millions of tons of rich topsoil being washed away each year, diminishing the productivity of prime agricultural land needed to grow food for future generations;

- depletion of the ozone layer increases the risk of members of future generations contracting cancer;

- environmental regulations fail to give recognition to the economic concerns of those affected by them, making it difficult for farmers, saw mill operators and others to make a living;

- parents live only for themselves, disregarding the impact the decisions they make have on their children;

- parents sacrifice everything for their children;

- sons and daughters who no longer live at home are indifferent to the well-being of their parents and never get around to doing something as simple as calling their parents to see how they are doing;

- sons and daughters give up their careers and sacrifice everything they have to look after their aged parents;

Sometimes questions of justice among generations involve public policy considerations. Sometimes they involve the personal decisions we make with respect to our own lives. But regardless of the context in which the issues are encountered, working to achieve justice among generations involves doing whatever we can to get things in balance as much as possible.

Fear

Fear is one of the most powerful of all motivating factors--fear of being rejected, fear of losing one's job, fear of not being able to maintain the standard of living one desires, fear of losing one's health, fear of dying, and fear of many other things. One cannot really understand other people (or oneself) without gaining an awareness of the fears and anxieties they experience. Fear causes one to be defensive. Fear, if allowed to gain the upper hand, results in people pulling their wagons in a circle and banging away at the rest of the world. The heavy-duty lobbying of government officials by various special-interest groups isn't simply the result of greed and selfishness, though such factors are often present. Intensive lobbying efforts are often motivated, at least in part, by fear and anxiety.

A greater measure of justice among generations is not likely unless we do a better job of responding to the fears and anxieties which are so prevalent today. Subsequent chapters suggest that measures such as restraint in the growth of Social Security benefits are necessary if at least some semblance of balance among generations is to be assured. None of this will happen, however, if those of us who comprise the rest of society fail to give recognition to the economic anxieties and other concerns which senior citizens and others experience. We all have fears and anxieties. Love for one's neighbor involves giving recognition to and responding to fears and anxieties within the context of a caring community.

An Experiential Dimension

There is a related point worth noting. Justice among generations cannot be accomplished simply by articulating complicated mathematical formulas or engaging in abstract intellectualizing. If a greater measure of justice among generations is to become a reality, there must be an experiential dimension. It must be rooted in the emotional bonds which tie individuals and communities together--bonds which, in many cases, have been allowed to wither in recent years. These emotional bonds must transcend generations, both in our families and in the broader communities in which we live. They must involve sensitivity and understanding, compassion and commitment.

Granted, in a nation of more than 260 million people, we must think in the abstract and the impersonal, as well as in the particular and the interpersonal. The point to be underscored, however, is that it is very difficult simply to think about the humanity of other people in the abstract. One of the ways we put a human face on others is to relate to them on the interpersonal level. Once we gain awareness of and are sensitive to the humanity of those with whom we personally come in contact, it is much easier to gain awareness of the humanity of those whose lives do not intersect with ours on a daily basis.

The Interpersonal, the Impersonal And Generations

A major theme in Reinhold Niebuhr's writings is the assertion that we are more likely to be moral in our dealings with people we know than in group relations that are impersonal.[16] There is something to that. It is not unusual for people who wouldn't think of harming the neighbor next door to be supportive of policies and programs which end up being very detrimental to people they don't know. There often is a difference between the way that people respond to the needs and concerns of identifiable individuals, on the one hand, and large groups of anonymous individuals, on the other. Many have noted, for example, the historical tendency of companies involved in mining operations to be reluctant to spend money on safety equipment but then spare no expense trying to rescue trapped miners once a disaster has occurred.

Quite obviously, there are some problems here as far as future generations are concerned. Breaking down age-segregation might help personalize a certain range of relations among existing generations. Personally relating to future generations, however, is beyond the range of the possible since by definition, members of future generations do not yet exist.

This problem might partially be mitigated by the fact that if we are considerate of younger generations, those not yet born are also likely to benefit. For example, if we exercise the self-discipline necessary to get the federal budget deficit under control, the future will be brighter for many generations down the road. But at best, this falls far short of being a satisfactory solution to the problem--although it might well be the best we can hope for, given the realities of human nature.

Even if we limit our concern to the six generations currently comprising the U.S. population, problems remain. Breaking down age-segregation might result in greater understanding between individuals from different generations. But that doesn't automatically translate into lifestyle choices and public policy decisions which take the well-being of all members of other generations into account. For example, time spent with a grandchild might result in the grandparent having increased concern about the well-being of that particular grandchild. But that concern could end up being expressed in the form of special provisions in the grandparent's will ensuring the financial security of that particular grandchild, rather than support for revisions in Social Security that would ensure the viability of Social Security for future generations.

Going from the particular to the general, from the personal to the impersonal, from the individual to the group, is seldom easy. Yet that is precisely the challenge which confronts us. As noted in the previous chapter, the Niebuhrian solution of trying to achieve a greater measure of justice by confronting power with power doesn't work when it comes to justice among generations since the youngest of those presently living and those yet to be born are powerless, as are, in many cases, the oldest members of society. Often all that we can do is appeal to the common sense and decency of members of the generations currently in the driver's seat and hope that a sufficient number will rise above narrowly-defined self-interest to make a greater measure of justice possible, while fully realizing that preoccupation with self-interest will blind many to the importance of doing so. Few tasks are so daunting or so crucial to the well-being of our children, our grandchildren and future generations.

Constructively dealing with difficult issues such as the federal budget deficit, Medicare and Social Security will be possible only if there is greater understanding of the needs and concerns of members of all generations. Listening is the first step toward understanding. Understanding is the cornerstone of justice.

Part II

Portraits of Generations

Chapter 3

The World War I Generation

(Born 1886-1905)

In the first year of the new century, Woodrow Wilson, professor of jurisprudence and political economy at Princeton University, observed, "Statesmen knew that it was to be their task to release the energies of the country for the great day of trade and manufacture which was to change the face of the world . . . ."[1]

The face of the world was changed but, to Wilson's great dismay, as a result of war of unprecedented proportions. On June 28, 1914, an assassin's bullet in the Bosnian town of Sarajevo lit a conflagration which was to snuff out the lives of more than 10 million human beings before it burned itself out. The conflagration brought the old order of Europe crashing down.

Wilson, who had assumed the responsibilities of the Oval Office seventeen months before the guns of war unleashed their fury in August of 1914, tried to keep the United States out of war. In 1916, he was re-elected on a platform proclaiming, "He Kept Us Out of War!" But nothing lasts forever--certainly not campaign promises. After a German U-boat torpedoed the British Cunard liner *Lusitania*, which sank in eighteen minutes off the coast of Ireland with the loss of 1198 lives, 128 of them Americans, public sentiment in the United States shifted in favor of intervention in the war in Europe. On April 2, 1917, a reluctant president asked Congress for a declaration of war against Germany.

American "doughboys," including many born during the years 1886-1905, were shipped to France. Under the command of Gen. John J. "Black Jack" Pershing, they provided a much-needed transfusion of blood for the weary Allies fighting Germany and the crumbling remains of the Austro-Hungarian and Ottoman empires. U.S. Marines, wearing Army uniforms, made Belleau Wood a celebrated chapter in U.S. military history. The Meuse-Argonne offensive, in which 1,200,000 American soldiers participated with one of every ten either killed or wounded, broke the German lines.[2] On November 11, 1918, the guns of war thundered one more time, shaking the earth with a final, furious barrage, and then fell silent as the armistice took effect at the eleventh hour of the eleventh day of the eleventh month of the year. With the outcome of the war already determined once the German high command accepted the terms of the armistice, no one was able to explain why one last orgy of killing was necessary.

When those in the generation born during the years 1886-1905 speak of "the war," they almost always are referring to World War I, a terrible slaughter which forever changed the way they were to look at things. The war remains deeply etched in their consciousness.

World War I, though, is not the only war they have witnessed. Those born before the turn of the century were children when President William McKinley, a Civil war veteran who knew what war was like, reluctantly yielded to the sentiments of a public eager to go to war and asked Congress to authorize using the armed forces of the United States to force

Spain to relinquish control of Cuba.³ Commodore George
Dewey, acting on orders cabled by Assistant Secretary of the
Navy Theodore Roosevelt while Secretary of the Navy John D.
Long was away for a weekend, sailed into Manila Bay in the
Philippines and destroyed the Spanish fleet without loss of a
single American life but had to wait for ground troops before the
city itself could be taken. Roosevelt used his political influence
to get an army commission, even though he was so near-sighted
he probably couldn't have passed an army physical. Followed
by his Rough Riders, who were on foot because the disorganized
U.S. Army hadn't sent their horses along with them, Roosevelt
charged up San Juan Heights near Santiago, Cuba, where he
captured the adoration of the American public. The Rough
Riders took heavy casualties. Roosevelt boasted that he had
personally killed a fleeing Spanish soldier, using a revolver
recovered from the sunken battleship *Maine*.⁴ On the other side
of the world, the ground troops needed to take Manila finally
arrived and the city was taken, though somewhat inconveniently
the day after the armistice was signed.⁵

World War I, which some naively believed would be "the
war to end war," was not to be the last war those of the World
War I generation were to experience. Wilson's idealism,
expressed in his Fourteen Points, was overshadowed by the
vindictiveness of the victorious European powers, who sowed the
seeds of the next war when they imposed the harsh Treaty of
Versailles on the defeated German nation. Two decades later,
the world, having endured a decade of economic disaster fertile
for the rise of fascism, was again convulsed in war. Some of the
World War I generation served in this war as well. Five years
after World War II came Korea and then, fifteen years later,
Vietnam, America's longest and least-successful war. A generation after Vietnam came lightning-fast victory in the Persian Gulf
War as American and other allied troops, using their high-tech
weapons, drove the Iraqi Army from Kuwait. The surviving
members of the World War I Generation who were born before
the turn of the century have witnessed six wars in which
American lives have been lost on foreign soil, as well as military

action of more limited scope in Beirut, Panama, Grenada and many other parts of the world.

A Breath-Taking Technological Revolution

Changes wrought by the devastation of war are not the only changes the World War I generation has witnessed. Their lives encompass a breath-taking technological revolution. Shortly before they arrived on the scene, Alexander Graham Bell, a teacher of the deaf, had introduced the telephone.[6] Telephone lines linking cities and farms, distant family members and neighbors down the road, spread across the nation. Thomas A. Edison, so deaf that little bothered or distracted him, perfected the incandescent electric light in 1879. Edison, a genius who as a child had been considered to be such a slow learner that he was taken out of school, then turned his attention to the phonograph, the mimeograph and the moving picture camera, all of which were successful. During a life which spanned nine decades (1847-1931), he received 1,093 patents--the most ever granted to one person.[7]

The automobile was not an American invention. But innovative American industrialists, among them Henry Ford and Ransom E. Olds, adapted and refined what their European counterparts had first developed. Ford's mass assembly techniques, used to perfection in the manufacture of the Model T, put America on wheels. In 1900, a year in which there were nearly eighteen million horses on farms, eight thousand motor vehicles were registered in the United States. In 1914, Ford produced his five hundred thousandth Model T. By 1930, he had produced twenty million automobiles--enough, if parked bumper-to-bumper, to encircle the globe. That year the number of registered motor vehicles in the United states totaled more than 26.5 million--nearly twice as many as the 13.7 million horses remaining on farms.[8] By 1993, the number of registered motor vehicles in the United States had increased to 194.1

million.[9]

On December 17, 1903, at Kitty Hawk, North Carolina, Orville and Wilbur Wright made history. With Orville at the controls, a flimsy six-hundred-pound contraption was pushed down a track in the face of a wind of more than twenty miles per hour and, powered by a gasoline engine, took to the air for a distance of 120 feet, attaining an altitude of ten feet before darting back to the ground. The flight lasted twelve seconds. The two brothers took turns at the controls of their flying machine as it became airborne three more times that windy winter day. The longest flight was the last one when, with Wilbur at the controls, the flying machine covered a distance of 852 feet in fifty-nine seconds.[10]

When the European continent erupted in flames in 1914, the airplane became a tool of destruction. Swarms of biplanes and triplanes buzzed over the muddy, blood-stained battlefields of the Somme, the Marne and Verdun, manned by pilots without parachutes shooting at each other with machine guns. Combat pilots who shot down five enemy planes gained the coveted title "ace." Very few aces lived to see the end of the war.

Biplanes gave way to monoplanes, piston-engine planes to jet-engine planes. Daring men sat in cramped nose cones perched on huge liquid-fueled rockets which blasted them into space. And on July 20, 1969, five months short of sixty-six years since the day Orville and Wilbur Wright made history, those of the World War I Generation still alive witnessed via the miracle of television Neil A. Armstrong and Edwin E. Aldrin, Jr., making history as they planted a metal American flag on the crater-pocked surface of the moon.

Communications satellites and fiber optics. Big-screen television sets and compact disc players. Several generations of computers, each making the preceding generation obsolete. Nuclear weapons of terrifying power and deadly nuclear-powered submarines lurking undetected below the surface of the ocean. Vaccines preventing once-dreaded diseases such as polio. Organ transplants offering renewed hope of life. Genetically-engineered varieties of wheat and corn. All of this and much more has happened since the World War I Generation was born. More technological innovation has occurred during their lifetimes *than in all preceding history combined.* That's how recent and how dramatic this technological revolution has been!

The Nineteenth Amendment

In 1848, Lucretia Mott and Elizabeth Cady Stanton organized a women's rights convention, held in Seneca Falls, New York, which called for including women on an equal basis in the democratic processes giving governance to the nation. The "Declaration of Sentiments" adopted by the convention stated:

> Now, in view of this entire disfranchisement of one-half the people of this country, their social and religious degradation . . . and because women do feel themselves aggrieved, oppressed, and fraudulently deprived of their most sacred rights, we insist that they have immediate admission to all the rights and privileges which belong to them as citizens of the United States.[11]

The struggle to secure the vote for women was a long and difficult one. In 1872, Susan B. Anthony, asserting that the Fourteenth Amendment to the United States Constitution did not allow excluding women from the voting booth, registered to vote and cast her vote for Ulysses S. Grant for president of the United States. Two weeks later she and fourteen other women who had voted were arrested and charged with having voted without having the lawful right to vote. When her case came to trial, she was convicted and fined $100 plus court costs.[12]

On March 3, 1913, the eve of Woodrow Wilson's first inauguration, eight thousand women marched up Pennsylvania Avenue past the White House. A huge crowd, in town for the inaugural festivities the next day, harassed and attacked the marchers. With police failing to protect the marchers, Secretary of War Henry Stimson was forced to send for Army troops.[13]

The January 23, 1914, edition of *The Suffragist* summarized some of the reasons suffragists had been told there should not be a constitutional amendment guaranteeing women the right to vote. They included the following:

That Woman Suffrage cannot be supported because of a man's respect, admiration, and reverence for womanhood.

That women must be protected against themselves. They think they want to vote. As a matter of fact, they do not want to vote, and man, being aware of this fact, is obliged to prevent them from getting the ballot that they do not want.

That the ballot would degrade women.

That no man would care to marry a Suffragist.

That women do not read newspapers on street cars.[14]

In 1917, Alice Paul, a Quaker from New Jersey, and other leaders of the women's rights movement, impatient with President Wilson's equivocation and delaying tactics, began picketing the White House, carrying banners asking "Mr. President, what will you do for woman suffrage?" and "How long must women wait for liberty?" The picketing continued for more than a year.[15] In October of that year, several of the protesters were arrested. Among them was Paul, who was sentenced to seven months in jail, where she went on a hunger strike and was force-fed. At the time she was arrested, she was carrying a banner which bore President Wilson's own words: "The time has come to conquer or submit. For us there can be but one choice. We have made it."[16]

By 1920, fifteen states, most of them west of the Mississippi, had legislatively provided for equal voting rights for women. Other states allowed women to vote for candidates some offices.[17] Finally, both houses of Congress passed a proposed constitutional amendment stating that "the right of citizens of the United States to vote shall not be denied or abridged by the

United States or by any States on Account of sex."[18] On August 18, 1920, Tennessee became the thirty-sixth state to ratify the Nineteenth Amendment to the United States Constitution. Eight days later, the amendment became the law of the land.[19] What Mott, Stanton, Anthony, Paul and many others had worked so hard for had finally been accomplished.

"Many That Are First Will Be Last . . . ."

On December 18, 1903 (the day after Orville and Wilbur Wright made history), Governor Charles B. Aycock of North Carolina spoke to an appreciative audience at a dinner in Baltimore, Maryland, outlining his views on race relations. He stated:

> I am proud of my State because there we have solved the negro problem, which recently seems to have given you some trouble. We have taken him out of politics and have thereby secured good government under any party and laid foundations for the future development of both races. We have secured peace and rendered prosperity a certainty.

He said that disenfranchisement of the negro as far as possible under the Fifteenth Amendment, the essential superiority of the white man, and the recognition by the negro of his own inferiority were responsible for the settlement of the question in his state. Governor Aycock concluded:

> Let the negro learn once for all that there is unending separation of the races; that the two peoples may develop side by side to their fullest, but that they cannot intermingle . . . . These things are not said in enmity to the negro, but in regard for him . . . . He has always been my personal friend.[20]

Four decades later, Martin Luther King, Jr., then in the

eleventh grade, entered and won an oratorical contest sponsored by the Negro Elks in a town in Georgia some distance from Atlanta. On the long bus ride back to Atlanta, King and a teacher who had accompanied him were reviewing the exciting events of the day when some white passengers boarded and demanded their seats. King refused to budge. The bus driver, who, like all bus drivers in the segregated South, was white, ordered King to give up his seat, subjecting him to demeaning racial epithets. He reluctantly complied. King later observed, "That night will never leave my mind. It was the angriest I have ever been in my life."[21]

On August 28, 1963, King stood on the steps of the Lincoln Memorial, addressing a crowd of more than a quarter of a million. "When the architects of our republic wrote the magnificent words of the Constitution and the Declaration of Independence," he stated, "they were signing a promissory note to which every American was to fall heir. This note was a promise that all men would be guaranteed the unalienable rights of life, liberty, and the pursuit of happiness."

Then, setting aside his prepared text and speaking from the heart, he went on to say that "in spite of the difficulties and frustrations of the moment I still have a dream." He continued:

> I have a dream that one day this nation will rise up and live out the true meaning of its creed: "We hold these truths to be self-evident--that all men are created equal." I have a dream that one day on the red hills of Georgia the sons of former slaves and the sons of former slave owners will be able to sit down together at the table of brotherhood . . . . I have a dream that my four little children will one day live in a nation where they will not be judged by the color of their skin but by the content of their character.[22]

The following year, Dr. King traveled to Oslo, Norway, where he received the Nobel Peace Prize. In this country, his birthday is now a national holiday.

And what of Gov. Aycock? As the nation moved toward

ensuring equal rights for all Americans, he was condemned to the eternal obscurity richly deserved by those who come out on the wrong side of history by failing to affirm the dignity of all humankind.

Centuries ago, a deeply-insightful teacher of ethics observed that "many that are first will be last, and the last first."[23]

Other Changes as Well

Grover Cleveland, the Democratic president who occupied the White House when the first of the World War I Generation were born, favored lowering tariffs, a major source of revenue during that era. He was embarrassed by the surplus building up in the federal government's coffers. Republicans in Congress, who favored protectionist policies, strenuously opposed the president.[24] Today, the surpluses are gone and the national debt is piling up at an alarming rate. The political winds have shifted. Many Democrats, supported by organized labor, advocate protectionist policies while most Republicans favor free trade.

The World War I Generation have witnessed many other changes as well:

• Prohibition has come and gone.

• Millions of Americans have moved from farms to cities and then to suburbs.

• The population of the country has grown from 76 million in 1900[25] to more than 260 million today.[26]

• The number graduating from colleges and universities increased from 29,375 in 1900[27] to more than 2 million in 1992.[28]

• The number of libraries has increased from 9,000 in 1900, each with at least 300 books,[29] to more than 35,000 today.[30]

• In 1900, there were 709,000 marriages and 55,751 divorces--a ratio of 13:1;[31] in 1993, 2,334,000 marriages and 1,187,000 divorces--a ratio of 2:1.[32]

• In 1900, the average cost of a pound of bacon was 14.3 cents, a 10 lb. bag of potatoes 14 cents, 5 lbs. of sugar 30.5 cents--a fraction of what these items cost today.[33]

• When wages are adjusted for inflation, today's factory workers make sixteen times as much as their counterparts did at the turn of the century.[34]

Hardy Survivors

In 1905, the World War I Generation (though, of course, they were not yet known as such) numbered slightly more than 18 million--nearly 24 percent of the population.[35] By 1994, the number had diminished to 1.2 million--0.5 percent of the population.[36] The life expectancy of a child born in the United States in 1900 was 47.3 years.[37] Those of the World War I Generation living today are hardy survivors, having beaten the odds twice over.

Their hands, once steady but now made hesitant by the ravages of time, no longer operate lathes and presses making parts of steel for automobiles and sewing machines, guide plows and cultivators preparing fields of springtime for planting wheat and corn, knead flour-covered dough to bake bread for families gathered around gingham-clad tables, or rock the cradles of weary children reluctant to sleep. They no longer toil as lumberjacks and lawyers, beauticians and bankers, ministers and mechanics, printers and plumbers, homemakers and harness makers, stevedores and surgeons, teachers and tailors. Such endeavors are but memories as they live a golden autumn of life extending far beyond what any dared hope. Their work now done, they quietly savor the gentle evening, saddened by the loss of spouses and friends but thankful for the gift of life.

"We Marched and Marched Right in Front of Those Men. "

Hope Doud Fender, who was born August 27, 1893, on a farm near Seton, Illinois, remembers what it was like when the law of the land didn't allow women to vote. "There would be political meetings before, like they have now, and the men would go off in another room somewhere to talk their business. I think that was because there are too many women--that's why they didn't want women voting. They were afraid they'd lose power."

Like other women, Fender didn't like being shut out. "It was kind of stinky of them to try to keep women from voting."

But the Nineteenth Amendment, which Fender's home state was among the first to ratify, changed all that. Fender has vivid memories of the election of 1920, the first election after the Nineteenth Amendment was ratified. "We had a parade that evening. We had such a good time that night. We marched and marched right in front of those men."

A couple of weeks later, the women of the community in which she lived had a potluck dinner for the men of the community to show that they didn't hold a grudge.

While it was not until the Nineteenth Amendment was ratified that women nation-wide were allowed to vote in all elections, Fender and other women living in Illinois could vote for candidates for some offices seven years prior to ratification of the Nineteenth Amendment. In 1913, Illinois Governor Edward F. Dunne signed into law a bill giving women the right to vote "for all political offices not constitutional in nature." Under this law, Illinois women were still excluded from voting for candidates for offices such as governor and lieutenant governor established by the state constitution but could vote for candidates for various county, city and township offices, as well as for electors for President and Vice-President of the United States.[38] In 1916, Fender cast her vote for electors committed to Woodrow Wilson.

Fender had eight older brothers and sisters. She recalls, "Mother always said that she named me 'Hope' because she hoped they wouldn't have any more children--but she had two after me, a boy and a girl."

Like many farm families of that era, they were dirt-poor. One of her earliest memories--dating back to when she was three years old--was of her mother hoping that she would get a pair of glasses for Christmas so that she could read. Every night Fender, while saying her prayers, asked God to help out with the glasses. Her prayers were answered. Somehow her father came up with enough money to buy a pair of glasses for her mother. On Christmas morning, her mother found the glasses hanging on the Christmas tree.

Other childhood memories include finally getting a drilled well, after several years of hauling water from a nearby spring. She was puzzled as to how the windmill attached to the pump drew the water from the well.

Fender has memories of her father and the neighbors talking about the Spanish-American War. Her memories of World War I are even more vivid. She had two brothers who served in the army during the war. One was sent over to France, where the weather caused problems. She recalls that he reported, "We crawled on our bellies in mud for miles." Both brothers survived the war.

When she saw a car for the first time, she "thought that would be a better way of going than with horses." She disliked the smell of the horse sweat on the harnesses.

She also likes trains. "I just loved trains, and they've done away with them all. I just loved to hear the sound of the whistle. It just fascinated me."

Airplanes are a different matter. "I would never ride in them. I never cared for them, though they are pretty to watch." She was twenty-seven when she married. She and her husband farmed for a few years and then moved to Alexis, a small town which straddles the line dividing Warren County and Mercer County in western Illinois. In Alexis, her husband ran a fuel oil business for thirty-two years. She and her husband had no children.

As for the Great Depression of the 1930s, she recalls, "It was terrible the way we had to mix things in the flour to make it go further." But, she adds, "I can't say things were hard with me because I had everything I wanted." Having grown up on a farm when times were tough, she was used to making do with very little.

The public works projects financed by the federal government as part of Roosevelt's New Deal included a new sewer line for the small town in which she and her husband lived. She felt sorry for the men working on the sewer line; the clothes they wore were "just ragged."

Fender has been a widow for nearly four decades. After her husband's death, she moved to a comfortable home in Aledo, Illinois, where she continues to maintain her residence. The living and dining rooms are filled with pictures of family and friends and the trophies she and her husband won at horse shows when they showed their prize-winning Tennessee walker horses, a variety of horses known for their classy gait. Though she has a cleaning lady come in to help with the cleaning, she still gets down on her hands and knees once a week to scrub the floor. That way, she "can be certain it is done right."

When she is not visiting friends or having lunch at the senior citizen center, she makes quilts, sewing together the patches of brightly colored pieces of cloth with tiny stitches that are almost invisible to the untrained eye. Between Christmas and Easter of last year, she made six quilts. In the course of the years, she has made several hundred.

On the walls of her home are pictures of Franklin Delano

Roosevelt and of both John F. and Robert Kennedy. She shook hands with John F. Kennedy when he was running for president. "He just looked like a kid to be running for president," she recalls.

With the exception of one year when ill health prevented her from voting, she has voted in every election since that long-awaited day in 1920 when the Nineteenth Amendment became the law of the land. "We fought so hard to get the vote, so I'm going to make sure to use it."

Politics today, she believes, has a harder edge to it. "We had a lot of fun," she observes. But today, "they seem nuts over it; they get in there and are like a bunch of wild kids."

She adds, "Today, there is a lot of lack of respect for the president. They just talk terrible things about him. That's no way to do it when he's our president."

She is also dismayed by the lack of respect shown by children for their parents. "I think it's terrible the way parents have let the children be the boss in place of themselves."

She believes that many people today are too preoccupied with having things. "People buy things they can't afford and it just leaves them in debt. They think it's the government piling up the debt, but it isn't just the government."

Her advice? "Don't try to keep up with the Jones's all the time." She adds, "My mother and father weren't that way. If the neighbors had something new, that was no sign you needed it. You just got yours when you needed it."[39]

"A Whole Century of Nothing But War"

Grover Cleveland was serving his second term as President of the United States when Conrad Bergendoff was born in Shickley, Nebraska, on December 3, 1895. There were no huge national or international crises dominating the news that day. The front page of the December 3, 1895, edition of *The New York Times* carried stories with headlines reading "Adulteration of Drugs: What Dr. Edward Squibb, Jr., Has to Say on the Subject", "Sing Sing's Big Whistle Tested: The Weather Was Rainy, But It Was Heard Ten Miles Distant," and "Purity Alliance to Meet." Speakers for the upcoming conference of the American Purity Alliance in Boston included Julia Ward Howe on "Moral Equality Between the Sexes" and William Lloyd Garrison on "The Relation of Poverty to Purity."[40]

When Bergendoff was five years old, he moved with his family to Middletown, Connecticut, located halfway between Boston and New York. Middletown dates back to Puritan times. When Bergendoff was spending his childhood years there, the Puritan traditions still defined the mold which gave form to the lives of the citizens of Middletown. In keeping with the ideals of entrepreneurship given expression in the values of the Protestant ethic, he peddled newspapers--issues of *The Penny Press!*--to the residents of the old colonial mansions which lined Middletown's elm-shaded High Street. Among his customers was Bishop Edward C. Acheson, the father of Dean Acheson, later to become Secretary of State during the Truman administration.

Though raised in an old Yankee community, Bergendoff was not of Puritan stock himself. His father, the pastor of the Swedish Tabor Lutheran Church, was an immigrant from Sweden. His mother was born in Princeton, Illinois, the daughter of deeply religious parents who had come from Sweden to till the rich soil to be found in that part of the country. The Bergendoff family took religion seriously with the Sunday service, still held in Swedish, being the central event of the week.

In the rear balcony of the church was a pipe organ, played by a part-time organist who spent the rest of the week working as a grocer. Some complained that the organist played too slowly, but the young Bergendoff, who often was called upon to pump the organ, was quite satisfied with the pace of the music. Other childhood memories include climbing up the dark belfry of the church with his father one night to view Halley's comet.

Bergendoff celebrated his eighth birthday two weeks before

the Wright brothers succeeding in getting their flimsy flying machine airborne on that momentous day in December of 1903. He followed reports of the flight with interest, recalling that it was viewed as "sort of a curiosity." As for its significance, "no one imagined what it might develop into."

As had his father, he went to college at far-away Augustana College, located on the banks of the Mississippi River in western Illinois. After completing his undergraduate studies at Augustana in 1915, he earned an M.A. at the University of Pennsylvania in 1916, studied at Columbia University for a year, followed by two years at the Lutheran Theological Seminary in Philadelphia, and then completed his seminary training in 1921 at Augustana Seminary, which at that time was organizationally linked to Augustana College. After a year spent studying in Uppsala, Sweden, and Berlin, Germany, he completed his graduate work at the University of Chicago, receiving the Ph.D. degree in 1928--one of 1,447 who received doctorates from U.S. universities that year. (Of those receiving doctorates, 1,249 were men, 198 women.[41]) Bergendoff returned to Augustana as dean of the seminary in 1931, retiring as president of the college thirty-one years later.

As he reflects about the changes he has observed, he speaks with great sadness of the impact of "a whole century of nothing but war." He recalls that early in the century, the Carnegie Endowment Fund for International Peace put out a pamphlet asking for ideas as to how to use their funds since it seemed unlikely that there would be any more major wars. The hope was short-lived, for it was not long until World War I enveloped Europe in flames. Bergendoff remembers vividly the August day in 1914 when he heard the news of war breaking out. A junior in college at the time, he was in Michigan helping the pastor of a church for the summer.

"To me, that was the turning point in my life," he states. "From that point on, war, rather than peace, became the background for my thinking." Referring to the millions killed in the wars of this century, he asks, "What does it do to the culture of humanity when the best of your youth are gone?

There's a link gone. They were the carriers of a culture to a new generation. And instead of being there to transmit this culture, there's a gap."

In a commencement address a few years ago, he called on the graduates to work for peace, expressing the hope that there could be a century of peace to succeed the century of war he has known.

As he reminisces about the slice of history he has experienced, he notes that there have been other changes as well, some of them more subtle. Among them, he suggests, has been "a gradual breaking down of all barriers as to freedom and the calling on the First Amendment to defend anything that you say or anything that you do. In Puritan New England, there were definite rules."

"As a child, I could not conceive of divorce being a normal thing. And yet the breakup of the marital relationship and the sexual freedom that now has come to be normal--there are no barriers anymore. Everything goes. And that is something that's radically changed from a time that the social bonds themselves held the society together. And with the loosening of the bonds, there's nothing to hold us together anymore."

While expressing dismay about some of the changes he has witnessed, he has always been supportive of constructive change. Few live to experience the tenth decade of life. Even fewer live ten decades without ever becoming part of the Old Guard. No one who knows Conrad Bergendoff would characterize him as being part of the Old Guard.

He notes that he doesn't know if there has been any greater change than in the relationship of men and women, adding that in his earlier years, it would have been unthinkable for women to be bishops or to be considered for the highest offices in the land. He observes, "This idea of women being able to take their place--men still resist it. I would admit that I welcome it. I still feel that men have oppressed women through the generations--still do, in some ways."

Three decades have passed since Bergendoff retired as president of Augustana College. His wife of fifty-seven years passed away several years ago. He lives by himself in an apartment in a retirement complex a little more than two miles from the campus of the college he served with distinction for so many years. His two daughters and son, none of whom live in the area, stay in touch with him and, in various combinations, spend holidays and share other special events with him. The latest issue of *The Atlantic Monthly*, which he has read regularly for the better part of a century, is to be found on the coffee table in his apartment.

It is a long journey from Connecticut to Illinois, from the last decade of the nineteenth century to the last decade of the twentieth century. The changes that Bergendoff has witnessed and experienced far exceed what anyone could have imagined on that December day in 1895 when he was born. Yet amidst all the change is a deep reservoir of constancy springing from the religious faith imparted by his parents--a faith given expression each day as he gives thanks for the blessings of the day. It is this faith which has sustained him for a century.[42]

"The War Was To Have Been the War To End War, But It Didn't. The Titanic Was Supposed To Be Unsinkable, But It Wasn't."

With American strength in France building rapidly, General Erich Ludendorff, realizing that time was running out for the Kaiser's armies, ordered a spring offensive in 1918, hoping to capture Paris before American troops were deployed in force. The German offensive pushed back the French armies along a sector stretching from Noyon, where four centuries earlier the theologian John Calvin had been born, to Rheims, the site of one of the most beautiful cathedrals ever constructed by human hands. In fierce fighting, German forces under the command of General Fritz von Below reached the River Marne at Chateau-Thierry, a scant thirty-nine miles from the French capital. For the French, the situation was desperate.

General John J. "Black Jack" Pershing welcomed the opportunity to break off the futile pursuit of Pancho Villa and his band of irregulars in northern Mexico in order to accept the more glorious task of commanding the American Expeditionary Force sent to France to help the beleaguered French and British armies. Upon assuming command of the American Expeditionary Force, General Pershing insisted that American troops fight as units, rather than as replacements assigned to depleted French and British units. He also insisted that they not be sent to the front until they were adequately trained. On March 28, 1918, General Pershing, satisfied that the American troops in France were ready to go into action, placed them at the disposal of Marshal Ferdinand Foch, who in the hour of desperation had been appointed supreme commander of allied forces. Marshal Foch ordered American troops into action at Cantigny, at Chateau-Thierry and at Belleau Wood.[43]

Meanwhile, American troops from the New World continued to stream across the Atlantic to fight the battles of the Old World. Among those making the crossing was Wesley W. Cathcart, who served in the 11th U.S. Infantry, which was part of the 5th Division. A farm boy of sturdy Scotch-Irish stock born October 11, 1897, in a sod house with a dirt floor near Palco, Kansas, Cathcart enlisted in the army in Davenport, Iowa, in August of 1917, five months after President Woodrow Wilson asked Congress to declare war on Germany to make the world "safe for democracy."[44]

The convoy which transported Cathcart and the other members of the 11th U.S. Infantry across the Atlantic had a rough crossing. But after fourteen days at sea, much of it in heavy weather, they landed in England.

On a Sunday evening prior to being transported across the English Channel to France, they were given sandwiches to eat. They received nothing more to eat until Tuesday afternoon when, after marching for several hours, they arrived in the camp in France to which they were assigned. There was no one in the camp to fix a meal for them, so they had to peel potatoes and prepare the meal themselves.

The first week in France, Cathcart recalls, "the officers got on this red and white wine and we didn't get much training, so we picked strawberries and helped women put up hay." But picking strawberries and putting up hay wasn't what they were sent to France to do. On October 14, 1918, as they were passing through the lines of the 3rd Division to take their position on the front during the thick of the Meuse-Argonne Offensive, they got hit with an artillery barrage, taking heavy casualties. But they kept moving forward. By the time darkness fell, they had pierced a heavily-fortified German defensive position which had been blocking the allied advance.[45]

The French and the Germans, Cathcart notes, would put up a white flag and take time off from fighting to do their laundry. "It changed when the Americans came."

Cathcart served on a mechanized ammunition train. To reduce the risk of being bombed or strafed by the German biplanes buzzing overhead or being hit by German artillery, they traveled at night. The headlights on the lead truck were taped so that only a small slit of light illuminated the road ahead. The other trucks in the convoy drove without headlights, with the driver following a small light under the bed of the truck ahead, reminiscent of the way circus elephants parade down Main Street, each holding on to the tail of the elephant immediately in front.

One night, the ammunition train traveled in heavy rain until 3:30 a.m., at which time their commanding officer dismissed them and told them to get some sleep, leaving them on their own to find some place to sleep. Cathcart and one of his fellow soldiers found shelter in a bakery wagon. When morning came, Cathcart recalls, they "must have been sleeping pretty sound" because they didn't hear the driver hook up a team of horses to the wagon. When they finally did wake up, they were no longer in camp and had to persuade the driver to return them to camp.

The armistice found the 5th Division knee-deep in mud in the Woevre forest near the village of Jametz.[46] Though there were a few shots fired after the armistice, Cathcart recalls, things pretty much quieted down once the armistice went into effect.

In contrast to other sectors along the front, there was no fraternizing with their German adversaries once the shooting stopped.

After the armistice, Cathcart drove a five-ton Packard truck to Belgium, where he remained for nearly a year as part of the army of occupation, returning to this country in September of 1919. The trip back was somewhat more pleasant than the trip over because having been promoted to first sergeant, he rated a private stateroom on the ship which brought him back. As a result of serving with the army of occupation in Belgium, he missed all of the welcome-home parades and other festivities honoring the victorious troops of the American Expeditionary Force.

After the war, he worked in a small factory in Galva, Illinois, until 1921, when he accompanied his grandfather's coffin to Kansas for burial. His grandfather, a Civil War veteran who served in the Union Army, married Cathcart's grandmother prior to going off to war. She was thirteen at the time.

Cathcart looked unsuccessfully for land to homestead in Wyoming and in Colorado and then returned to Kansas, where he worked for a livestock dealer. From 1923-25, he farmed in Kansas, getting only one crop in three years but making enough that year to come out a little ahead. In 1927, he moved back to western Illinois, where he married and took up carpentry, which supported his family during the lean years of the Depression. He has two children, a son and a daughter.

In 1963, he and his wife moved to Arkansas, where they lived for several years. Their circle of friends in Arkansas included Sam Walton, the founder of Wal-Mart. "Sam was a good fellow," Cathcart notes. "The whole family was. His wife worked with the ladies at church."

Cathcart's wife passed away five years after they celebrated their golden wedding anniversary. In 1984, he remarried. His second wife is in failing health and is now in a nursing home. Though slowed down a bit by the wear and tear of nearly a century, he continues to live by himself in an apartment in a senior citizen high-rise in Galva, Illinois.

Who is the best president to serve in the Oval Office during the years encompassed by Cathcart's life? "Roosevelt," he says without hesitation. "Teddy Roosevelt. He got things done."

He has keen recollections of the news reports of the sinking of the *Titanic*. "The war," he notes with soft-spoken wisdom gained from years of practical experience, "was to have been the war to end war, but it didn't. The *Titanic* was supposed to be unsinkable, but it wasn't."

And that's pretty much the way the first part of this century was--grandiose optimism shattered by brutal reality.[47]

"These Are the People Who Built Our Society"

Ida Will, Frances Woltman, Frances Schellpfeffer and Martha Voss get together almost every day for coffee at the Clearview Nursing Home in Juneau, Wisconsin, where they have lived for a number of years. Their ages add up to nearly four centuries. All have Wisconsin roots dating back to their childhood years. They were all born on farms--Will on a farm between Marshall and Waterloo June 17, 1893, Woltman on a farm near Lebanon May 14, 1899, Schellpfeffer on a farm near Horicon February 28, 1904, and Voss, the "young one" in the bunch, on a farm near Marshfield July 11, 1904. As have many other women their age, all four have outlived their husbands.

The sands of time soften the edges and cover many of the details of days gone by. But even after decades have passed, there are memories of the people, places, and events intertwined in life's experiences.

Will has memories of riding in horse-drawn buggies on dusty roads. She was nineteen when she first saw a car. During the war, she and her husband lived in Milwaukee, where he was a baker for a delicatessen. She has two daughters and one son.

Woltman's twenty-first birthday was a very special day for her: that was the day she and her husband were married. Her husband was a mason, building walls and buildings of brick and stone. She reports that she has "been lucky" all her life, rarely being ill. She has two sons, both of whom live in the Juneau area.

Schellpfeffer, who married in 1927, had two sons, one of whom one was killed in a car accident when he was twenty-nine years old, leaving his widow and four small children. Schellpfeffer and her husband farmed. During the depression years of the 1930s, they couldn't sell the milk their cows produced, so they made butter of the cream from the milk.

Voss also married a farmer. She also made butter, but instead of using a churn to agitate the cream until the milk fat solidified into butter, she found it was much easier to use her washing machine to get the job done. Her husband was a veteran of World War I but would never talk about the war, so terrible was the experience. She has vivid memories of a huge snowstorm in 1935 which kept them snowed in for an entire week. She had six children, one of whom passed away. The family lived in a log house without indoor plumbing.

Clearview Nursing Home, owned and operated by Dodge County in the central part of Wisconsin, is a good place to live when one is no longer able to live by oneself. The facility is modern and well-maintained. The staff is cheerful and helpful. Nursing services are available around the clock. A physician makes rounds five days a week and is on call for emergencies. There are a wide range of activities to encourage residents to remain active, including horseshoes and more varieties of bingo than most people realize exist. And on Fridays there are freshly-baked cookies--scrumptiously wonderful gourmet delights which add quality to the lives of all who have the good fortune of partaking of them.

Medicaid helps pay the costs for more than eighty percent of the residents of Clearview. Fifteen percent are private pay; the remainder receive Medicare coverage.

Proposed reductions in federal funding for Medicaid are of great concern to David Howard, a retired career Army officer who is the administrator of Clearview. He comments, "I have great moral and ethical concerns about our society turning its back on those who are older. These are the people who built our society--the farmers, the merchants, the factory workers and others who are now in need of our help."

The revenues derived from Medicaid, Medicare and private pay leave a $2 million shortfall in Clearview's $20 million annual budget. This is covered by intergovernmental transfer payments utilizing federal matching funds and by a tax levy on county residents. Howard fears that Clearview might lose the federal matching funds as a result of the block grant proposals now in Congress. If this happens, Clearview will either have to cut back on services or ask for an increase in the tax levy on Dodge County residents.[48]

Will, Woltman, Schellpfeffer and Voss are happy to leave worrying about complex financial matters to others. When the centenarian and three nonagenarians get together, the conversation ranges from sad events such as the loss of a roommate to news and events of a more cheerful nature. And on Fridays, there are the freshly-baked cookies, which Woltman takes from the cookie sheets with a spatula as she helps with the serving. Will is very fond of the double-chocolate cookies, though she thinks the chocolate chip cookies are pretty good, too. Voss highly recommends the peanut butter cookies, which remind her of the ones she used to make. Schellpfeffer puts in a good word for all of the varieties available, knowing that you can't go wrong with any of them.[49]

Chapter 4

The World War II Generation

(Born 1906-25)

They were mechanics and machinists, college students and carpenters, farmers and pharmacists, lawyers and linemen. Some were fresh out of high school and had never held a full-time job. Others interrupted busy careers. Some were married and had left their parents' homes to establish their own homes. Others had never left home before. They were sent to places like Anzio and Salerno, Omaha Beach and Bastogne, Guadacanal and Guam, Iwo Jima and Okinawa. Most had never heard of any of these places. None thought of themselves as heroes. But they did what was asked of them as they fought the forces of tyranny in Western Europe and in the Pacific, endeavors which culminated in victory. For those who lived through the war years, whether serving in uniform or working long hours in factories or on farms back home, it was an experience never to be forgotten.

The Dance Was the Charleston
And the Drink Was Gin

The oldest of the World War II Generation were children when Europe was torn apart by World War I, which at that time was known as "The Great War" because no one then knew that there would be an even more terrible war less than thirty years later. Some saw their fathers and their uncles go to war filled with idealism and optimism, only to return deeply disillusioned after encountering the brutal realities of mechanized warfare-- disillusionment which gave rise to rampant cynicism in the post-war years. The costs of World War I extended far beyond the lives lost on the battlefield. The casualties included the traditional beliefs and values which had given shape to people's lives prior to the war.

The oldest of the generation which was to bear the brunt of the costs of World War II spent their teenage years and early years of adulthood in the "Roaring Twenties," when the dance was the Charleston and the drink was gin. In theory, the Eighteenth Amendment to the United States Constitution, ratified January 29, 1919, prohibited "the manufacture, sale, or transportation of intoxicating liquors within, the importation thereof into, or the exportation thereof from the United States and all territory subject to its jurisdiction . . . ." But in practice, gin and other alcoholic beverages were readily available in speakeasies and from bootleggers in an era of inverted values in which many viewed as heroes Al Capone and others who lived outside the law.

From the speakeasies and the private parties, which proliferated in an age given to merriment, came the sexy, syncopated sounds of jazz, which drowned out music of a more conventional sort. For many younger Americans, the saxophone became the national instrument, the inane popular song, "Yes, We Have No Bananas," the new national anthem.

To the consternation of parents who adhered to the values

and traditions of a different era, young women bobbed their hair and wore skirts which were shockingly short. Many of the "flappers," as they came to be known, brazenly violated social convention by smoking cigarettes, stylishly held in long-stemmed cigarette holders. And in the urban east, there were reports of co-ed swimming parties in the buff, even in Boston, once the domain of the stern Puritans who founded the Massachusetts Bay Colony. The erosion of traditional values among younger Americans resulted in a generation gap of unprecedented proportions.

Occupying the Oval Office, as flappers and their friends danced their way through the first part of the Roaring Twenties, was Warren Harding, a man of mediocre abilities given to endless games of bridge. His scandal-ridden administration ended when he died unexpectedly on August 2, 1923, while returning from a tour of the Pacific coast states. "Harding was not a bad man," Alice Roosevelt Longworth, who was Theodore Roosevelt's eldest daughter, said after Harding's death. "He was just a slob."[1]

Calvin Coolidge, a plain-spoken Vermonter who was the complete antithesis both of his predecessor and of those engaged in the non-stop frivolity sweeping across the nation, succeeded Harding. "Silent Cal," as he was tagged by the press because he was just as parsimonious with words as with assets of a more tangible nature, summarized his political philosophy in just six words, "The business of America is business."[2] Longworth, always ready with a sharp-tongued comment, described Coolidge as having been "weaned on a pickle."[3]

Heroes and Years of Prosperity

There were nationally-known figures far more compelling than Coolidge. In a decade many consider to be the golden age of baseball, millions idolized George Herman Ruth, better known simply as "Babe." In 1927, Ruth hit sixty home runs, a record which would stand until Roger Maris topped it in 1961. The 1927 World Series, which the New York Yankees took in four games after having won 110 games in the regular season, was the first to be broadcast nationwide on radio. An estimated thirty-five million Americans listened to the World Series that year.[4]

By the 1920s, the flying contraption Orville and Wilbur Wright managed to get airborne at Kitty Hawk, North Carolina, December 17, 1903, had been obsolete for more than a decade. New airplanes, many of them sleek monoplanes with powerful rotary engines, pushed aviation to new heights and ever-greater distances. At 7:54 a.m. on May 20, 1927, Charles A. Lindbergh, in pursuit of a cash prize of $25,000 for the first solo flight across the Atlantic, managed to get his heavily-loaded single-engine monoplane, *The Spirit of St. Louis*, airborne from Roosevelt Field on Long Island, clearing the telephone lines at the end of the runway by only twenty feet. Thirty-three and a half hours later, he landed at Paris's Le Bourget Field.[5]

Lindbergh received the Cross of the Légion d'Honneur from the President of France. King George V of England sent word that he wanted to receive him in audience. After meeting with Lindbergh, the king described him as "quite a feller."[6] When Lindbergh returned to this country, making the return trip as a passenger on the *U.S.S. Memphis* along with *The Spirit of St. Louis*, which had been dissembled and crated, he was unable to escape the adulation of an adoring public. When he was honored with a ticker tape parade in New York, his motorcade was showered with eighteen hundred tons of ticker tape, shredded telephone directories, and anything else that could be torn up to make confetti.[7]

It was quite a year--Lindbergh crossing the Atlantic in *The Spirit of St. Louis* and Babe Ruth hitting sixty home runs. The economy was booming, jobs were plentiful and millions of Americans were enjoying unprecedented levels of prosperity.

And then, less than two years later, it all came apart.

"Hoovervilles" and "Okies"

On October 22, 1928, Herbert Hoover, the Republican candidate for president that year, wrapped up his campaign with a speech in New York in which he declared, "We are nearer today to the ideal of the abolition of poverty and fear from the lives of men and women than ever before in any land."[8] Notwithstanding the fact that Babe Ruth supported Democratic presidential candidate Al Smith (who was not a keen supporter of prohibition), Hoover won in a landslide. When he took the oath of office March 4, 1929, the nation was prosperous. "I have no fears about the future of our country," Hoover confidently declared. "It is bright with hope."[9]

As far as most Americans were concerned, there was no reason to disagree with Hoover's optimistic assessment. The stock market continued to climb to new heights. Apart from the farm belt, where the heavy indebtedness of many farmers was a problem, the future looked brighter than it ever had at any previous time in the nation's century-and-a-half of existence.

The picture was far different after Tuesday, October 29, 1929, which, in the words of economist John Kenneth Galbraith, "combined all of the bad features of all of the bad days before."[10] It was on this day that the stock market suffered the greatest crash in its history, a crash which was a harbinger of the greatest economic crisis this country has ever experienced.

Industrial production plummeted. As factories were shuttered, workers lost their jobs. By the end of 1930, nearly seven million workers in the United States were unemployed; two years later, the figure had doubled.[11] Thousands of banks collapsed as panicked depositors rushed to withdraw their savings; many didn't get there in time, losing their savings when bank doors slammed shut in their faces.

And as if the bad economic news wasn't trouble enough, nature stirred up more trouble. A terrible drought parched the Great Plains. With the soil stripped of its protective cover as crops withered and died, hot winds blew away half of Oklahoma and surrounding states. Desperate and distressed people, having lost their farms, their jobs and their homes, packed whatever they could on rattle-trap automobiles and trucks and headed wherever they thought they might find work. Over a five-year period, more than a quarter million "Okies" and "Arkies" from Oklahoma and Arkansas made their way to southern California, where, rumor had it, there were jobs to be found picking fruit in the orchards and vineyards of "a land flowing with milk and honey." There were very few jobs, and such jobs as there were paid very little and didn't last very long. Mostly, what those traveling to California found was still more shattered dreams, a heart-breaking human drama vividly portrayed by John Steinbeck in his 1939 novel, *The Grapes of Wrath*, which was awarded a Nobel Prize.

Thousands of previously-prosperous Americans found themselves cooking what little food they could scrounge up on converted oil drums in shanty towns, which they bitterly called "Hoovervilles." World War I veterans marched on Washington, demanding immediate payment of the bonus Congress had promised them in 1924. President Hoover ordered the army to move them out of the camp they had set up. Federal troops with fixed bayonets and tear gas canisters routed them from their camp and torched their shanties, injuring several of the protesting veterans in the process. The federal troops were under the command of General Douglas MacArthur.[12]

From today's perspective, we know that the Great Depression didn't last forever and that economic recovery eventually occurred. But for those who experienced the terrible times of the 1930s, there was no assurance that would happen. Notwithstanding the election of Franklin Delano Roosevelt in 1932 with his bold assurance that "the only thing we have to fear is fear itself" and his alphabet soup of New Deal programs, recovery was distressingly slow. Many doubted that recovery would ever occur. Some were ready to junk capitalism for socialism or some other type of economic system.

While economists and politicians today continue to debate

the efficacy of New Deal programs, the historical reality is that full recovery did not occur until war once again broke out in Europe and American factories geared up to supply the British and their allies. It is one of the greatest ironies of history that it took the terrible disaster of war to bring an end to the most devastating economic disaster the United States has ever known.

The Dogs of War Unleashed

Today, in an era in which a sense of historical perspective is often lacking, there are those who assume that the United States was involved in World War II from start to finish. But like so many other things that are widely believed, that is not true. The war in Europe, which lasted nearly six years, had been devouring Europe for more than two years before the United States entered the war. In the Far East, the war had been going on even longer--nearly a decade.

Many today who are too young to remember World II, but who know from first-hand experience how deeply divided the nation was during the Vietnam era, falsely assume that the American people were of one mind when it came to getting involved in World War II. While the American people were united once the United States entered the war, prior to Pearl Harbor there were sharply differing views as to whether the United States should join Great Britain and her allies in the desperate struggle to prevent all of Europe from being crushed under the heel of Adolf Hitler.

Among those opposing any type of U.S. involvement was Charles Lindbergh, who became the most prominent spokesperson for the America First Committee, a group which insisted that the United States should keep its distance from the war in Europe. In a speech Lindbergh made on April 17, 1941, he asserted that "it is physically impossible to base enough aircraft in the British Isles alone to equal in strength the aircraft that can be based on the continent of Europe."[13] In a speech in St.Louis two weeks later, he stated, "I have seen France fall, I see England falling, and now America is being led into the same morass."[14]

Among those favoring U.S. intervention was Reinhold Niebuhr, who had been a pacifist in the years immediately following World War I. Writing in the December 18, 1940, issue of *The Christian Century*, he called for the U.S. intervention "to prevent the triumph of an intolerable tyranny." Those opposing military intervention, he asserted, must be challenged "lest we deliver the last ramparts of civilization into the hands of the new barbarians."[15]

Roosevelt, who favored helping the embattled British, managed to get his lend-lease bill through Congress in March of 1941. Officially titled "An Act Further to Promote the Defense of the United States," the lend-lease bill for all practical purposes ended neutrality by making the United States, as Roosevelt put it, "the arsenal of democracy" supporting the British, who, after the fall of France, stood alone in the face of Hitler's juggernaut.[16]

Pearl Harbor ended any pretense of neutrality. Hitler, it turned out, was as surprised by the attack on Pearl Harbor as were Roosevelt and British Prime Minister Winston Churchill. After temporizing for a few days, Hitler abandoned his policy of trying to avoid war with the New World and, on December 11, 1941, declared war on the United States, which resulted in the U.S. Congress declaring war with Germany later the same day.[17]

Roosevelt boldly stated in his message to Congress asking for a declaration of war with Japan, "With confidence in our armed forces--with the unbounding determination of our people-- we will gain the inevitable triumph--so help us God."[18] In a "fireside chat" to the nation following the declaration of war with Japan, he stated, "We are going to win the war and we are going to win the peace that follows."[19]

But notwithstanding the President's brimming optimism, the outcome of the war was far from certain. In the weeks and months which followed Pearl Harbor, the war news was almost all bad. Front-page headlines in *The New York Times* the first five months of 1942 tell the story:

> *Manila in Peril as Reinforced Foe Closes In* (January 1); *Manila and Cavite Base Fall, Army Fights On;* (January 3); *Foe Gains in Malaya and Borneo* (January 5); *Enemy Pushes within 150 Miles of Singapore* (January 13); *Third Ship Torpedoed off the Atlantic Coast* (January 19); *Two More Ships Torpedoed off Coast, 46 Dead* (January 22); *Enemy 40 Miles from Singapore* (January 29); *Axis Regains Derna on Libyan Coast; Rommel Advances* (February 5); *Japanese Land on Singapore Isle* (February 9); *15th Ship Is Sunk off Our Atlantic Coast* (February 12); *Singapore Surrenders Unconditionally; Churchill Asks Unity in Hour of Defeat; Foe Pours into Sumatra, Strikes in Burma* (February 16); *U.S., Norwegian Ships New U-Boat Victims off Atlantic Coast; Twenty Die in Blazing Sea* (February 22); *Submarine Shells California Oil Plant* (February 24); *Japanese Invade New Guinea at 2 Points; Claim Rangoon and Push West in Burma* (March 9); *Armed Ship Victim of U-Boat; 31 Lost in a Sea of Flame* (March 16); *Foe Takes Outposts in Bataan Attack* (April 2); *Corregidor Surrenders under Land Attack after Withstanding 300 Raids from the Air* (May 6); *Philippines Lost; Wainright a Prisoner with End of Organized Resistance on Isles* (May 7)

But as Admiral Isoroku Yamamoto, who had masterminded the attack on Pearl Harbor, had predicted, the tide of the war turned once the United States mobilized its immense industrial capacity and began producing airplanes, tanks and ships in unprecedented numbers. In a very basic sense, World War II was won in U.S. factories and shipyards, as much as on the battlefield.

In North Africa, a successful allied campaign proved that German Field Marshall Erwin Rommel, known as "The Desert

Fox" for his prowess, was not invincible. Allied landings at Salerno and Anzio put Hitler's *Wehrmacht* on the defensive in Italy. Meanwhile, the Red Army continued to hammer away at Hitler's once-unstoppable legions on the eastern front. More airplanes than anyone had imagined could be in one place at one time swarmed from landing fields in the British Isles and knocked the vaunted *Luftwaffe* out of the sky over Europe, dramatically proving false Lindbergh's pessimistic prediction. Huge quantities of ammunition and supplies piled up in England as the allies prepared to invade occupied France. "If it were not for the barrage balloons holding things up," a one-liner making the rounds ran, "England would sink into the sea." On June 6, 1944, allied forces landed on the beaches of Normandy and began the advance which, though halted temporarily during the hard-fought Battle of the Bulge in December of that year, took them to Germany and the end of the war.

By then the tide had turned in the Pacific as well--in May and June of 1942 at the battles of Coral Sea and Midway, and at Guadacanal later that year. Then, after nearly a year spent building up strength, it was on to the Gilbert Islands in November, 1943, where bloody Tarawa underscored the need for improved tactics for amphibious landings. The bitter lessons learned at Tarawa were put to use in the Marshall Islands and the Marianas Islands the following year. Gaining control of the Marianas, which included Guam (a U.S. territory Japan had occupied three days after Pearl Harbor), put long-range B-29 bombers within striking distance of Japan itself. The next spring, the bloody conquest of Iwo Jima provided a landing site for crippled bombers returning bombing runs over Japan and bases for fighters to protect them.

When Germany surrendered on May 7, 1945, U.S. forces in the Pacific were involved in a bitter fight for Okinawa, with *kamikaze* pilots raining destruction from the sky on naval units supporting the invasion. Meanwhile, preparations were underway for the invasion of Japan, which everyone expected to be a bloodbath. On August 6, 1945, a lone B-29--the *Enola Gay*--

flew over Hiroshima, Japan, and dropped the most devastating and terrifying weapon ever devised by human hands, ushering in the nuclear age. On August 9, a second atomic bomb was dropped on Nagasaki. The next day, the Japanese government sued for peace, with hostilities ending August 14. Formal surrender ceremonies took place on the *U.S.S. Missouri* in Tokyo Bay September 2. The war was over.

The Post-War Years

For many in the World War II Generation, the post-war years have been both anticlimactic and filled with unexpected blessings. During the Great Depression of the 1930s and the war years which followed, they went through two terrible experiences in which life was very precarious. But in both cases, they persevered.

When called upon to fight in the war or work in the factories and on the farms supporting the war effort, they discovered a mission and a sense of purpose which contrasted sharply with the uncertainty and lack of direction which characterized the preceding two decades. They made great sacrifices during the war years; victory came with a stiff price tag attached to it. But it was sacrifice for something worth fighting for--a cause which touched the very heart of what it was to be an American. Even though few entered the war with banners flying, it was a war with a purpose, a war which was fought to protect the ideals on which this nation was founded. And most important of all, it ended with victory. Few days in the history of all of humankind have been filled with as much jubilation and relief as V-E Day and V-J Day.

Given the emotionally-intense nature of the war experience, it was inevitable that the war years would be anticlimactic for the World War II Generation. But, though low-keyed compared with what had preceded them, the post-war years brought a whole new set of unexpected experiences. For many of the

World War II Generation, the post-war years were years of prosperity. Just as few expected the 1930s to be years of economic disaster, most did not expect the post-war years to turn out the way they did. For the World War II Generation, many of whom had spent their childhood years or their early years of adulthood experiencing the poverty and deprivation of the Great Depression, they were years of blessings beyond their wildest expectations.

The post-war prosperity that many members of the World War II generation came to experience, of course, did not just happen. Returning veterans and those who had served on the home front worked hard, bringing to the work place the dedication and determination which had characterized their participation in the war effort. Many were aided by government programs, such as the G.I. bill which enabled them to continue their education and Veterans Administration loan programs which helped them purchase homes.

Today, most members of the World War II generation are retired from the work force. They benefit greatly from Social Security and Medicare and from other publicly-funded programs oriented toward older Americans. During the war years, they made great sacrifices for their country. In the post-war years, their country has been generous to them.

"I Try Not To Think about It"

In contrast to 1939, when Hitler ordered German U-boats to take pre-assigned positions along British shipping lanes in anticipation of hostilities breaking out, there were no U-boats prowling the coastal shipping lanes on the U.S. side of the Atlantic when Japanese naval forces launched their attack on Pearl Harbor. But once hostilities had been declared, Admiral Karl Dönitz, who commanded German submarine forces, lost no time putting together an attack plan which targeted shipping along the U.S. Atlantic coast--an operation code-named *Pauken-*

schlag (Drumroll). After the war, Admiral Dönitz became a devout Christian. But that was to come later. During the war, his devotion was to Adolf Hitler, his obsession destroying Germany's adversaries.[20]

Columns of black smoke from torpedoed ships became familiar sights along the U.S. coast from New York to Florida. To the astonishment of the German U-boat skippers, the U.S. cities along the coast did not blacken out their lights at night. Brightly-lit cities silhouetted the freighters and tankers hugging the shoreline, making them easy targets for the U-boats loitering offshore. When U.S. naval authorities asked cities along the coast to dim their lights at night, the owners of the luxury hotels in Atlantic City, Miami and other popular resort areas protested that "the tourist season would be ruined." And so to avoid interfering with the tourist season, the lives of hundreds of seamen were lost as marauding U-boats sank the ships on which they were serving. It was not until April 18 that the order went out to dim waterfront lights, with the order mandating a complete blackout not being issued until May 18.[21]

The 3rd Naval Construction Battalion, a unit of "Seabees" based in Norfolk, Virginia, had the job of salvaging torpedoed ships. Among the divers assigned to the 3rd Naval Construction Battalion was T.D. "Dale" Vinette. Born on June 18, 1915, in Nahma, Michigan, to a family of French origins whose history in North America dates back nearly four centuries, he was somewhat older than many of the recruits who volunteered to serve in the Navy after Pearl Harbor. Because of his prior diving experience and having graduated in 1936 from the Merchant Marine Academy, then located in Washington, D.C., he was offered a rating of first class diver when he enlisted. When he went to the Great Lakes Naval Training Station for basic training, he was assigned to a company which included other older recruits--a company which proved nearly impossible to teach the finer points of marching in step or standing in a straight line when at parade rest. When graduation day arrived, Vinette's company was ordered to sit in the grandstand and watch the graduation ceremony, rather than march in it.

But marching wasn't why the Navy had recruited him. He was recruited because of his skills as a diver, developed over a period of several years prior to the war. The Navy had work for him to do up and down the Atlantic Coast--more work than the brass really wanted to have since when a call went out to the 3rd Naval Construction Battalion, it was often because a ship had been torpedoed or something else had gone wrong.

In November of 1942, Vinette was assigned to a joint U.S.-British underwater demolition team which participated in the landing at Oran as American, British, Canadian and Free French troops under the command of General Dwight D. Eisenhower opened a second front in North Africa, linking up with British forces under the command of General Bernard "Monty" Montgomery at Tunis six months later. Vinette received a Sliver Star for his role in the landing at Oran. The months following the landing at Oran found Vinette, who was promoted to chief petty officer in December of 1942, degaussing magnetic mines laid by German submarines off the shore of Bermuda, doing salvage work on the *Normandie*, which had burned and rolled over on its side while moored at Pier 89 in New York Harbor, and attending Officer Candidate School in Williamsburg, Virginia. After completing Officer Candidate School, he was promoted to warrant officer and assigned to the newly-formed 301st Naval Construction Battalion in the Pacific theater.

Vinette spent the rest of the war in the Pacific. He was at Kwajalein, where he did salvage work. Then it was on to Saipan, where he was part of an underwater demolition team. Then Guam, where his detachment went in ahead of the 77th Army Infantry Division to blow up underwater obstacles which might impede their landing. He was with an underwater demolition group at Pelau and at Iwo Jima, where he landed four hours before the initial wave went ashore. While pinned down by heavy Japanese machine gun fire coming from the heights overlooking the beach, Vinette crawled over to help a Navy medic tend to the wounds of a Marine who had been hit. The Marine turned out to be from Escanaba, Michigan, where Vinette had lived prior to the war.

During the battle for Okinawa, his detachment was sent in to clear a harbor needed to supply American troops. They landed at the major airport on Okinawa before it was secured. Their plane crashed when landing, but the passengers and crew escaped with only minor injuries. Then it was back to Guam, where he was based between special assignments.

Vinnette's recollections of wartime experiences include a rescue operation to save crew members trapped in a U.S. submarine which struck a reef while on patrol approximately two hundred miles south of Japan. Vinette and three of the divers working for him were assigned to the rescue operation. Using a diving bell lowered from a rescue vessel, they descended to the disabled submarine eight times over a period of twenty-eight hours, saving the thirty-three surviving crew members. The display of medals on Vinette's office wall includes a Navy Cross for this mission.

In the early days of August, while still at Guam, he was asked to take two fully-equipped divers to the neighboring island of Tinian and stand by while some "valuable cargo" was unloaded from a heavy cruiser. Their job was to recover as quickly as possible the crates containing the cargo in the event that it was lost overboard during the unloading process. The cargo was unloaded without incident, so they didn't have to do any diving that day. The heavy cruiser was the *U.S.S. Indianapolis*.

A few days later when he came up from a dive, he heard news of a huge explosion over a Japanese city caused by a new weapon of some type that had been dropped from an airplane. That new weapon was the valuable cargo which had been unloaded from the *U.S.S. Indianapolis*.

When the war ended, Vinette and other men in his unit thought they would be going home. But there was still salvage work to be done. It was not until Christmas Eve of 1945 that he returned to his hometown of Escanaba, Michigan. He was released from active duty two months later.

Vinnette's wife--they were married in June of 1941-- remained in Michigan during the war, where she taught school.

She passed away in 1968. Vinette remarried in 1971.

After the war, Vinette established a boat-building and marine storage firm in Escanaba, located on Little Bay de Noc on Michigan's Upper Peninsula. In the five decades which have passed since the firm was established, the T.D. Vinette Company has built more than three hundred steel and aluminum boats of various sizes. Two of his step-sons now operate the boat yard, though he still stops by the office almost every day to see how things are going.

Even after half a century, he cannot escape the war. He still has nightmares about removing bodies from sunken ships. When he awakens in the middle of the night, he cannot expunge from his mind the smell of decomposing bodies.

"I try not to think about it," he says, knowing full well that it is impossible for him to forget the war.[22]

"It Was a Terrible, Frightening Sight to See"

When it became clear that the Pacific fleet would be based at Pearl Harbor for extended operations, Joe Giovenazzo's wife borrowed money from her parents and notified him that she would be joining him in Honolulu. Though he didn't think that was such a good idea with tensions in the Pacific growing, he found a small bungalow for them to live in, and she joined him there.

Born in Johnstown, Pennsylvania, April 28, 1916, Giovenazzo, the son of Italian immigrants, moved with his family to Silvis, Illinois, while still a child. When Giovenazzo was old enough to go to work, his father, who worked for the fabled Rock Island Line, got him set up with a job in the round house servicing steam locomotives. But with the nation in the midst of the Great Depression and work rules favoring those with more seniority, he was frequently laid off. In December of 1935, he joined the Navy.

He was one of fifty in his class at the Great Lakes Naval

Training Station to be assigned to the *U.S.S. Arizona*, where he served for four-and-a-half years. In 1939, Joe got a letter from his younger brother, Mike, who had also joined the Navy. Joe encouraged Mike to put in for the *Arizona* so the two of them could serve together, which they did until Joe was transferred to a destroyer that had been converted to a minesweeper, where he served for a year until transferring to the repair ship *U.S.S. Vestal* in August of 1941.

On the first Saturday in December of that year, the *Vestal* was tied up to the *Arizona*, moored on battleship row on the southeast side of Ford Island right in the middle of Pearl Harbor. Both the *Vestal* and the *Arizona* had personnel inspections that day. When Joe completed his, he boarded the *Arizona* and waited for Mike. When Mike was free to go on liberty, the two brothers, joined by a marine who shared the same home town, went to Joe's bungalow, where his wife had lunch waiting.

Joe had tickets for the football game that afternoon--the University of Hawaii was playing Willamette in the annual Shrine game. Because he was feeling a bit under the weather from the shots he was required to have after signing up for another hitch in the Navy, he gave his ticket to Mike.

The previous week at the Army-Navy game back in the States, the game program included a picture of the *Arizona*. The caption alongside the picture boasted, "It is significant that despite the claims of air enthusiasts no battleship has yet been sunk by bombs."[23]

Mike joined Joe and his wife at their bungalow for dinner after the game. Joe tried to talk Mike into staying at the bungalow that night, but Mike decided to head back to the *Arizona*.

Giovenazzo was awakened the next morning by a neighbor pounding at the door, saying that Pearl Harbor was under attack. Giovenazzo quickly put on his uniform and headed for the harbor. At the landing for the liberty boat, he met two of his shipmates from the *Vestal*, who were also hoping to return to their ship. That was not possible. The *Vestal* had been cut loose from the *Arizona* and towed away from the burning battleship.

Giovenazzo heard later that the skipper of the *Vestal*, Commander Cassin Young, had been blown overboard when the *Arizona* exploded but climbed back on board and resumed command of the ship, giving the order to cast off from the *Arizona*.

Since it was not possible for Giovenazzo and the two shipmates he met at the landing to return to the *Vestal*, they boarded a small rescue craft which was departing for Ford Island. As they made their way to Ford Island, they could see the *Arizona* in flames, the *Oklahoma* turned over on its side, and heavy smoke rolling up from several other ships.

"It was a terrible, frightening sight to see," Giovenazzo sadly recalls.

When Giovenazzo and his two shipmates from the *Vestal* landed on Ford Island, a chief gunner's mate ordered them to draw three .50 caliber machine guns from the armory located on the island. Even though they had no prior experience with machine guns, they were ordered to take positions on the roof of the enlisted men's mess hall. By now (9:00 a.m.), the attacking Japanese planes were dropping armor-piercing bombs from altitudes well beyond the range of their machine guns. But they fired at the attacking planes anyhow, hoping to hit one. Two hours later, they were ordered to leave the mess hall roof and reposition their machine guns on the nearby Ford Island radio tower. They remained on alert until 1:00 a.m. the next morning, when they were finally relieved and instructed to get some sleep in the barracks.

Barely had Giovenazzo stretched out on a bunk and closed his eyes when he was awakened by a petty officer who ordered him to go back on duty. He was given a pistol and a boat hook and taken to the overturned hull of the *Oklahoma*, where he was assigned to security while work crews cut through the hull to rescue those trapped inside, some of whom were tapping against the hull of the overturned battleship to help rescuers locate them.

The boat hook, Giovenazzo was told, was to pull from the water the bodies of those who hadn't made it. He shuddered at the thought that his brother might be among them.

The next day, when he was finally able to get back to the *Vestal*, his commanding officer let him take some time off to look for his brother. Giovenazzo talked with a chief petty officer from the *Arizona* who had the list of names of those who had been rescued from the ship and those who had reported to other ships. Mike's name was not on either list. The chief petty officer, who himself had lost two brothers on the *Arizona*, talked about the situation with Giovenazzo, noting that it would have been very difficult to get out of the area on the ship in which Mike was likely to be sleeping, given the way the ship was constructed and where it had been hit. To Giovenazzo fell the sad duty of calling his parents to inform them that Mike hadn't made it.

Shortly after Christmas, the Giovenazzo family back in Illinois got a telegram from the Navy Department stating that Mike had survived. Overjoyed with the news, they bought a turkey on credit at a local grocery store and had a special family dinner celebrating the wonderful turn of events. It was a false report. Someone somewhere in the military bureaucracy had apparently confused the two brothers.

Giovenazzo served on several other ships during the war, including an escort carrier that nearly got hit by kamikaze pilots during the Battle of Okinawa. The escort carrier on which he was serving when the war ended was anchored offshore when the formal surrender ceremonies took place in Tokyo Bay.

After the war, Giovenazzo legally changed his name to "Givens" to simplify the spelling. He stayed in the Navy until 1955, when he was eligible to retire after twenty years of service. He worked five years at Ryan Aeronautical Company in San Diego building KC-135 tankers (an Air Force tanker built on the Boeing 707 airframe). In 1965, he "fully retired."

He has three daughters, a son, eleven grandchildren and four great-grandchildren. On May 17, 1980, he married for the third time. His wife, Iris, framed their marriage certificate and hung it on the living room wall of their home in Silvis, Illinois. "This one's permanent," he says with a good-natured smile covering his congenial face.

Events have taken him to many parts of the world. Overshadowing all of his life experiences, however, is a December day which, in the words of Franklin Delano Roosevelt, will forever be remembered as "a day of infamy."[24]

"I Am Not Hateful"

In 1915 near the town of León, Mexico, located in the state of Guanajuato about 150 miles north of Mexico City, a terrible series of battles lasting more than a month took place between the opposing forces of Francisco "Pancho" Villa and General Alvara Obregón. The two had fought together to overthrow the brutal dictatorship of Porfirio Díaz in 1910 but were now bitter rivals.[25] Several thousand men lost their lives in this senseless slaughter, which devastated the crops and the lives of the families who made Guanajuato their home. Homeless and hungry and having had enough of the havoc of war, many left their farms and villages and headed north, some walking, others riding whatever they could find, all hoping to find a better life across the border.

Among those making the journey was Juan Pompa, who, along with his young wife, Jesus Maria Segura, made his way to Dodge City, Kansas. Dodge City was a rough-and-tumble cow town where just a few years earlier hell-raising cowboys shot up the town with abandon when unwinding after long days on dusty trails driving herds of cattle up from Texas.

Clara Pompa Knox was born in Dodge City. When she was two years old, the family moved back to Mexico--back to the León area where there had been so much trouble less than a decade earlier. Her younger brother and sister were born while the family was in Mexico--an accident of birth which was to cause problems for Knox's brother, Tony, in subsequent years.

In 1927, the Pompa family was on the move again, this time to Silvis, Illinois, where Clara's father found work with the Rock Island Line building and repairing track. Because housing was not available elsewhere, the Pompas and several other Mexican-American families lived in the Silvis railroad yard, some in boxcars, others in small company-owned houses. The Pompa family, along with two other families, lived in a very crowded boxcar. Coming from a culture in which family and church are very important, the Mexican-American families living in the railroad yard moved two boxcars together to make a church where the families comprising the congregation of Our Lady of Guadalupe Mission could worship together.

In 1928, the citizens of Silvis, outraged that the Mexican-American families living in the railroad yard weren't paying city taxes since they weren't living within the city limits, pressured the railroad into evicting the Mexican-American families from the railroad yard.[26] So the Pompa family had to move again.

Finding another place to live, however, was no simple manner in an era in which prejudice was rampant. The Pompas were turned away from many places. Finally, they and twenty-one other Mexican-American families built small homes along an unpaved two-block street on the west side of Silvis where no one else wanted to live. Billy Goat Hill, which overlooks the street, became a playground of sorts where the children of the families living along the street played war games, threw green apples at each other, and tumbled and slid down the hill.

When the United States became involved in World War II, Tony Pompa was the first one from Second Street to leave to go to war. Having lost a job at nearby Rock Island Arsenal when it was discovered that he was not a U.S. citizen since, unlike his older sister, he was born in Mexico, he lied about his age and enlisted under a false name in the Army Air Corps, having heard that one could become a U.S. citizen by serving in the armed forces. After completing training, he became a tail gunner on a B-24 Liberator.

The Pompa family didn't know what had happened to him until at long last, a letter from him arrived in the mail. Like many others serving in the military, he was less than enthusiastic about the food in the mess hall and more than a little homesick.

Tony Pompa was the first of six young men from Second Street to lose his life during the war. His B-24, which the crew had nicknamed "Sinner's Dream," was hit January 31, 1944, while flying over northern Italy. Pompa's parachute got tangled up and he went down with the plane, which burst into flames when it hit the ground.

Two more young men from Second Street lost their lives in Korea. Today, in honor of the eight who gave their lives for their country, the street is known as "Hero Street USA" and has been featured on network television and in national publications. The street is now paved, and Billy Goat Hill has been made into a park honoring all the young men and women from Hero Street USA who have served in uniform. A committee of area residents is raising funds to build a monument to honor the memory of the eight who gave their lives and to give recognition to all who have served in uniform.

In 1948, Clara Pompa Knox married and moved to a house just a few blocks away from Hero Street USA, where she lives today. Her husband, who passed away in 1982 a couple of years after retiring from one of the Deere & Co. plants located in the area, was Dutch and Irish and, as he used to put it, "a little bit bulldog."

One of Knox's three sons now lives in the house on Hero Street USA in which she once lived. Her sons have all experienced educational opportunities far beyond those available to her. And unlike her, they have not had to go without shoes or worry about whether there would be enough to eat.

Times have changed in other ways as well. Knox has painful memories of being forced to eat outside because restaurants would not allow Mexican-Americans to eat inside and of being forced to sleep in her family's car because no hotel or motel would rent a room to Mexican-Americans. But she does not allow anger to get the better of her.

"I am not hateful," she quietly states.[27]

"That's the Way It Was"

When Carl Harrell of Beaumont, Texas, answered the telephone, he began the interview by asking, "Have you read that book *Grapes of Wrath* or seen that movie with Henry Fonda in it? Well, that's the way it was."

Harrell was born November 12, 1922, in Broken Bow, Oklahoma. His father, a "jack-of-all-trades" who from time-to-time worked as a cabinet maker or did some carpentry, "always wanted to be a farmer, but didn't have much success at it." When Harrell was a year old, the family moved to Oklahoma City, where his father worked in a blacksmith shop. Then they moved to Tulsa, Oklahoma, where they lived for a brief period of time before moving to Pine Bluff, Arkansas, where his father worked for a cabinet maker. Though skilled as a cabinet maker, his father always "had this itch for farming" and went back to sharecropping, buying everything on credit with the hope that he would be able to pay off the loans when the cotton was ready to be picked and could be sold. When Harrell was six, the family loaded everything in their Model T touring car and moved to Columbus, Georgia, for another try at farming, and then back again to Pine Bluff in 1929.

"That's when all them California people put out flyers about wanting fruit pickers," he recounts. So the Harrell family once again loaded everything they owned in their Model T touring car and headed for California. Harrell and his three younger sisters (his younger brother was born later) slept in the car while his parents slept on pallets by the car. It took them three months to get to California since they would "run out of gas and money and pick cotton to get moving again." But when they finally got to Stockton, California, they had no trouble finding work.

They stayed in Stockton until the summer of 1932, when his father "got that farming itch again." It took them three months of traveling and picking cotton to get back to Pine Bluff, where his father once again tried his hand at sharecropping--this time just as the Great Depression was wreaking havoc with the American people.

Roosevelt managed to get Congress to approve the Civilian Conservation Corps (CCC) as part of the New Deal legislation enacted during his first hundred days in office. The CCC employed young men to work on projects such as reforestation, flood control and swamp drainage. They were paid $30 a month, $5 of which they got to keep, the remaining $25 sent back to their families.

Harrell's father decided to sign him up for the CCC, even though he was only fourteen at the time and the minimum age was seventeen. But he was tall for his age, and his father decided to "swear to a lie" and say he was seventeen. Harrell spent six months in a work camp on the banks of the Clearwater River in Idaho and another six months in Oregon fighting forest fires and building fences, before transferring back to Sulphur Springs, Arkansas, so that he could spend the last year in what was listed as his home state.

After doing odd jobs in Georgia and Arkansas for awhile, Harrell went back to California, where he got a job working for a brother-in-law as a bookkeeper in a linoleum store. On December 7, 1941, he was "sitting in a picture show" to which he had taken his nephews when the stunning news about Pearl Harbor was announced.

After Christmas, he left California for Beaumont, Texas, and went to work in a shipyard building cargo and transport ships. In July of 1942, he enlisted in the Navy. After completing basic training at Great Lakes Naval Training Station in Illinois, he received orders to report to a destroyer based in Norfolk, Virginia. The day after he reported aboard, it left for the invasion of North Africa.

After completing escort duties in support of Allied operations in North Africa, Harrell's ship returned to its home port, where he had six days leave. The ship then headed for Plymouth, England, as part of the build-up of naval forces for the Normandy landing. On D-Day, they were assigned shore support duties off Omaha Beach, with orders to help evacuate the troops who had gone ashore, should the need arise. After Normandy, they were involved in the landing in southern France near Marseille. Between invasions, they made runs to Norway and Iceland.

On October 13, 1945, Harrell was honorably discharged from the Navy. After the war, he returned to Beaumont, joined the ironworkers union, and spent thirty-seven years building prefabricated buildings, twenty of these years traveling to various parts of the country. He is active in his local Veterans of Foreign Wars Post, serving as quartermaster after having been through the rotation of officers twice.

He has four grown sons and seven grandchildren. With sadness in his voice, he notes that he and the boys' mother "didn't see eye to eye." Their marriage, which began in 1947, ended in 1967.

The post-war years have been good to him--he had a good job as an ironworker and has enjoyed a degree of financial security which far exceeded what his parents experienced. Yet, like others who endured the depression and fought to defeat the forces of tyranny during the World War II, the good times are not what he talks about. It is in times of difficulty that one discovers the true measure of a person. For Harrell, the war years and the difficult times which preceded them were his finest hour.[28]

"The Statue of Liberty Looked Great!"

Born on a farm near Harvard, Nebraska, on September 14, 1922, Wayne Ross worked as an auto mechanic before enlisting in the Army Air Corps in September of 1943. After completing training, he served as a waist gunner on a B-24 Liberator nicknamed "Sinner's Dream", which was part of the 449th Bomber Group based in southern Italy. On January 31, 1944, "Sinner's Dream" lifted off the runway for a bombing mission in northern Italy, which was still held by the *Wehrmacht*. It was

Ross's twelfth mission.

It was also his last mission. "Sinner's Dream" was hit while flying over Aviano, Italy. When it became apparent that the plane was going down, the crew prepared to bail out.

Tony Pompa, the tail gunner (see page 72-74), had snagged the rip cord of his parachute on something, resulting in his parachute opening inside the plane, and had been knocked unconscious when the plane went into a dive. Ross and the other waist gunner tried to stuff Pompa's parachute through the door of the plane and help him get out but were unable to do so. Finally, they had to jump if they were not to go down with the plane.

"Sinner's Dream" usually flew with a crew of ten. But that day, there was an extra crew member along--someone who wanted to get in an additional mission. Nine of the eleven bailed out of the crippled heavy bomber. The radiotelephone operator's chute didn't open. The other eight made it down.

"I hit the ground with such force," Ross recalls, "that I broke a bone in a foot and injured my back. I tried to crawl over to help another guy who had been injured, but the Germans were firing at us so I got down again and stayed where I was."

Their captors put them on a passenger train heading north. Most of the other passengers on the train were civilians who "gave us dirty looks because we still had our flying suits on." The train took them to Frankfurt, where they were put in solitary confinement and subjected to interrogation. While they were in Frankfurt, the city was bombed several times. "The bombs were so close they were shaking loose dirt."

Then Ross and the others who had been captured with him were put on a cattle car without any sanitary facilities and transported to Berlin, where they narrowly missed being hit by Allied bombers pounding the city. From there, they were transported to a prisoner-of-war camp somewhere in the eastern part of Germany or the western part of Poland, where they remained until the approaching Red Army forced Ross's German captors to evacuate the camp. Ross could hear the thunder of Russian artillery as he and the other prisoners were marched from the camp.

They were moved to a German town on the North Sea, where they spent a night on an old coal barge. After leaving the barge, the young German marines guarding the prisoners-of-war handcuffed them together, three to a group. Ross could understand some German and overheard the German marines talking about bayonetting stragglers and turning the guard dogs loose on them, whereupon Ross suggested to the two men to whom he was handcuffed that they move into the middle of the group of prisoners. On the march to the next camp, many in the rear of the formation were bloodied by the bayonets of the German marines prodding them on.

Ross and his fellow prisoners remained at the next camp--*Stalag Luft No. 4*--until early in 1945, a year after he had been shot down. Once again the sound of the big guns of the Red Army could be heard. And once again, the prisoners were forced to leave the camp to be moved elsewhere.

The march that followed was "one of the most horrible experiences imaginable." Food was scarce. Body lice tormented them. The winter weather was often terrible. "I don't know how many we lost on that march," Ross sadly recalls. "They'd fall out and we'd never see them again."

Day after day, forced on by their German guards, those who survived slogged on, covering a distance of nearly five hundred miles over a period of several months as they marched away from the advancing Red Army.

Then one day in early May, they were ordered to turn around and march the other way. The next day--May 6, 1945--British troops made a big push, overtaking the prisoners-of-war slowly marching back toward the east. For Ross and the others who survived, their captivity was over.

The ordeal which they had to endure, however, was not over. Malnourished and weakened by the deprivation to which they had been subjected, many became seriously ill when they started eating good food. Some died. Ross and several others were put on an eggnog diet. In time, they regained their strength, but never a taste for eggnog.

When Ross recovered enough to travel, he and other former prisoners-of-war were put on a Liberty ship which, after stopping at Southhampton, England, headed out to sea. They had several days of terrible weather, but finally reached New York, where Ross saw the Statue of Liberty for the first time. "The Statue of Liberty looked great!" Ross recalls, his voice cracking with emotion. The ordeal was over.

From New York, he traveled by train--this time under more pleasant circumstances--to Ft. Leavenworth, Kansas, where his parents met him. Then, after having been gone for nearly two years and enduring more than most endure in a lifetime, he returned to the family's farm near Harvard, Nebraska, for thirty days of leave.

Though the war in Europe was now over, the fighting in the Pacific continued. With attention shifting from Europe to the Pacific, Ross received orders to go to Santa Monica, California, which he expected would only be a brief stop on his way to the Far East. But this time, fate dealt him a better hand. While he was in the train station at Santa Monica waiting for a train, word came that the Empire of Japan had surrendered.

A spontaneous, joyous celebration erupted as a war-weary nation welcomed the end of the war. Some carried their celebrating too far. Two sailors in the Santa Monica train station started lighting firecrackers and throwing them around. One exploded where Ross was standing. "Flak-happy" after having been shot at and shot down, he instinctively grabbed the two sailors and knocked their heads together.

After the war, Ross worked as a mechanic for a few months. Then his father, who was injured in a farm accident, asked him to come back to the farm, where he has been ever since. He and his wife were married May 23, 1946. They have two daughters and a son. Their son is a Vietnam veteran. Now semi-retired, Ross and his wife spend the winters in Texas.

There was one bit of unfinished business. Though Ross was eligible for a Purple Heart as a result of the injuries he sustaining when he hit the ground after bailing out of "Sinner's Dream," the government didn't get around to presenting it to him until September 2, 1995--more than fifty-one years after the fact. Senator James Exon of Nebraska pinned the Purple Heart on him at a meeting of former prisoners-of-war held in Omaha.[29]

"The Group Got Real Close"

Carlisle "Ki" Evans, who was born July 27, 1925, in Rock Island, Illinois, was eighteen days short of his eighteenth birthday when he enlisted in the U.S. Marine Corps on July 9, 1943, a month after graduating from high school. His nineteenth birthday found him on Guam in the thick of the fight to wrest control of the island from the Japanese invaders.

Prior to Pearl Harbor, Guam was U.S. territory. An hour after the attack on Pearl Harbor, Japanese bombers based in Saipan began bombing the island. A Japanese invasion force landed in the early morning hours of December 10, 1941, and quickly took control of the lightly defended island. It remained under Japanese control until July 21, 1944, when fifty-five thousand U.S. combat troops from the 3rd Marine Division, the 1st Provisional Marine Brigade and the 305th Regimental Combat Team of the 77th Army Infantry Division made an amphibious landing and began the liberation of Guam.

Evans, who served in the 1st Provisional Marine Brigade, was among those who went ashore at Agat Beach in the face of devastating fire from Imperial Japanese Army troops deployed in heavily fortified pillboxes and other defensive placements strategically located on the hills overlooking the beach. The terrain over which the marines had to advance in order to put the pillboxes out of action was (and still is) covered with scrubby trees which impeded their progress while offering little protection. Casualties were heavy.

In this hostile environment, the men in Evans' company looked out for each other, helping those who were wounded and offering covering fire when someone was pinned down or when a buddy was dashing ahead to the next tree or rock. "The group got real close," Evans notes. They had to get close, because they had to depend on each other if they were to survive.

"The Japanese were good fighters," Evans observes. "They didn't care about human lives."

At night, the weary marines dug foxholes, two men to a foxhole. Evans recalls that it rained almost every night, filling the bottom of the foxholes with water and forcing the marines to rest their heads on their helmets in order to keep their faces above water. Sleep was hard to come by.

He also has less-than-pleasant memories of wading through chin-deep water in swamps, holding his Browning Automatic Rifle above his head while watching out of the corner of his eye for snakes.

On the third day of fighting, Evans' assistant, Thomas Manning from Youngstown, Ohio, was killed. He was right next to Evans when he got hit. "It shook me up when my assistant got killed," Evans sadly notes as he relives the painful memories.

As the struggle for the island continued, the casualty list grew longer. Evans' name was added to the list when a round from a Japanese mortar hit him on July 29--two days after his nineteenth birthday. Don LeVie, one of Evans' closest friends in the unit, started dragging Evans back from the front line to a place of relative safety where medics could get to him and try to stop the bleeding. They hadn't gone far when a Japanese machine gun opened fire on them. LeVie quickly pushed Evans into a shell hole and lay over him, protecting his friend with his own body while other members of their unit put the Japanese machine gun out of action.

Evans wasn't expected to live. But he defied the odds. He spent the next year in military hospitals in Hawaii and California recovering from the damage the mortar shell did to his body. While he was in the San Leandro Naval Hospital in California, his fiancee and his parents came to visit him. Evans and his fiancee were married while he was still in the hospital.

When he had recovered enough to be released from the

hospital, he and his wife, Barbara, returned to Illinois, where he took some additional time for recovery and then continued his education. After completing his degree in architectural engineering at the University of Illinois, he worked for the federal government in various positions until retiring in 1987.

In the summer of 1994, Evans, accompanied by his wife, returned to Guam for a special commemoration of the fiftieth anniversary of the liberation of the island. It was a time for words of appreciation from the Chamorro people, who had been brutalized by the Japanese invaders, and for tear-filled eyes while remembering fallen comrades and the terrible events which had devastated so many lives. On July 22, 1994, as the marines and their families prepared to leave Guam to return home, a large crowd gathered at the airport to see them off, holding signs saying "Thank You," "God Bless You," "We Love You," and "Guam is Grateful."[30]

Chapter 5

The Silent Generation

(Born 1926-45)

In many respects, the Silent Generation, so named because most have had relatively little to complain about, might have been called "The Lucky Generation." While some of the leading edge members of the generation found themselves in Korea and some who are part of the trailing edge got caught up in Vietnam (as did some older Silent Generation members who made a career of the military), most came of age during peacetime.

They have been fortunate in other ways as well. The United States was the only major industrial power to come through World War II with its factories and cities intact. All other major combatants--Great Britain, France and the Soviet Union on the side of the victorious Allies and Japan, Germany and Italy on the side of the defeated Axis powers--suffered terrible damage. While they struggled to rebuild their shattered economies, the U.S. economy experienced tremendous growth as pent-up consumer demand for everything from automobiles to saddle oxfords kept factories humming. For many Americans, the post-war years were a time of prosperity.

"An Iron Curtain"

The post-war years were very good ones for the United States in most respects. But every silver lining has a cloud behind it. Notwithstanding the hopes of the visionaries who founded the United Nations in 1945, the wartime marriage of convenience between the western industrial democracies and the Soviet Union did not last. With the Red Army occupying much of eastern Europe when the war ended, Joseph Stalin, the iron-handed Soviet dictator, imposed communism on Poland, Hungary, Rumania, Bulgaria, Czechoslovakia and the Soviet occupation zone in Germany, ignoring pledges he had made at Yalta and elsewhere. On March 5, 1946, Winston Churchill, speaking at Westminster College in Fulton, Missouri, observed with great regret, "An iron curtain has descended across the Continent."[1]

With public sentiment strongly in favor of "bringing the boys home" once Germany and Japan were defeated, the United States rapidly demobilized. Stalin kept his army intact. The United States, though, did have the atomic bomb. The Truman administration threatened Stalin with nuclear annihilation if the Red Army attacked the European countries which were not already under his control.

Realizing that the war-shattered countries of western Europe were vulnerable to Soviet expansion, Congress, at the urging of the Truman administration, passed the Marshall Plan, which pumped into the countries of western Europe billions of dollars of aid desperately needed to rebuild their devastated economies. As the industrial democracies got back on their feet and stood firm in the face of Soviet expansionism, many came to view the Marshall Plan as one of the best investments this country has ever made.

But Stalin was not finished. In 1948, Stalin cut off road and rail access to Berlin, located deep in the portion of Germany occupied by the Red Army. For nearly a year, a huge American and British airlift supplied the beleaguered city, which, in keeping with the post-war partition agreement, was jointly occupied by the United States, Great Britain, France and the Soviet Union. In May of 1949, Stalin conceded defeat by lifting the barriers to supplying the city by road and rail.[2]

Later that year, Stalin had his own moment of triumph when Soviet scientists, utilizing highly-classified materials pilfered from the West, exploded an atomic bomb. The United States no longer had a nuclear monopoly. The world had entered a dangerous and terrifying new era.[3]

Trouble on the Other Side of the World

Meanwhile, there was trouble brewing on the other side of the world. Chinese communists led by Mao Tse-tung defeated the Nationalist government of Chiang Kai-shek, who was forced to flee to the island of Formosa. The world's most populous nation was now allied with the Soviet Union.

More trouble came on June 25, 1950, when the Soviet-trained and equipped North Korean Army swept across the thirty-eighth parallel and attacked South Korea. The attack occurred while the Soviet Union was boycotting the United Nations to protest the refusal of the Security Council to seat the People's Republic of China in the seat reserved for China. Not having to worry about the threat of a Soviet veto, the Security Council authorized military action to stop the North Korean invasion. Acting under the authority extended to him by the United Nations, President Harry S. Truman placed General Douglas MacArthur in charge of the United Nations forces deployed to counter North Korean aggression.

Those who expected the United Nations forces to have an easy go of it were in for an unpleasant surprise. North Korean columns, spearheaded by Soviet-made tanks, pushed South Korean and American troops back to a narrow defense perimeter on the southeastern tip of the Korean Peninsula. The tide of battle shifted dramatically in September, however, when General MacArthur turned the North Korean flank by executing a brilliant amphibious landing at Inchon, a short distance from Seoul, the South Korean capital city. Suddenly, the North Korean forces were in full retreat.

Though there was a case to be made for arguing that United Nations authorization for military action in Korea ended once the North Korean army was pushed back across the thirty-eighth parallel, General MacArthur ordered United Nations forces to continue pursuing the fleeing North Koreans. By the end of November, most of North Korea was in United Nations hands and there was talk of "bringing the boys home by Christmas."

But then the tide of battle changed once again. Large numbers of Chinese "volunteers" poured across the Yalu River, which separates North Korea from Chinese-controlled Manchuria, and pushed the United Nations forces southward in a bitterly-cold winter retreat. On April 11, 1951, President Truman removed General MacArthur from command, replacing him with General Matthew Ridgeway.

By June, United Nations forces were slowly moving northward again in the vicinity of the thirty-eighth parallel when word came that the Soviet Union favored peace negotiations to end the fighting. It took two years of hard negotiating before a cease-fire could be put in place.[4]

A Destructive Demagogue

On February 9, 1950, Senator Joseph R. McCarthy of Wisconsin was the featured speaker at a Republican Lincoln Day celebration in Wheeling, West Virginia. In his speech, he charged that there were communists in the State Department who were betraying the United States.[5] It was the beginning of a witch hunt that was to destroy the reputations and careers of many conscientious and patriotic Americans.

McCarthy was joined by other Republicans who charged that Democrats were "soft on communism." The hard-liners asserted that Dean Acheson, who was Truman's Secretary of State when Mao Tse-tung defeated Chiang Kai-shek's Nationalist forces, had "lost China." No one was able to explain how the United States could lose something that didn't belong to it.

McCarthy, who liked to think of himself as a back-alley fighter, which he was, would gulp down a water glass filled with Scotch in one swallow, followed by a chaser of bicarbonate of soda. During binges of heavy drinking, he would eat butter, a quarter-pound stick at a time, which he believed would help him hold his liquor.[6]

The senator from Wisconsin did not go unchallenged. Among the first to publicly take issue with him was a fellow Republican, Margaret Chase Smith, a former schoolteacher from Maine who was the only woman in the Senate at that time. On June 1, 1950, she rose unannounced on the floor of the Senate to give a speech on political morality. She stated:

> The American people are sick and tired of being afraid to speak their minds lest they be politically smeared as "communists" or "fascists." The American people are sick and tired of seeing innocent people smeared and guilty people whitewashed.[7]

Chastised but not deterred, McCarthy continued his attacks. "The job will be a long and difficult one," he asserted, "in view of the fact that all of the power of the administration is dedicated to the task of protecting the traitors, communists, and fellow travelers in our government."[8]

The fact that the Truman administration had deployed American troops to stop communist aggression on the Korean Peninsula was of no significance to McCarthy, who continued to allege that the Truman administration was full of communists.

By the time the shooting in Korea finally stopped, Truman

was no longer in the White House, having decided in 1952 not to run for re-election. His successor, Dwight D. Eisenhower, while staunchly anti-communist himself, deplored McCarthy's tactics and style.[9] In 1954, McCarthy was censured by the U.S. Senate after nationally-televised hearings in which he overplayed his hand going after the army, making unfounded accusations of disloyalty in the ranks and among the top brass. Three years after being censured by the Senate, McCarthy died of cirrhosis of the liver at the age of forty-eight.[10]

Peace and Quiet

Eisenhower identified with and gave expression to the nation's desire to have some peace and quiet to raise families and enjoy the good life.   Once McCarthy disappeared from newspaper headlines, the Eisenhower years were a time of good will and growing affluence for many Americans.   Eisenhower believed that what the American people needed most was to be left alone to pursue their own goals and objectives and to spend time with their families. The 1956 Republican platform, quoting Eisenhower who, though recovering from a heart attack, agreed to run for a second term, stated:

> In all those things which deal with people, be liberal, be human. In all those things which deal with people's money, or their economy, or their form of government, be conservative.[11]

Lucille Ball, whose CBS television debut in 1951 marked the beginning of one of the longest running situation comedies on television, entertained the nation with her well-meaning, thoroughly-unpredictable antics.   At Ball's insistence, Desi Arnaz, her husband in real life, played the role of her husband on television. When she became pregnant in 1952, CBS broke new ground by writing her pregnancy into the script. Week by week, the nation went through the pregnancy with her. When the time came for her to go to the hospital to have the baby, the program which ran that week depicted Lucy, who was calmly in control of the situation, pushing her nervous husband in a wheelchair as they arrived at the hospital. Forty-four million Americans watched that particular episode--twice as many as watched Eisenhower's inauguration the next day.[12]

Lucille Ball and Desi Arnaz were not the only ones to bring their real-life family to the screen. *The Adventures of Ozzie and Harriet* starred Ozzie and Harriet Nelson and their sons David and Ricky. Ozzie, who had some type of a white-collar job, "brought home the bacon." Harriet was a dutiful wife, tending the home fires and not complaining at all when Ozzie limited her phone calls to thirty seconds. An idyllic view of the family, laced with heavy doses of male chauvinism in an era in which feminism attracted few supporters, was portrayed on other television programs as well, among them *Leave it to Beaver* featuring the Cleaver family with their suburbanized lifestyle.[13]

Joe DiMaggio, the smooth-hitting center fielder for the New York Yankees, retired in 1952 and handed over center field to a hard-hitting Oklahoman by the name of Mickey Mantle. In 1954, DiMaggio married film star and sex symbol Marilyn Monroe. They traveled to Japan for their honeymoon. Monroe took time off from their honeymoon to entertain American troops in Korea.

"Joe, you've never heard such cheering," she reportedly said to DiMaggio upon rejoining him after her performance.

"Yes, I have," he answered.[14]

Unlike the storybook marriages portrayed on television, the Monroe-DiMaggio marriage was not destined to last. A year later they were divorced.[15]

As the population exploded with the birth of the post-war baby boomers, growing families moved to the suburbs. Houses with front porches, which promoted neighborliness as people sat on them to escape the heat on summer evenings and visited with neighbors and those passing by, gave way to air-conditioned homes with fenced-in back yards. Automobiles, with different styles of tail fins and grills giving a distinctive appearance to each model year, were central to the suburban lifestyle.

In 1952, Dick and Maurice (Mac) MacDonald, two brothers who had failed in almost everything they had attempted, sold a franchise right to the only thing they had ever done that succeeded, a fast food restaurant selling hamburgers for fifteen cents apiece. Within a few years, the distinctive yellow MacDonald arches spread throughout the nation.[16]

Fast food restaurants. Drive-in movie theaters. Shopping malls. Suburban sprawl. Traffic jams as suburbanites returned home from their places of employment in the cities. PTA meetings. Little League baseball. A never-ending stream of activities. Peace and quiet were pursued at a very hectic pace.

Racial Justice

Life in the 1950s was good for most Americans--as long as they were white. For African Americans and other minorities, the 1950s were an entirely different story.

On December 1, 1955, Rosa Parks paid the ten cent fare and boarded a bus in Montgomery, Alabama, exhausted after a long day working as a tailor's assistant at a Montgomery department store. In Montgomery, as in other cities in the segregated south, the front seats on the bus were reserved for whites. Parks took a seat in the first row designated for African Americans. As the bus continued on its route and additional passengers boarded, all of the seats reserved for whites were filled. When another white passenger boarded, the driver ordered Parks and the three other African Americans sitting in the row in which she was seated to give up their seats. Parks refused. The driver, after subjecting her to verbal abuse, got off the bus and phoned the police, who arrested her for violating the city's laws mandating racial segregation.[17]

The African American community in Montgomery, groaning under the burden of Jim Crow laws and incensed at the humiliation to which they were subjected, decided the time had come to stand up and be counted. African American pastors and civic leaders gathered at Dexter Avenue Baptist Church to devise a strategy for challenging the white power structure. Knowing that African Americans comprised a substantial majority of the passengers on the city's mass transit system, the assembled pastors and civic leaders decided to hit the white city fathers where it hurt the most--in the pocketbook--by organizing a boycott of all city busses. Martin Luther King, Jr., the articulate and energetic young pastor of Dexter Avenue Baptist Church, recalled that when the meeting ended, "the clock on the wall read almost midnight, but the clock in our souls revealed that it was daybreak."[18]

Despite the efforts of city officials to undermine the boycott and fragment the African American community, the boycott was a resounding success which exceeded all expectations. African Americans walked to work or rode in make-shift car pools throughout the dreary days of winter, the warmer days of spring, the hot days of summer and the crisp days of autumn. On November 13, 1956--almost a year after the boycott had begun-- word came that the U.S. Supreme Court had ruled that the Montgomery bus-segregation law was unconstitutional.

On December 21, as the city prepared to desegregate its busses, an empty bus stopped at a corner near King's house. The white bus driver greeted the passenger who boarded with a friendly smile and said, "I believe you are Reverend King."

"Yes, I am," King acknowledged.

"We are glad to have you with us this morning," the driver replied.[19]

The boycott was over. The African American community had pulled together to challenge a brutally oppressive system. They had willingly put up with the inconvenience of not using public transportation, letting their tired feet send a powerful message to city hall. Justice never comes cheap. They had paid the cost.

The Montgomery bus boycott was not the first step in the march toward racial equality. A year before the boycott began, the U.S. Supreme Court's *Brown v. Board of Education of*

Topeka struck a blow for racial equality by reversing *Plessy v. Ferguson*, the 1896 Supreme Court Decision which allowed racially segregated schools. However, Rosa Parks, Martin Luther King, Jr., and the others who participated in the dignified and courageous protest in Montgomery captured the attention of the nation by putting a human face on what was happening. It was the beginning of the end for Jim Crow laws and racial segregation imposed by the white majority.

Other Cultural Changes

There were other cultural changes during the 1950s, including some which were far less dignified. In 1949, an aspiring young actress struggling to make ends meet bared her bosom in front of a photographer's camera. She was paid fifty dollars, which happened to be exactly the amount she needed to make the monthly payment on a second-hand car she had purchased. The result was a calendar picture which did not go unnoticed in neighborhood garages, bars and barbershops throughout the nation.[20]

Three years later, when an anonymous caller threatened to reveal the identity of the nude model, Marilyn Monroe, whose career was gaining momentum, acknowledged that she was the model. "Sure, I posed," she stated. "I was hungry." When asked if she had anything on when posing for the shot, she replied that she had the radio on.[21]

In the fall of 1953, twenty-seven-year-old Hugh Hefner drove to suburban Chicago and bought the rights to the Monroe photograph, along with several other photographs of nudes, for $500. Monroe received none of the money. Hefner used the photograph to launch *Playboy*, which reached a circulation of 100,000 within a year. Hefner became the well-known proponent of a sexual ethic which, in sharp contrast to the Victorian values many defended, boldly proclaimed that sex ought to be enjoyed by consenting adults, whether married or unmarried, as part of an ethic dedicated to the pursuit of pleasure. *Playboy* made Hefner a millionaire.[22]

Elvis

Born in 1935 in the hill country of northeast Missouri, Elvis Aron Presley experienced a troubled childhood. His father was convicted of forgery and spent two-and-a-half years in prison while Presley was a child. The Presley family lived on the brink of poverty and the edge of despair.

Shy and unsure of himself, Presley had few friends in high school. He couldn't read a note of music, but he had almost perfect pitch. And he could pick up a guitar and make the most incredible music flow out of it.

When he graduated from high school, he decided to become a gospel singer. He sang with a local group from his church while supporting himself working at a small plant in Memphis making artillery shell casings, a position he left when he got a job driving a truck for an electric company.[23]

In 1953, Presley walked into Sam Phillips' recording studio in Memphis and told the proprietor that he wanted to cut a record to give his mother for her birthday. Presley paid the three dollar fee and sang two songs for Phillips' little record-making machine. Phillips liked what he heard and invited Presley to come back.

After listening to Presley a few more times, Phillips recruited a couple of instrumentalists to work with Presley to see what they could put together. In July of 1954, Presley, accompanied by the two instrumentalists, returned to Phillips' studio for a recording session. The first few pieces didn't go particularly well. Then Presley started playing and singing his rendition of "I'm All Right, Mama," a piece recorded several years earlier by a well-known African American blues singer by the name of Arthur Crudup. The instrumentalists joined in. Phillips had the piece he wanted for the record, which came out with

Presley's rendition of bluegrass singer Bill Monroe's "Blue Moon of Kentucky" on the other side.[24]

Phillips sent the record to Dewey Phillips (no relation), a local disc jockey who played the record on his show on radio station WHBQ. The switchboard at the radio station "lit up like a Christmas tree" as listeners asked Phillips to play the pieces on the two sides of the record again and again, which he did for the rest of his show that night. Almost overnight, Presley became the idol of millions of teenagers.[25]

Several years later, Leonard Bernstein, one of this country's most distinguished conductors and composers, said of Presley, "Elvis Presley is the greatest cultural force in the twentieth century."[26]

A Formative Decade

Contrary to what some younger Americans might believe, those who comprise the Silent Generation have not lived their entire lives in the 1950s. They have experienced much both before and after the 1950s. Yet, for all members of the Silent Generation, the 1950s have particular poignancy. For those who are older, it was the decade in which they came of age and began their careers. For those who were schoolchildren during the 1950s, there are haunting memories of classroom drills instructing them what to do in the event of a nuclear attack and fears that lightning flashes on the horizon were nuclear bombs exploding. Notwithstanding the veneer of serenity, the 1950s were a time of great anxiety for many.

The 1950s are of significance for the Silent Generation in another way as well. Sandwiched between the cataclysmic events of the 1940s and the tumultuous years of the 1960s, the 1950s are, comparatively speaking, quiet and subdued, as are many members of the Silent Generation. Perhaps because of their quietness, they have often gone unnoticed.

One member of the Silent Generation put it this way:

"During the ferment of the 1960s, a period of the famous 'generation gap,' we occupied, unnoticed as usual, the gap itself."[27]

"The Only Decisions We Had to Make Were Where We Wanted to Live and Which Offer To Accept"

Ralph Risdal was born in Sidney, Montana, May 13, 1928, which happened to be Mother's Day that year. His parents had immigrated from Norway to this country, where they homesteaded in the eastern part of Montana just a few miles from the North Dakota state line. He was the youngest of nine children. In an era in which a good deal of the work on farms was done by muscle-power, large families provided much-needed help when the hay was being put up and when the crops were being harvested.

In 1938, the Risdal family, with most of their belongings loaded in a four-wheel trailer pulled behind the family car, moved to a farm in the Flathead Valley in northwestern Montana near Glacier Park. Risdal's father, who greatly enjoyed hunting and fishing, missed the mountains and fjords of Norway and welcomed the opportunity to leave the semi-arid terrain of eastern Montana for country more to his liking.

Upon graduating from high school, Risdal enlisted in the Navy's V-5 program and completed two years at Montana State College at Bozeman before going on active duty in 1948. In a sense, enlisting in the Navy was continuing a family tradition. His father had served as a deck hand for several years on sailing ships in the Norwegian merchant marine, rounding the Horn and traveling to many parts of the world before immigrating to this country. The elder Risdal had spent countless hours in the rigging high above the water furling and unfurling sails. The young Risdal aimed higher, applying for and being accepted into the Navy's flight program.

After completing flight training, Risdal was assigned to the photographic squadron VC-61, where he was the navigator on a PB4Y-1 (a Navy version of the B-24 Liberator which had been equipped for photo-reconnaissance). He spent a summer in Nome, Alaska, where his detachment mapped the entire Seward Peninsula. After completing his assignment in Alaska, he switched to single-engine planes, training as a fighter-photo pilot.

A year after the North Korean army crossed the thirty-eighth parallel and invaded South Korea, Risdal was sent to Korea as part of a F9F-2P Panther detachment operating from the *U.S.S. Essex*. By then, the war was stalemated and efforts were being made to negotiate an end to the fighting, though it was still to be two years before a cease-fire would be in place. Meanwhile, the fighting continued.

The *Essex* was stationed off the east coast of the Korean Peninsula, where Risdal's Panther was launched for the photo-reconnaissance missions he flew. Though no match for the MiG-15s which were appearing in growing numbers on the other side of the Korean Peninsula, the straight-winged, single-engine Panther was a good plane for the job it was assigned. Other fighters provided protection as the Panthers flew straight and level photographing rail lines or swooped down low to photograph bridges and other targets of military significance. One of the fighter pilots providing air cover was a fellow by the name of Neil Armstrong, who made history seventeen years later when he planted an American flag on the moon.

Risdal was fortunate. His plane did not take a hit on any of the seventy-four combat missions he flew, even though on more than one occasion he had the unpleasant experience of seeing tracer bullets headed his way or was warned by those flying fighter cover that flak bursts were creeping up behind him.

After being released from active duty in August of 1952, Risdal went back to school, completing both his baccalaureate and masters degrees in aeronautical engineering at the University of Washington. Jobs were readily available for those with degrees in aeronautical engineering. "The only decisions we had to make," he recalls, "were where we wanted to live and which offer to accept."

Risdal and his wife, Jackie (they were married in 1955), chose Los Angeles, where he spent five years working for Douglas Aircraft. While in California, they became homeowners and bought a turquoise 1957 Chevrolet Bel Air convertible with a white top. Their two children were born while they were living in California.

In 1960, the Risdals moved to the Seattle area, where he went to work for Boeing as an aerospace engineer. His specialty was conducting performance and trajectory analyses of space vehicles. Projects on which he worked during his thirty years at Boeing included the Lunar Orbiter Program, which on five missions photographed the moon in detail prior to the manned landings, and the Inertial Upper Stage, an upper stage booster rocket used on the space shuttle and its Titan launch vehicle. This rocket was developed to transport satellites to high earth orbit or to send space vehicles on interplanetary missions.

Watching the live television pictures of Neil Armstrong setting foot on the moon was an unforgettable experience which he describes as "a very emotional time." He recalls, "I don't think I have ever been moved by anything as much as watching those pictures."

Risdal retired from Boeing in 1990 and is actively enjoying retirement. He and his wife are both avid golfers who play golf whenever possible. Since moving to a house immediately adjacent to the country club to which they belong in Redmond, Washington, opportunities to play golf have not been hard to come by.

When he retired, they purchased a recreational vehicle, which they have used extensively touring the country. He describes himself as "very happy being retired."

Keenly aware that life has been very good to him, he is dismayed that young people today face so many problems. He is also concerned about lack of discipline, deterioration of community values and the increase of violence. "We hear about a drive-by shooting just about every week," he notes.

Risdal was not born to wealth and privilege. When the rains did not come and the crops were poor on the farm in eastern

Montana on which he spent his early childhood years, money was scarce. The crowded house in which he and the other members of his family lived was little more than two small cabins connected together (one cabin had been moved adjacent to another cabin, with a small dining room connecting the two). But the American Dream, as he came to understand and envision it, promised that by working hard and taking advantage of the educational opportunities that were available, a better life was possible.

For Risdal, this vision of the American Dream became a reality.[28]

"Inward Values and Self-Discipline In the Classic Sense"

Bob Ballentine was born in Missouri July 26, 1930, but spent most of his childhood years on a farm in Iowa, where he was raised by an Irish grandfather after his parents divorced. After graduating from high school, he enrolled in an aviation institute, becoming a licensed aviation mechanic upon completing his studies there. When Uncle Sam, represented by his local draft board, started indicating an interest in his services, he enlisted in the Air Force. After twenty years of active duty as a flight mechanic, he retired in 1972, having attained the rank of master sergeant.

The Korean War was winding down when he went on active duty on December 7, 1951. But sixteen years later, he found himself in Vietnam, arriving at the air base at Bien Hoa in 1968 just in time for the Tet Offensive. Though Bien Hoa was hit, the Viet Cong did not succeed in curtailing air operations. The base continued launching planes throughout the offensive.

Ballentine was surprised to discover when he returned to this country that the Tet Offensive was viewed by many as a defeat for the United States. "I came home thinking we had really blown them out on the Tet Offensive because tactically, they never accomplished totally any of their missions. And then I came home to find out that we'd lost the Tet Offensive. That was really discouraging." He adds, "I did not come home embittered. I was very embittered after I came home." Reflecting on his experiences in Vietnam, he observes that those in combat situations "go through a dehumanizing process" which, he suggests, "is very necessary to maintain your sanity." He recalls, "You never called in an air strike on people. You neutralized the zone; you eliminated a target." This dehumanization process "to me, in retrospect, is what is dangerous." The experience in Vietnam, he notes, changed him. When he returned home, where the styles of dress and length of hair contrasted sharply with what he had been used to, he came to realize that it's not how one looks that makes the difference. Rather, "outward appearances weren't as meaningful as inward values."

He also returned with a deepened appreciation for the gift of life. He "religiously celebrates birthdays" because he is keenly aware of how close he came in Vietnam to not having any more birthdays. On July 25, 1968, Bien Hoa got hit with a ground attack. They were still fighting off the attackers when midnight, which marked the beginning of his thirty-eighth birthday, arrived. He promised that if he lived to see the sun come up, he would celebrate every birthday "with joy and enthusiasm because, you know, the alternatives are just not good."

During the Vietnam era, the standard tour of duty in Vietnam for those who escaped injury was twelve months. Ballentine served the entire twelve months. Official records indicate that he was not injured. The facts are otherwise. He is carrying around a piece of shrapnel in his left hand but did not put in for a Purple Heart because he felt that his injury was not of sufficient magnitude to merit one.

After retiring from the Air Force in 1972, he went back to school, earning both a baccalaureate degree and an M.B.A. "I'm a firm believer that college should not be wasted on youth," he says with a smile on his face. "People should have to be forty years old before they start college. You get so much more out of it."

M.B.A. in hand, he began a second career as a corporate accountant with GTE. He retired from GTE in 1991. "It was one of those downsizings. They made me an offer I couldn't refuse."

He and his wife live in San Angelo, Texas, a very enjoyable community that many career military families find out about sooner or later. He and his wife "just liked the people" there and decided to make San Angelo their retirement home. They have three children--a daughter who is a schoolteacher, a son who has recovered from a serious auto accident and is now a registered nurse, and a son who is a motorcycle mechanic.

As he thinks about the future, he is concerned about the erosion of "inward values and self-discipline in the classic sense," which he defines as "that instilled desire to do what is right without a bunch of rules saying what you can get away with." Trying to get away with as much as one can, he adds, is "what seems to be prevailing today."[29]

"I've Always Been Very Fortunate In Terms of Employment."

Just about everyone in western Illinois and eastern Iowa knows who Silas "Si" Howard is. Most, however, don't know him by his given name. As often as not, folks simply refer to him as "Uncle Sam."

There's a reason for that. A distinguished-looking gentleman with a lean face and long gray hair and a goatee turned almost white, he's the spitting image of the way Uncle Sam looks on the posters. Since nature went to all the trouble of creating him to look like the gentleman on the posters, Howard decided there was no point in letting all that effort go to waste. He dresses up in an Uncle Sam outfit--long-tailed blue coat, red bow tie and the works--and marches in parades, visits veterans hospitals and convalescent homes, and participates in all sorts of ceremonies and events in which there is a need for the type of patriotic dimension he brings.

When dressed up in his Uncle Sam outfit, he attracts a lot of attention. On one occasion, as a group of veterans were about to get in a van and drive to Iowa City to visit with the patients in the Veterans Administration hospital located there, a girl, who appeared to be about six years old, rode up on her bicycle and sat there looking at Howard. "Are you the President?" she asked, once she had summoned up the courage to address the very distinguished-looking gentleman standing in front of her.

"I'm Uncle Sam," Howard replied.

The girl pointed her right index finger at Howard, just the way Uncle Sam does in the posters, and said, "Now, you just stay right there while I go get my sister."

Howard's appearance at the Veterans Administration hospital always elicits good-natured banter--comments such as "Hey, I've already served my hitch" and "Tryin' ta get me ta re-up?" But most important of all, his being there brings smiles of warm appreciation to the faces of some very lonely people. When Howard visits nursing homes during the holiday season, he elicits a similar response. His voice chokes with emotion as he tells of lonely people who grasp his hand and won't let go.

A deeply thoughtful and caring person, Howard is dismayed that many people never get around to registering to vote. "A lot of people paid a lot so that we can have the right to vote," he notes, painfully aware of how great the costs have been to many of the veterans he knows and with whom he spends time.

Howard was born February 27, 1933, in Sulligent, Alabama, a small town not far from Birmingham. His father was a share-cropper who spent the winter months working at a sawmill or in the small, underground coal mines known locally as "gopher mines." In 1940, at which time Howard, the youngest of the four surviving children in the family, was seven, the family "made the harvest," getting in their car and following the harvest north. In Arkansas and Missouri, they picked cotton. Howard was "barely old enough to pull a small sack but picked cotton anyway." The family picked tomatoes in Indiana and apples and cherries in Michigan that year. When picking apples, Howard's job was to climb up in the trees and shake the higher limbs so the apples which couldn't be reached from the ladders would fall to the ground, where they could be picked up.

In the early 1940s, Howard's father ran a small sawmill, making lumber from trees cut in various small tracts of timber scattered around Alabama. Because lumber production was considered critical to the war effort, he received a draft deferment but had to report to the draft board the amount of lumber he produced in order to maintain his deferment.

In 1943, the elder Howard hired an African American man to work with him in the mill. Tracts with good timber on them became less available, resulting in a drop in production.

When Howard's father went to the county courthouse to make his lumber production report, a member of the draft board happen to meet him on the lawn outside the courthouse and asked how the sawmill was doing. The draft board member, upon hearing that lumber production from the mill had declined, said, "You know what this means." Howard's father acknowledged that he did. As the draft board member walked away, he turned and said over his shoulder that if Howard's father would fire the African American man working for him, he would get better timber to cut and wouldn't be drafted.

It would have been easy to do what the draft-board member suggested. Some might have rationalized firing the African American employee by noting that he would have lost his job anyway if Howard's father was drafted. With the availability of timber declining, firing the African American man might even have been represented to him as an economic necessity. But that's not the way Howard's father operated. Firmly believing that principle is more important than expediency, Howard's father refused to conform with the racist practices of the segregated South. He was drafted and spent two years in the South Pacific assigned to grave-digging details.

The incident had a tremendous impact on Howard. When he dresses up in his Uncle Sam outfit and marches in parades, it is not simply because he happens to look like Uncle Sam. It is because Uncle Sam means something to him. Part of what Uncle Sam means to him is the affirmation of the dignity of all persons--a principle given eloquent expression in his father's courageous decision to suffer the consequences of refusing to fire the African American employee, rather than perpetrate an injustice.

In 1948, one of Howard's older brothers and an uncle heard from the local John Deere dealer that there were jobs at the Deere & Company plant in Moline, Illinois, and moved there. Other family members, including Howard and his parents, followed them to Illinois. Howard got a summer job with a roofing contractor, working as a helper for the hourly wage of ninety cents an hour. The contractor let him work evenings and weekends when he went back to school for his senior year in high school. The day after his eighteenth birthday, he interviewed at the Deere plant where his brother and uncle worked. He went to work at the plant the following Monday.

About to be drafted, he enlisted in the Marine Corps. After completing training, he was assigned to a unit involved in nuclear bomb tests in Nevada. His unit was ordered to dress in full battle gear and take their positions in a trench a mile from where the nuclear bomb was to be exploded. To prepare for the blast, they stuffed their ears with cotton "as hard as we could get it in." They were instructed to sit on the bottom of the trench with their knees bent up, cross their arms on top of their knees, and bend over and shield their faces behind their arms. When the bomb went off, it was "just like thousands of light bulbs in your eyes" even though their eyes were closed and hidden behind their arms. A fraction of a second later when the sound of the explosion got there, their cotton-stuffed ears were hit with a tremendous roar.

After the nuclear tests, he was sent to Korea. This time, good fortune smiled on him. The cease-fire was in place by the time he arrived there.

When he had completed his tour of duty with the Marine Corps, he returned to Illinois and went back to work for Deere & Company. He retired in 1990 after thirty-six years of service.

Since retiring, he has had more time to spend playing the role of Uncle Sam at various events.

He and his wife were married in 1977. It is the second marriage for both of them. They have one daughter and a granddaughter. Howard also has two children from his first marriage.

As he thinks about what he has experienced, he observes, "There was always work available if anyone had any type of skills at all. I've always been very fortunate in terms of employment." But, he adds, it is not as easy for younger people today. So many things are changing that it is harder to keep updated. And, he notes, "Jobs aren't as readily available as they used to be."[30]

"We've Got to Depend on the Land And on the Marketplace"

Kingsley, Iowa, was the place of Sally Puttmann's birth on June 7, 1935. She was a "tail-ender"--several years younger than her sister and two brothers.

Though only a few years old at the time, Puttmann has vivid memories of the depression. Her mother kept chickens on the farm. Some were stolen by those desperate for a meal, who had to walk half a mile to get to the chickens. From time to time, hitchhikers would stop by the farmhouse and ask for a meal. Puttmann's mother always gave them something to eat.

December 7, 1941, is a day she vividly recalls. They were listening to the radio in the alcove in their dining room when the news about Pearl Harbor was announced. Her father, a World War I veteran who had come face-to-face with the devastation of war, responded to the news with anger. He had lost a brother in World War I and didn't want to see another generation of young men become "cannon fodder."

One of Puttmann's older brothers served in the army in France. He was one of the fortunate ones who escaped injury.

After the war, he and Puttmann's other brother took over the family farm, enabling her parents to retire and move to Kingsley.

Puttmann married in 1953. Her husband was a junior at Iowa State College in Ames, Iowa, at the time. After he graduated, he taught vocational agriculture at Stanhope, Iowa, for a year, and then went on active duty in the army for two years to fulfill his military obligation, having been in ROTC in college. When his two years of active duty were completed, he returned to the farm on which he had been raised and took over the farming operation so that his father could retire.

While many other farmers have specialized, devoting all of their land to crops such as corn and soybeans, the Puttmanns have maintained a diversified operation, raising hogs and cattle as well as corn and soybeans. The manure from the livestock is worked into the soil to maintain the high levels of organic matter necessary for good soil.

The Puttmanns have also retained such traditional practices as raising crops for "green manure"--crops such as red clover which are plowed down to enrich the soil. They believe that traditional farming practices are much better for the soil than modern practices involving heavy applications of pesticides and artificial fertilizers.

Many farmers today, she believes, "want to whip in and whip out to get the crop in, and the land suffers." The fact that a lot of farm land today is rented, she believes, is part of the problem. Those who farm rented land, many of whom have short-term contracts rather than contracts extending over several years, have less incentive to take care of the land. "Cash rent being what it is," Puttmann observes, "they are between the rock and the hard place." Economic pressures force those who farm rented land to get as much out of it as quickly as possible. That usually means piling on large amounts of artificial fertilizer and pesticides, even though that isn't good for the land in the long run.

Because of her strong commitment to taking good care of the land, Iowa Governor Terry Branstad appointed her to the State

Soil Conservation District in her part of the state, where she served for eight years. She now serves on the advisory board for the Leopold Center for Sustainable Agriculture at Iowa State University in Ames. The advisory board appointment gives her the opportunity to encourage and promote agricultural practices "that will not only economically sustain the family that farms the land, but that will enhance the land long after my family is gone."

With all of the talk about deficit reduction in Washington, what about the federal farm program? She states, "We can't depend on the government to be a safety net for us. We've got to depend on the land and on the marketplace." To the extent that federal funds are available, she notes, "I would see payments made to people who are using good conservation practices and would be willing to do more." She favors "retiring marginal land for wetlands or for tree planting."

Largely unnoticed outside farming communities is a sociological fact of life which, in coming years, is likely to substantially transform the agricultural sector. Many farmers (including the Puttmanns) are approaching retirement but, in contrast to their parents' generation, do not have sons or daughters who wish to go into farming. As a result, land ownership and farming practices are likely to be restructured significantly in the next decade.

The Puttmanns have two daughters, both married. Both daughters and their husbands have made career commitments in areas other than agriculture. Wanting to see their farming operation continue once they retire, the Puttmanns found a novel solution. They arranged to have a job notice posted in the placement office at Iowa State University, announcing their interest in bringing a young farmer into their operation. Thirteen Iowa State students applied for the position. The Puttmanns interviewed seven of the thirteen, and, after the interviews, invited one of the applicants to work for them during the summer between his junior and senior years at Iowa State. The trial run was successful. He joined them on a full-time basis after graduating from Iowa State. In 1989, the Puttmanns built a new house three miles away from the home place. The young farmer and his family now live on the home place.

On September 7, 1995, Puttmann was one of four Master Farm Homemakers honored by *Wallaces Farmer* magazine. The award was given in recognition of work with family, home and community. The citation accompanying the award takes particular note of the work she did on the state soil conservation committee and her commitment to environmental preservation.[31]

"People in Our Age Group Grew up with An Entirely Different Work Ethic."

Betty Baumgardner and her husband live in a spacious house in Palm Springs, California, overlooking Bob Hope's palatial estate. They also have a home in San Felipe, Mexico, and a cabin in the San Bernadino Mountains a little more than an hour from Palm Springs. They own property on an island in the Caribbean but have not yet built there since they are uncertain how much time they will be able to spend there, given the extensive entertaining they do in their home in Palm Springs. When they are able to get away from Palm Springs, they usually go to their place in San Felipe, which is right across the street from a beautiful beach on the Sea of Cortez, or to their cabin up in the mountains.

Baumgardner wasn't born in Palm Springs. Very few people who live in Palm Springs have been there since their childhood years. She was born on September 16, 1936, in a very different sort of place--Dawson, Minnesota, a small farm town in west-central Minnesota not far from the South Dakota state line. Her mother taught school; her father drove trucks, though when times were tough during the depression he took any type of work he could find, including a stint as a short-order cook.

After graduating from high school, Baumgardner worked in Minneapolis, where she found a job as a secretary. In the early

1960s, she moved to southern California. Her younger sister was there and encouraged Baumgardner to join her. In California, Baumgardner found a job with a small company which manufactures computer hardware. In keeping with the work ethic she learned as a child, she worked hard and received several promotions, retiring as director of personnel in 1987.

In 1970, she married the owner of the company, who retired in 1994. As are many others in their age-group, they are very busy in retirement, entertaining guests almost every weekend.

As she reflects about the path she has traveled from rural Minnesota to Palm Springs, she observes, "People in our age group grew up with an entirely different work ethic. When we looked for a job, we were willing to start low, with the understanding that with hard work, we could get promotions and raises." Recalling her experiences as a personnel director, she comments, "Some kids today believe they should start out at least as a manager."

She is also concerned about the state of affairs in her adopted state. "California is a welfare state. It's killing us. Many on welfare have no intention of going to work. If they need more money, they have another child and hide assets to receive aid."

Like many others who are part of the Silent Generation, Baumgardner has enjoyed a high degree of success. But as she looks at the value shifts which have occurred and what she views as an erosion of the work ethic and of personal responsibility, she is skeptical about the prospects for younger generations experiencing the level of affluence she has attained.[32]

"Unlike Us, They Will Not Be Denied!"

When the program committee needed to come up with a speaker for the 1995 Martin Luther King Day celebration in Rock Island, Illinois, Clara Jenkins was an obvious choice. A highly-respected community leader and educator, she has this way of saying what needs to be said in a thoughtful, engaging manner.

The person who introduced her listed her academic degrees and other accomplishments and all of the other things typically included in introductions and then added a comment which was the only introduction that really needed to be made, "But we all know her as 'Clara.'" She was greeted with a warm round of applause.

In keeping with the theme of the day, her speech was entitled "A Time for Reflection." She began by giving an overview of race relations in the post-war years. She spoke of the returning African American G.I.s who "sought a piece of the pie they had risked their lives defending." She talked about the momentous events of the 1960s and of the tremendously significant contributions of Martin Luther King, Jr. She made reference to recent political developments and, lest anyone succumb to complacency, cautioned, "The gains of the movement can be lost, taken away or simply not recognized."

The crowd of three hundred listened carefully to what she had to say, nodding their heads in agreement.

She spoke of a "clear erosion of employment opportunities" in recent years contributing to a sense of hopelessness and a rise in "young people turning to crime." She stated, "We have watched more than ten years of the train going backwards."

"All Americans must work to break the cycles of despair," she emphasized, "and, as usual, we as African Americans must work harder than others." She talked about the way that racism and discrimination have been ever-present factors to be dealt with in the quest for equality. "But," she added, "we must not use racism as an excuse for not striving."

She called for greater self-discipline and a greater sense of responsibility. "We must eliminate drugs. We must get tough on our own community. We need to get our act together. We need to take our streets back."

The audience signaled its approval with a spontaneous round of applause, accompanied by comments such as "That's right, sister!" and "We're with you!"

Her voice rising in intensity as she reached the conclusion of her speech, Jenkins continued, "Family-oriented, drug-free, well-educated children--they are the key to our future. And unlike us, they will not be denied!"

The crowd leapt to their feet and gave her a thunderous standing ovation.

Jenkins was born in Hannibal, Missouri. While still a child, she moved with her family to Rock Island, Illinois, where she received her elementary and secondary education in the public school system. She received a scholarship to attend Illinois State University, where she majored in education.

Upon graduating from Illinois State in 1957, she wanted to return to Rock Island to teach but was told that "Rock Island was not yet ready for a colored teacher." So she took a job in St. Louis in a school which, though not officially segregated--the U.S. Supreme Court had stated in *Brown v. Board of Education of Topeka* that segregated schools were illegal--had only African American students. While teaching there, she discovered that what she had been taught in school had very little to do with the real world. She learned much, however, from an outstanding principal who gave her encouragement and support.

When Jenkins had been teaching in St. Louis for a little more than a year, school officials back in Rock Island decided that perhaps the school system was ready for an African American teacher after all and sent her an application form, which she refused to fill out. Her principal, unbeknownst to her, highly recommended her. A few weeks later, a teaching contract arrived in the mail. She accepted the offer and returned to Rock Island.

In a career that stretched over more than thirty years, she taught on the elementary level, served as a counselor at a junior high school, and was instrumental in setting up a vocationally-oriented career education program on the high school level. Along the way, she completed the requirements of a M.S. in education at Illinois State University and an E.D.S. in educational administration at Western Illinois University.

While she was on vacation one year, she was named to a

position for which she had not applied--the job of director of guidance and career education. Though she had explicitly said she didn't want the job, she accepted the position, recognizing that there was work which needed to be done, and went about it with the dedication and enthusiasm which typify everything she does.

A particular concern of hers was the middle group of students--those who were not part of either the honors programs or the special education programs. This middle group of students, which included a number of minority students, tended to get overlooked. Much of her work was directed toward helping this middle group of students.

Jenkins retired in 1992 and then immediately went to work again, this time as coordinator of Quad-Cities Scholars, a privately-funded program in Rock Island and surrounding areas established to encourage minority students to stay in school and aim for college. Minority students with college potential are identified on the elementary and junior high levels. When they enter high school, they are invited to join the Quad-Cities Scholars Program. Both parental permission and parental involvement are required for the program.

Jenkins notes that trying to keep students with college potential "on track is getting harder and harder because there is so much going on out in the community which distracts them from what they should be doing."

Yet there are many successes to celebrate. Each year between seven and ten of the students who complete the program receive college scholarships. Jenkins reports with pride that a recently-completed follow-up study indicates that almost all of the scholarship recipients graduate from college.

Jenkins plans to retire from her position of coordinator of Quad-Cities Scholars, though, given her energy level and enthusiasm, retirement is a relative term.

She has two children, both of them graduates of Jackson State University in Mississippi, both of them doing very well in their careers. Her husband passed away in 1992. Her mother, who is in her late seventies, lives with her.

"I'm going to care for her," Jenkins states. "There's no way she's going to a nursing home."[33]

"Another Way of Caring"

Arlene Lowney was born February 22, 1939, in New York City. Her mother, a single parent, worked for others as a domestic. Lowney spent the first few years of her life in foster homes, all in the New York area. She came home to live with her mother when she was five. Her mother married a first-generation Italian-American laborer. Lowney was with him when he died. She was six at the time.

Lowney's maternal grandparents, who were born in the Ukraine, came to this country when they were children, growing up in Johnstown, Pennsylvania. Her grandfather was a coal miner and a farmer, her grandmother a housewife. They were the parents of nine children, four of whom died during childhood. A couple of years ago, Lowney accompanied one of her aunts (her mother is no longer living) to Johnstown, where they retraced the family roots. The house in which her grandparents had lived is no longer standing. But they found the church in which her aunt and her grandparents had worshiped. "The church was a very important part of their life," Lowney notes.

Lowney attended public schools in New York City, graduating from high school in 1955 when she was sixteen. The following year, she began nursing school at Bellevue Hospital, graduating in 1959. While there, she discovered that Bellevue was the hospital where she was born. After completing her training, she continued working at Bellevue for four years in an acute care setting where many early innovative technologies were being developed in areas such as cardiac catheterization and open heart surgery.

She married in 1963 and accompanied her husband, a surgeon, to The Netherlands, where she worked for three years in an open heart unit. The parents of three children, Lowney and her husband were divorced in 1990 after twenty-seven years of marriage and after having been through two very critical life events. At age twenty, their eldest daughter was diagnosed with cancer, but after treatment is a survivor and today is in good health. Their son went through a drug treatment program at nearly the same time and is now in recovery. "So I have much to be grateful for every day of my life," Lowney comments, "and I never forget it."

Her son now lives in Alaska. When she visited him, she shared with him their family history. He shared with her the outdoor activities he so greatly enjoys. While in Alaska, Lowney, a New York native who has always lived in cities, went backpacking for the first time, joining her son on a trip he planned.

During the late 1970s and early 1980s, Lowney went back to school, continuing her training in nursing and also picking up a degree from Wellesley in art history and philosophy, two areas which had always interested her. She is now working on an M.B.A. Her daughters tell her that she is "the perennial student."

When she returned to this country from The Netherlands, she went to work in an intensive care unit. During this time, her second stepfather, whom her mother had married while Lowney was overseas, became terminally ill. Her stepfather wanted to be at home, rather than in the hospital, once it became apparent his condition was terminal. Coming from an acute care background, Lowney had questions about whether home care was workable. But she supported her stepfather in this decision.

Lowney observes, "He died at home in my mother's arms on Palm Sunday in a very peaceful place, having had the absolute best care. Although my mother was not a nurse, nor was she trained in that area, she knew what needed to be done and what his needs were. And although they did not have lengthy conversations about death and dying, it was a very basic sense of community--caring about each other--that unfortunately did not extend at that time to the health care system."

The experience taught Lowney about "another way of caring" that she had not experienced in intensive care units. As a result, she changed the direction of her career, leaving the high-tech world of intensive care for work in hospice programs, which are oriented toward making the final days, weeks and months of the lives of terminally-ill patients and their families as rich and meaningful as possible. For three years, she was the director of the Hospice of Cambridge, located in the Boston area. She is continuing her mission of caring as a consultant working with various hospice programs in Boston and surrounding areas.[34]

"Everything Is So Hurried"

Susan Mondshein Tejada was born in Providence, Rhode Island, December 16, 1945, which, as the generations have been defined in this volume, is almost as close to being a baby boomer as is possible without actually being one. Like many of the trailing-edge members of the Silent Generation, she has more in common with the leading-edge baby boomers than with the older members of the Silent Generation.

Her father was in sales; her mother worked for a telephone answering service. The family of four (she has one older sister) lived in an ethnically-diverse neighborhood.   Both sets of grandparents were devout Orthodox Jews. Her paternal grandparents came to this country from Austria, her maternal grandparents from Russia the early part of this century to escape the prejudice and mistreatment which were rampant in Europe long before the Holocaust shocked the conscience of the world.

Tejada attended Hebrew school two afternoons a week and on Sundays. She received her secular education in the public school system, graduating in 1963 from Classical High School in Providence. At Classical, which she describes as "a strict and old-fashioned school," she took four years of Latin, along with French and her other studies. After graduating from Classical, she attended Barnard College of Columbia University, located in Manhattan. At Barnard, she majored in French.

By her senior year, opposition to the war in Vietnam--a war which she strongly opposed--was gaining momentum. While she did not join the Weathermen or any of the other radical anti-war groups which had substantial support at Columbia and Barnard, she marched in several anti-war demonstrations. One day while passing a storefront near Columbia, she happened to notice a poster which stated, "Don't send money to Vietnam. Send yourself." It was a recruiting poster for a private volunteer organization which worked on economic and community development projects in countries with which the United States did not maintain diplomatic relations. She decided to apply.

Her academic advisor was not enthused about the idea, suggesting that "war is no place for a woman" and adding that "soldiers in war degenerate and go crazy." Her advisor instead encouraged her to apply for the Peace Corps. She applied for both.

The Peace Corps responded first. She stated a preference for going to Thailand, which was as close to Vietnam as she could get in the Peace Corps. She was assigned to the Philippines, instead.

She was trained to teach at the elementary level. But when she arrived in the Philippines, she ended up teaching English in a high school in Manila, replacing a teacher who was on leave getting a master's degree. She taught four classes each day with fifty students in each class--but with only forty-eight desks and chairs in the classroom and forty-five books for the students to use. The students she taught were from working-class families which she describes as "just scraping by."

Though Manila was a rest-and-recreation stop for military personnel assigned to Vietnam, she had little contact with them other than seeing them (and the "hostesses" who followed American military personnel) at a hotel swimming pool to which she had access.

Wanting to stay in Manila for the second year of her Peace Corps assignment, she managed to line up a job at a university medical school developing a family planning program for use in rural areas. She wrote a script and put together a slide show. But after much work, nothing came of it. While working on the family planning program, she also worked at a day-care center.

During the summer between her two Peace Corps jobs in Manila, she worked in a more rural setting on Catanduanes Island south of Luzon. There was only one air-conditioner on the island, located in the bank in the capital city of Virac. While in Virac, she met Rey Tejada, who was practicing law there. They were married the following May, a development that did not entirely please her Jewish relatives.

When she completed her Peace Corps assignment and returned to this country with her husband, she worked for a few months in a clerical position at Children's Hospital in Washington, D.C., a job of which she has fond memories. She left Children's Hospital to take a staff job with the Peace Corps. She held a series of writing jobs with the federal government, transferring from the Peace Corps to the Foster Grandparent Program, then to the Civil Service Commission just in time for Watergate, and to the Environmental Protection Agency just in time for the Reagan years, when efforts were made to emasculate the agency. She left the Environmental Protection Agency to work for the National Geographic organization, where she is the editor of *World*, a magazine oriented toward children.

She and her husband, who works for the Foster Grandparent Program, have one son--Justin, born in 1976, the year of the nation's bicentennial. More than seventy-five members of her family, many of whom she hadn't seen for years, came to Justin's *bar mitzvah* in 1989.

As she reflects about life today, she notes, "The good news is that younger generations have been brought up with increased environmental awareness. The unfortunate thing about post-Watergate is that they have also grown up with a great distrust of government without knowing that this wasn't always the case-- that there was a time when people were proud to be civil servants."

Investigative journalism, she suggests, "though good, has given rise to a pervasive cynicism in the media."

She is dismayed about "the way life is not integrated but is so segmented and fragmented." While appreciative of the fact that she was able to work part-time while raising her son, she sees many two-career families forced to drop off their children at day-care centers and then rush off to their jobs.

"Everything is so hurried. There just doesn't seem to be an accommodation to families." And, she adds, "The stresses are even greater in single-parent households."

She recalls, "When I was a kid, you could wander around without fear. And you could just do nothing, if that's what you wanted to do. Now children have to be programmed all year around."

We are all, she suggests, "moving on a conveyer belt from one activity to another. The feeling of lack of control is so hard."

"I have this fantasy," she states, "that outside big cities, the pace of life is more reasonable--that people don't have to work sixty hours a week, that people have more time to spend with their families and to be involved in religious institutions."

"But," she adds, "I'm not certain it is true."[35]

Chapter 6

The Baby Boom Generation

(Born 1946-65)

January 30, 1968, was the first day of Tet, the Vietnamese New Year. A thirty-six hour cease-fire had been announced to allow war-weary combatants a much-needed respite from fighting and an opportunity to celebrate Tet. North Vietnamese and Viet Cong forces, knowing that their South Vietnamese adversaries had relaxed their guard and hoping that American forces would do the same, launched assaults on seven South Vietnamese cities and scores of smaller population centers and military installations. In Saigon, Viet Cong commandos blasted their way through the outer defense perimeter of the U.S. Embassy. It took six hours of hard fighting for American troops, who landed by helicopter on the embassy roof, to regain control the embassy grounds.[1]

The Tet Offensive shocked the American public. Many

were appalled that the North Vietnamese and Viet Cong would use a holiday truce to launch an offensive. The press made no mention of the fact that in 1776, General George Washington, aware that the Hessian troops hired by the British were accustomed to the European practice of refraining from fighting on holidays, moved his tattered army across the icy Delaware River during the evening hours of Christmas Day and routed the Hessian troops at Trenton when daylight came.[2]

Even more shocking to the American public was the fact that North Vietnamese and Viet Cong forces had sufficient strength to strike at the heart of South Vietnam's largest cities, which seemed to contradict Pentagon claims that there was "light at the end of the tunnel." Within a few days, American and South Vietnamese forces reclaimed most of the real estate the North Vietnamese and Viet Cong had gained during the offensive. Tactically, the Tet Offensive was a significant defeat for the North Vietnamese and Viet Cong, who suffered heavy casualties.[3] But on the battlefield of public opinion, it was a huge victory for them. Growing numbers of Americans came to the conclusion that if the Viet Cong could penetrate the grounds of the U.S. Embassy in Saigon, the war was an exercise in futility.

Meanwhile, in the highlands in the northern part of South Vietnam, the U.S. Marine outpost at Khe Sanh remained under siege, dangerously exposed to North Vietnamese artillery units bombarding the beleaguered marines from the surrounding hills.[4]

On March 31--a Sunday evening--millions of Americans gathered around their television sets for a special address by Lyndon Baines Johnson, President of the United States. The president announced that he had ordered a halt in the air and naval bombardment of most of North Vietnam and had invited the North Vietnamese government to join him in "a series of mutual moves toward peace."[5] Then, looking straight into the television cameras with his Basset-hound face framed by the long-lobed ears cartoonists loved to satirize, he stated, "I shall not seek and I will not accept the nomination of my party as your President."[6]

Spontaneous celebrations broke out at college and university campuses throughout the nation. Many thought the war in Vietnam was over. It wasn't. More Americans and Vietnamese, both North and South, were killed after President Johnson's announcement than before.

President Johnson's surprise announcement started the week on a note of optimism. The week ended amidst great grief, anger and despair. On Thursday evening, April 4, Martin Luther King, Jr., was fatally shot as he chatted with friends and staff members on the second-floor balcony near his room at the Lorraine Motel in Memphis, Tennessee. Immediately prior to being struck by the assassin's bullet, he had asked one of his friends, who was a musician, to play the spiritual, "Precious Lord, Take My Hand," at a rally that was to have been held that evening to support striking Memphis sanitation workers.[7]

As the nation mourned King's death, a relief column of twenty thousand U.S. troops moved toward Khe Sanh. U.S. officials reported on April 6 that the siege had been lifted.[8]

The terrible violence which typified so much of the year was not yet over. In the early morning hours of Wednesday, June 5, Senator Robert F. Kennedy, the winner of California's Democratic presidential primary, spoke to an exhausted but exhilarated group of campaign workers and supporters in the ballroom of the Ambassador Hotel in Los Angeles. Moments later, as he left through a kitchen corridor outside the ballroom, he was gunned down by an assailant with a handgun.[9] Despite emergency surgery and intensive efforts to save his life, Senator he died at 1:44 a.m. the following morning--the second Kennedy brother to be assassinated in less than five years.[10]

On June 27, as preparations were underway for the evacuation of Khe Sanh, U.S. officials in Saigon announced they had decided to use a "mobile offense" rather than fixed fire bases. *The New York Times* reported that during the ten weeks that Khe Sanh was under attack, U.S. planes dropped 220 million pounds of bombs on North Vietnamese positions in the surrounding hills.[11]

The first six months of 1968 were to leading-edge baby

boomers, and many who are younger as well, what the 1950s were to members of the Silent Generation--defining moments which left an indelible impression on their consciousness. There were other times that were happier--January 11, 1969, when Joe Namath and the upstart New York Jets defeated the heavily-favored Baltimore Colts in Super Bowl III, July 20, 1969, when Neil A. Armstrong and Edwin E. Aldrin, Jr., made history on the moon, and August 15-17, 1969, when a multitude of fans gathered for a rock festival held on a farm near Woodstock, New York--so many that organizers of the event gave up trying to determine who had tickets. There were also other times of tragedy--November 22, 1963, when President John F. Kennedy was assassinated as his motorcade wound its way past the Texas School Book Depository in Dallas, and May 4, 1970, when a National Guard detachment opened fired on student demonstrators at Kent State University, killing four and wounding nine. But though there were other times both happy and tragic, the first six months of 1968, with their awful brutality, cast a far longer shadow over subsequent years and events than any other period of time during the 1960s or 1970s.

The Biggest and the Best

The most salient characteristic of the Baby Boom Generation, it is often suggested, is its sheer size. It represents a bulge on the population curve unequaled by any generation either before or after--a bulge which continued to grow until the early 1990s as immigrants swelled the ranks of boomers in numbers more than sufficient to offset those claimed by mortality.[12]

There is a widely-held assumption that the post-war baby boom was the result of returning G.I.s catching up on things they had missed while away at war. There is a kernel of truth in this hypothesis. The birth rate in the United States did increase in the two years immediately following World War II. But then, for a three-year period, it tailed off until, in 1951, it started going up again.[13]

The explosion in the birth rate during the 1950s, for the most part, did not occur because couples decided to have large families, as was common in the previous century and during the first part of this century. Rather, the baby boom was the result of more women having children--and at a younger age. The percentage of women giving birth to two or more children rose from 55 percent in the 1930s to 85 percent in the 1950s. Many women in the 1950s married at a younger age than had their mothers (or, in later years, did their daughters). During the early part of the baby boom, half of all women marrying for the first time had not reached their twentieth birthday. In 1960, as the baby boom moved toward its conclusion, 71 percent of women 20-24 years of age either were married or had been married, compared with 54 percent in 1940 and 37 percent in 1990.[14] Some of the trailing-edge baby boomers (those born as the baby boom came to its conclusion in the mid-1960s) were born to teenage mothers who themselves were baby boomers, born in the years immediately following World War II.

For the most part, the 1950s and 1960s were years of prosperity. Jobs were readily available. Wages and salaries were high enough to enable the family bread-winner to provide a decent living for a growing family on a single income. Many women chose to be full-time homemakers. Parents carefully heeded the gentle advice of America's best-known baby doctor, Dr. Benjamin Spock, who favored permissiveness and positive reinforcement rather than harsh discipline. Millions of dollars were pumped into education on all levels, both to accommodate the flood of baby boomers and to expand educational opportunities. The Salk and Sabin vaccines made polio, which in previous generations had crippled thousands of children, a rare occurrence. Baby boomers had more toys, more recreational opportunities, more leisure time and more money to spend than had their predecessors. They were, in substantial measure, a privileged generation. Some might say that many were pampered during their childhood years.

A Revolt of the Privileged

And then something unexpected happened: the privileged rebelled. The first rumblings of the rebellion were discernible long before Vietnam dominated newspaper headlines. The rebellion began when the sexual revolution, facilitated by the introduction of "the pill," swept across college campuses. As the rebellion gained momentum, authority of all types was questioned. Anyone over the age of thirty was viewed with suspicion. Baby boomers flocked to concerts by the Beatles, the Rolling Stones and other groups who challenged convention as they redefined aesthetic standards. Children of affluence rejected the values of their parents--and the affluence their parents had worked hard to acquire. Some of the rebellious children of affluence experimented with drugs. Some joined communes. Some did both.

Since this rejection of authority was already well on its way toward transforming the cultural landscape before the United States got bogged down in the Vietnam quagmire, it should have been apparent to President Johnson and others in positions of responsibility that baby boomers could not be led docilely into a war for which no coherent explanation was ever given. But many things which should be obvious go unnoticed by those who should take heed of them. The result was anger and anguish of unprecedented proportions as the nation was torn apart by a bitterly-controversial war that, as it divided the nation, pitted fathers against sons, college students against "hard hats," friends against friends, and neighbors against neighbors.

Trailing-Edge Baby Boomers

Because so much has been written about baby boomers and the Vietnam experience, it is easy to assume that the Vietnam era was a formative period for all baby boomers. While it is difficult to overstate the impact of Vietnam on older baby boomers, many younger baby boomers came of age after the last U.S. troops had been withdrawn from Vietnam and the war had disappeared from newspaper headlines. For them, the war is but a distant memory, if they remember it at all. Their formative years encompassed the post-Watergate years, the rather colorless presidency of Gerald Ford, the Arab oil embargo, the Iran hostage crisis, the "malaise" during the Carter years and the election of Ronald Reagan. As with the trailing-edge members of every generation, they often have more in common with the leading-edge members of the generation which follows them than with older members of the generation of which they are a part.

The Middle Years of Life

Leading-edge baby boomers are no longer rebellious college students--nor are trailing-edge baby boomers. In the middle years of life, many baby boomers have become part of what they once derisively labeled "the establishment." They are investment bankers and entrepreneurs, corporation executives and lawyers, sales managers and plumbing contractors, physicians and pharmacists. They live in comfortable homes in upscale housing developments, in pricey condominiums in urban areas undergoing gentrification and in rural areas from which they commute to their jobs in the cities. Many voted for Ronald Reagan in 1980 and for Republican candidates in 1994 as Republicans gained control of both houses of Congress. Some are grandparents.

The urge to reform society has not entirely disappeared. Some middle-aged boomers are committed environmentalists, animal rights advocates or anti-smoking zealots. Some advocate reform of our educational system and of the work place. Even as the march of time mellows the indignation of youth, a perception that all is not right with the world persists in the minds of many.

"We Were into Small Acts of Kindness"

There wasn't much diversity in Glen Ellyn, the upper-middle class Chicago suburb where Nancy Stengel, who was born May 19, 1947, spent her childhood years. Her father, a dentist, brought home sufficient income to enable the family of six to have just about everything they wanted. But in conservative DuPage County, where Glen Ellyn is located, there was (and still is) a lot of pressure to conform. Not wanting to conform, Stengel, after completing two years of nurses' training, welcomed the opportunity to go to California with a friend who had arranged to drive a car there for someone who wanted the car moved to California.

Stengel had planned to visit California for a few days and then return. But one thing led to another and she ended up spending four years there, staying in various places up and down the coast in the Huntington Beach and Laguna Beach areas. In the California flower culture Stengel encountered and of which she became a part, there were no rules other than "nothing plastic and nothing old." Plastic symbolized "the system" which Stengel and her friends viewed as phony. "Old" was defined as anyone and anything over thirty.

"Anything establishment was out," Stengel recalls. Ostentatiously showing wealth was considered to be highly inappropriate. "If you had money, you didn't show it." One girl's father gave her an expensive convertible for her birthday. She refused to drive it.

Though Stengel and her friends worked when necessary to buy food and pay the rent, "money wasn't part of our culture at all."

"The lifestyle was very unique," she notes. People came and people left. The door was always open to anyone who wanted to "crash" there. "When you met someone, they were automatically your friend."

"The first love-in I went to, I was really blown away.

People would come up to you and give you a flower. The essence was giving something to make others happy."

Stengel visited Haight-Ashbury in San Francisco but didn't like what she encountered there. She saw a sharp contrast between the communes of northern California, which she describes as placing women in subordinate roles and exploiting them, and the "flower child" culture of Southern California.

"Hippies were into dropping out of society. They were real scary children. As flower children, we were the complete opposite."

There was also more drug use in Haight-Ashbury than in the circles she traveled. While marijuana "was not considered illegal," heroin and cocaine weren't widely used "though someone would occasionally get hold of LSD."

Although Stengel and her friends opposed the war in Vietnam, they weren't involved in anti-war protests. Most anti-war activists, she notes, were college students "who were still locked into the system."

"No one thought the war was right. We were absolute pacifists. But we weren't the protesting type. We were into small acts of kindness."

Stengel and other flower children refrained from being judgmental about those who went to Vietnam, viewing those who were drafted as victims of the war. "Most of the guys who went to Vietnam were in a very bad spot."

She spent six months in Hawaii, joining some friends who were already there, but decided it was "too idyllic to stay any longer."

She and a friend, who had family members living in Rome, decided to try the Mediterranean lifestyle. On the way to Rome, Stengel stopped by to visit her parents at their cabin in northern Wisconsin. While there, she met a Vietnam veteran who had been in the thick of the fighting in Vietnam. They were married one year later.

Her husband is a stockbroker who heads up the local office of a major brokerage firm in Davenport, Iowa. They recently moved out into the country on the Illinois side of the Mississippi

River, where they have a spacious home and plenty of room for their daughter's horse. In addition to their daughter, born in 1980, they have two sons, born in 1974 and 1975. They also raised the son of a close friend from Stengel's California days, who died when her son was thirteen. In a somewhat ironic twist of events, the son of the close friend, who spent most of his childhood years in the flower culture of southern California, "turned out very materialistic."

She characterizes herself as having "held true to the same values learned in California." As she reflects about these values, she observes, "I never attributed them to anything other than the here, the now and the present. But now I view it in a more religious sense. Now I realize that God is the center of it all."[16]

"Just Tell Him That It's a Gift from You"

Dan Carothers, a Leap Year baby born February 29, 1948, received his draft notice during the tumultuous summer of 1968. Even though college students were the ones marching in the anti-war demonstrations, it was those who were not fortunate enough to be in school who were more likely to be drafted and who bore the brunt of the costs of the war. Carothers had gone to work for Ozark Airlines after graduating from high school; his job didn't come equipped with a draft deferment.

After basic and advanced training at Ft. Polk, Louisiana, he spent two months at noncommissioned officers school at Ft. Benning, Georgia. There he got his sergeant's stripes and then put in a stint at Ft. Lewis, Washington, as an instructor at infantry school.

During the late 1960s, there were three categories of soldiers in the U.S. Army--those who were going to Vietnam, those who were in Vietnam, and those who had been in Vietnam. Carothers moved from the first category to the second on April 1, 1969--April Fool's Day--when he joined other replacement troops on an airplane which took them to Vietnam, where he was assigned to the elite 82nd Airborne Division.

Shortly after joining his unit in the field, he observed to his commanding officer that the map coordinates for the place his squad was ordered to go appeared to be in Cambodia. Carothers asked his commanding officer, "We're supposed to be in Vietnam, right?"

"Absolutely."

"These grid coordinates you gave me are on the west side of the Cambodian-Vietnam border; it looks to me as if we're in Cambodia," Carothers noted.

"Sergeant Carothers, we're in Vietnam," his commanding officer replied. "We're not allowed to be in Cambodia."

Carothers looked at his commanding officer, who looked back at him with a look in his eyes which said, "I can't tell you, but do you get it?"

Life in the field in Vietnam (and Cambodia) was a hellish routine of search-and-destroy missions, punctuated by guard duty on the defense perimeter of the fire base from which they operated and night ambushes set up to thwart anyone inclined to attack the fire base. For weeks, they operated on no more than three to four hours of sleep a night.

Dealing with the steamy jungle environment, teeming with leeches and other unfriendly creatures, added to the exhaustion. In an effort to keep leeches from crawling into their boots and up their pant legs, they taped everything that could be taped, which, instead of keeping the leeches out, sometimes simply made them harder to get to when they started digging in.

Though Carothers' squad was frequently under fire and several in his squad took hits, Carothers lost but one man--his radiotelephone operator, an African American by the name of Alton Ellison who hailed from a back-woods area in Georgia. When the squad stopped for a brief rest while on a search-and-destroy mission, Ellison took off the radiotelephone and inadvertently placed it on top of a Viet Cong mine which blew his leg off. Carothers, who had gone forward to check with the point man, came back to Ellison to see if anything could be done for him. He was bleeding so profusely that all Carothers could do was be with him as he died.

Though Carothers had intended to write to Ellison's family to let them know what had happened to him, the exhausting combat schedule didn't allow time to do that. When he returned from Vietnam, he tried to put the war out of his mind. After quite a few years had passed and he was able to deal with the war again, he decided he'd better take care of unfinished business. He left a message which the army personnel office passed on to Ellison's mother inviting her to call him collect, which she did a few weeks later.

After Carothers had filled her in on what had happened, she asked, "Would you like to speak with Alton's son?"

Though Carothers thought he knew Ellison quite well, he had heard no mention of a son. Ellison's mother explained that his girlfriend was pregnant when he left for Vietnam and he died not knowing that he had a child on the way.

Among those in Carothers' squad who got hit was Doug Peterson, who carried the M-60 machine gun assigned to the squad. Peterson was hit by rounds fired by two Viet Cong they unexpectedly met face-to-face on a jungle trail while setting up an ambush. Peterson's spinal column was severed. Though he survived the war, he was paralyzed from the waist down. Carothers was invited to attend Peterson's wedding several years after they had both returned from Vietnam.

Although Carothers was frequently exposed to bullets and flying shrapnel, he escaped without injury. "It just wasn't meant to be," he muses.

While the standard tour of duty in Vietnam was twelve months, Carothers returned after eight months and twelve days when the 82nd Airborne Division was withdrawn from combat. Everyone who served in Vietnam worried about getting hit when they were "short"--when their tour of duty was nearly over and they were about to leave. Everyone on Carothers' plane was quiet until they left Vietnamese air space. Then, once they were beyond the range of Viet Cong and North Vietnamese rifles and artillery, once the realization hit them that they were going to make it, the most joyous celebration any of them had ever experienced spontaneously broke out on the plane.

Carothers was released from active duty shortly after returning from Vietnam and went back to work at the job with Ozark Airlines he had prior to going into the service.

Carothers married in February of 1970. Carothers' wife, Sue, gave birth to their first child--a daughter--later that year. Their daughter went on to become the first college graduate in the family. In 1994, she married a plant engineer for a major grain processing company. The Carothers' son was born in 1972. He is now married and has three children.

While working for Ozark Airlines, Carothers started a small construction firm. Beginning with an investment of $1500, the company grew to a $2.5 million operation, providing full-time employment for Carothers and a number of others. But then, a business deal that went sour undercut the viability of the company. In 1989, Carothers made one of the toughest decisions he has ever made--the decision to shut down the company in which he had invested so much, both emotionally and financially. "To me," Carothers observes, "the loss of the company was like the death of a child."

Carothers went to work as a heavy equipment operator for a construction company which had been one of his major competitors. He continues to work for the company, as does his son, who works with him. The Carothers have recovered financially from the loss of the company and have nearly worked through the grief process resulting from the decision to dissolve the company.

The Carothers are restoring a grand old Victorian-era house in Rock Island, Illinois, carefully saving the painstakingly-crafted woodwork and stained glass windows. For both of them, it has become a labor of love. The house is located in a transitional area which had been experiencing urban decay, with older houses turned into rental units for low-income families. Many of the houses continue to be rental property while others, such as the one in which the Carothers live, are being renovated.

As in other low-income neighborhoods, there are many children without fathers. Carothers worries about them and does what he can to be a surrogate father. Now that he no longer has the construction company, he has time to be a neighbor. The Carothers' front porch has become "The Front Porch Club," where neighborhood kids and others from the community gather to visit and talk about whatever needs to be talked about. To make sitting on the front porch more comfortable on hot summer days, he installed a large ceiling fan to circulate the air.

Discovering that one of the neighborhood kids wanted a bicycle, Carothers bought a used bicycle, fixed it up and gave it to the boy's mother to give to him as a gift. The boy's mother, who knew that her son wanted a bicycle but wasn't able to come up with the money for one, said to Carothers, "I'll let my boy know that it's a gift from you."

"No," Carothers responded, "This is my gift to you to give to your son. You just tell him that it's a gift from you."[16]

"A Land of Opportunity"

Bee-Lan Wang was born January 23, 1949, in Penang, Malaysia, where she was part of the sizable Chinese minority. She was adopted by a widow who had two older sons. Since Bee-Lan was several years younger, she was, for all practical purposes, an only child.

Though growing up fatherless in a very poor family, she was able to attend an English-speaking school which had been founded by Methodist missionaries. By the time Bee-Lan finished primary school, the government had assumed the responsibility for running it, though Christian humanitarian values still played a prominent role in the curriculum.

Like many other schools in Asia, the school placed strong emphasis on achievement. Bee-Lan was a star student, excelling in every area. She was at the top of her class academically, president of the student government, captain of the Red Cross Society, leader of the debate squad, and much more. As a result of her academic success, she won a scholarship to attend

Radcliffe College, where she planned to study biology and chemistry in preparation for a career in medicine.

The move from Malaysia to Radcliffe in 1967 was quite a culture shock. She recalls, "I got to Radcliffe when the anti-war, anti-establishment and counter-culture movement was at its height. I responded with utter confusion."

"I grew up in a very anti-communist environment," she notes, adding that she did not respond positively to those who were protesting the war in Vietnam. "My reaction was that these kids were spoiled and crazy. How could anyone in his or her right mind be a communist sympathizer? As a Malaysian, I wanted the United States to win the war in Vietnam."

Radcliffe was unsettling for her in other ways as well. During the three years she spent at Radcliffe, she began to question the preoccupation with achievement which had obsessed her every step of the way up to that point. While she had considered herself a true convert to Christianity prior to coming to this country, participating in the Harvard-Radcliffe Christian Fellowship changed her life and the direction her career was headed.

"I learned that the most important thing is to exhibit love," she notes. "A sense of personal inadequacy drove me to achieve in every aspect of life. In the Harvard-Radcliffe Christian Fellowship, I learned that the mark of a Christian is love."

She adds, "So in true 'Bee-Lan' fashion, I set about to exhibit this love for others but didn't have it, because it's not something you can just trump up."

Despair overwhelmed her. "I felt as if my prayers were bouncing off the wall."

Then one day she picked up an out-of-print book of poetry based on events in the life of Christ. One of the poems was about the love commandment: "You shall love the Lord your God with all your heart, and with all your soul, and with all your mind. This is the great and first commandment. And a second is like it, You shall love your neighbor as yourself." Matthew 22.37-39 (RSV)[17]

Bee-Lan recalls, "The poet asked how one can love one's

neighbor as oneself without loving oneself. In order to love others, we must have a sense of self-worth based on the fact that God placed so much worth on each of us. He gave his only Son in order that *I* can become his child!"

The poem opened Bee-Lan's eyes. She was suddenly aware that she "was full of self-rejection." She discovered that "the crux of the Christian gospel is that we cannot make ourselves worth something but rather our worth is the result of the infinite God putting an infinite value on each of us." She came to experience great joy as the discovery of grace replaced a religion of works.

Bee-Lan realized that her preoccupation with success was the result of a deeply-ingrained sense of personal inadequacy and that her decision to pursue a career in medicine had more to do with the prestige associated with the practice of medicine than with any sense of a call to serve. But burning the bridges to medical school proved to be terribly difficult. She applied for admission both to schools of medicine and to schools of educa-tion. She was invited for interviews and was in the final stages of the admission process for Harvard School of Medicine when, after praying with two friends, she called the admissions office and withdrew from consideration.

In 1972, Bee-Lan married Timothy Wang, a physician who is also from Penang, Malaysia. Along with their three sons, born in 1977, 1979 and 1983, they live in St. Charles, Illinois, an upscale community on the Fox River within commuting distance of Chicago.

In 1975, she received a Ph.D. in education from the University of Chicago. From 1974-82, she taught at Wheaton College, dropping to part-time in 1977 when her first son was born. In 1990, she became a U.S. citizen.

Today, she is considering various options for resuming her career. "Now that my child-raising years are drawing to a close," she states, "I want to do something which will make use of my skills and education and will have a positive impact on people."

As an immigrant, Bee-Lan has a perspective which many

Americans lack. "I cannot impress on my three sons enough how privileged they are to be born in this country and in this generation. They have never known poverty and probably never will. All the opportunities which they want are here for them. Truly, America is a land of opportunity. Those of us who are immigrants can see it better than those who were born here."

She emphasizes, "The opportunity is not just for immigrants but for everyone who lives here. Most Americans just don't realize how privileged they are."

Does she have concerns about America? She states, "We as Americans have a tendency to emphasize our rights--you know, we have a right to this and a right to that--but we are failing to balance this with a sense of our responsibilities."

She is also concerned about the limited range of opportunities in the public school system for gifted students. "We as a society are going to lose out because we are loath to provide anything extra for our brightest minds. We are failing to challenge our young people academically. We over-emphasize sports."

At the same time, she in no way wants to place today's students under the pressure to achieve which she experienced. Rather, she sees a need for a greater number of opportunities to learn that will engage the interests of the brightest minds, without in any way pressuring them to succeed.[18]

"We Use Way Too Much Of Our Natural Resources"

Palma Jorgenson, who was born January 28, 1951, in Lebanon, New Hampshire, spent her childhood years in Fairlee, Vermont, where her parents owned and operated a country store. Her mother, who taught dance, named her after a former dance instructor. Like the nation, Jorgenson's family history combines a native American heritage with traditions coming from Europe. Her father was English and Sioux, her mother half Cherokee on both sides of her family.

Foster children augmented the family of seven. (Jorgenson has three sisters and one brother.) To respond to an important community need, as well as to help make ends meet, her mother ran a nursery for mentally-handicapped children in their home, with as many as fourteen children joining them for the day. Both her parents strongly emphasized the importance of helping those in need. One Christmas Eve, her father invited a stranded motorist, who happened to be African American, a rarity in Fairlee at that time, to spend Christmas with them. The family tradition called for putting on an impromptu play on Christmas morning, illustrating a Biblical story. After the play, they would open their gifts, which, given the limited financial resources of the family, were few in number. After the play had been presented the year the stranded motorist joined them, her father announced, "No one can have Christmas until we each make one present for our guest." Jorgenson wrapped fifty pennies she had saved and gave them to the guest as her gift to him.

In 1972, Jorgenson completed her training as a nurse and moved to Palo Alto, California. The first head nurse for whom she worked was a native American with an active interest in native American culture. After working in California for a couple of years, Jorgenson returned to Vermont and married. Her first child, Travis, was born in 1975. And then, as has happened to others, her marriage ended when her husband developed other interests.

With $400 to her name, she and Travis moved to Florida, where an aunt was living. In Florida, she resumed her career in nursing. In 1983, she married Lance Jorgenson, who works for a regional telephone country. He brings a Swedish-American dimension to their multi-cultural family. Their son, Kurtis, was born on Christmas Eve in 1984. After having worked for a plastic surgeon for several years, she now works in the emergency room of a community hospital.

When she and her husband were building their home in Destin (located in the Florida panhandle on the Gulf coast), she discovered a large spearhead in dirt that had been excavated from the construction site and another in shallow water right offshore a short distance away. She later learned there had been a Seminole ceremonial site on the shore within sight of where they built their house.

When her father, who strongly identified with his native American heritage, visited her the last time before he passed away, they walked together along the beach. He left his walking stick leaning against a tree and said to her, "Don't worry. I will be back."

In 1990, after several years of planning, she was part of a team of twelve who went on a ten-day medical mission to Guatemala. They raised the money themselves for the project, which was developed in cooperation with the Agency for Central American Development (ACAD). A gigantic recycling project helped fund the trip.

They set up a clinic in a hospital built by the Guatemalan government in Joyabaj, located in the highlands northwest of Guatemala City fifty-three kilometers from Utatlán (the capital of the Quiché Mayan nation which flourished in the area prior to the Spanish conquest).[19] The building in which the medical team set up their clinic had no electricity or running water.

When Jorgenson returned to Guatemala the following year as part of another medical team, they set up clinics in several Quiché villages in the mountains surrounding Joyabaj, where the conditions were even more primitive. In most cases, communicating with villagers necessitated the use of two translators--one to translate the Quiché language to Spanish and a second to translate from Spanish to English.

In a certain symbolic sense, the recycling project which helped finance the medical missions to Guatemala brought together three important strands in Jorgenson's life--concern about the environment, a commitment to responding to the needs of others and active interest in native American culture, both in this country and elsewhere in the Western hemisphere. Underlying all of this is a very strong commitment to family.

As she thinks about the future her sons will experience, she expresses concern about the environmental costs being imposed on future generations. "We use way too much of our natural resources--for example, excessive packaging for toothpaste and other products. People are not asked to pay the environmental costs of the products they use. Future generations will pay the price." She is similarly concerned about loss of wilderness areas, noting that future generations "will not be able to see, hear or smell wilderness." She also laments the fact that "trains are no longer operating because people didn't support them," noting that trains release far less pollution into the environment than do the number of automobiles required to move a similar number of people. On the positive side, she believes that when it comes to respecting and preserving the environment, "our next generation is much smarter than we are."

Giving expression to her strong commitment to family, she states, "It's essential children have a family nucleus." As for the extended family, she emphasizes, "We have to take care of our own. When grandmother is sick, don't make the government take care of her."

Her life is the story of putting into practice the ideals to which she is committed.[20]

"God Gave Me the Strength to Change"

Glenn Surgest was born April 17, 1956, in Sewickley, Pennsylvania, the son of a professional cleaner and a clerical worker. After graduating from high school, he attended a welding school for six months and then got a job with a company that reconstructed barges. Married in 1977, he has three children--two daughters and a son.

In the early 1980s, his life started coming apart. His job ended and so did his marriage. "It was me," he recalls. "I didn't have the motivation. I was running away from problems-- myself, everything."

His life disintegrated even more when he was incarcerated

after having been convicted of a homicide "having to do with money." Today, he deeply regrets having taken the life of another human being. "I know I can't bring that guy back," he acknowledges and then adds, "I took a life; now I want to give something back."

He recalls telling himself while in prison, "I want out of this prison. Anger is not the way to go." He reports that he got along well with people at the prison. "I met a lot of good people there."

Music played a key role in turning his life around. As a child, he played the trumpet. While in prison, he managed to get his hands on a trumpet and started playing again. He notes with a smile on his face that when he first started playing, the guards would let him have the trumpet for only a few minutes each day. But as he got better, the guards would bring the trumpet to him and ask him to play. Soon he was playing several hours each day. "The horn was a lifeline," he recalls. Now that he is out of prison, he shares the gift of music with others, playing at clubs and wherever folks want to hear him play.

Religion has come to play an important role in Surgest's life. "God gave me the strength to change," he observes, adding that "we live too much by man's laws and not enough by God's laws." While taking pride in his African American heritage, he does not set himself up above other people. "I humble myself. God wants me to be like that."

While in prison, he got some additional training in welding. After being released from prison, he found a job in Pittsburgh. He likes Pittsburgh. "People are friendly here."

"I'm lucky; I'm blessed," he observes. "The friends I've got, I cherish them."

"The main thing now," he says, reflecting on his life, "is to be a good parent. I ask God what to do."

He also spends time being a good friend. When interviewed for this book, he was visiting with a friend struggling to deal with paralysis resulting from multiple sclerosis. (For a profile of the friend, see pages 148-50.)

"We all have crossroads," he said to his friend as he shared with him words of encouragement. "Out of the negative can come the positive."

Surgest would be the first to admit that what he did was terribly wrong. And he knows that for years to come, he will continue paying for the crime he committed. There is, however, a sense of forgiveness which involves seeing the person behind the fault, while in no way excusing the fault. It is that sense of forgiveness that Surgest is seeking and hopes to experience.[21]

"It's So Hard to Find Security and Stability"

Born on June 11, 1956, in Muscatine, Iowa, Kris Rame was thirteen months old when she moved with her two older sisters and her parents to Columbus, Ohio, where they spent the next four years. Then it was on to Staten Island, New York, for four years and Foster, Rhode Island, for eight years. In Rhode Island, her father was the director of a home for unmarried mothers while her mother was the director of a Red Cross program for military families. In Rhode Island, they lived on a thirty-acre farm where they raised collies and had a boarding kennel and grooming business.

Much of her mother's work involved the families of those serving in Vietnam. "Vietnam was all around me," Rame recalls. "I felt my mother's pain every night."

The U.S. Supreme Court's 1973 *Roe v. Wade* decision, which legalized abortion, reduced the number of unmarried mothers needing the services of the home Rame's father ran. And with the war in Vietnam winding down, her mother's case load diminished significantly. When Pearl Buck called Rame's father and asked him to run an adoption agency in Pennsylvania for Amerasian children from Southeast Asia, her parents sold the farm and moved to Pennsylvania.

A junior in high school when the family moved to Pennsylvania, Rame finished high school at Palisades High School in

Kintnersville, Pennsylvania. After graduating from high school, she attended Bucks County Community College and Philadelphia College of the Performing Arts, where she studied oboe. Contemplating a career in music, she found herself pulled in different directions. Playing principle oboe in orchestras, doing chamber work, and premiering new works for aspiring composers, which was her real passion, all appealed to her. None of them, however, provided a steady income.

To pay the rent, she worked at a barn in Cherry Hill, New Jersey, teaching riding lessons and training and showing horses. Things were going very well until the barn was sold in 1980. Though there were investors willing to help her set up her own barn, the high interest rates then being charged made that impractical.

As she was trying to sort things out, one of her Norwegian bachelor uncles called from Minnesota and asked her to move to Minnesota to help him on the family farm. He had worked on Great Lakes ore boats prior to retiring and returning to the family farm. He offered to help her start her own barn if she would promise that he would never have to go to a nursing home. After numerous calls from her uncle, begging her to join him in Minnesota, she accepted the offer. In March of 1981, she loaded her piano, her books, two bridles, a saddle, a few clothes, two dogs and her oboe into her pickup and a small U-Haul trailer, and, with her father accompanying her to help with the driving, moved to her uncle's farm near Bricelyn in southern Minnesota, not far from the Iowa state line.

Both she and her uncle kept their ends of the bargain. He helped her get set up in business and he never went to a nursing home. He passed away in 1992.

She met her future husband playing softball the first summer she was in Minnesota. They were married December of that year. He farms a thousand acres of fertile Minnesota farmland, raising corn and soybeans. They have one son, who was born in 1990.

In 1985, she added managing horse shows to her busy schedule of activities. She manages five major shows--the

Midstates Spring, Summer and Fall Shows in Mason City, Iowa, and the Minnesota Hunter/Jumper and Minnesota Harvest Shows. When not running horse shows, she judges shows, trains horses and gives riding lessons, though she has had to cut back on the number of students she has because managing shows takes so much of her time.

Reflecting on the move to Minnesota, Rame observes, "When I came out here, the phone wasn't ringing off the hook. I had some time to think. I needed that." She also needed some stability in her life, noting that she "had moved a lot and had no roots prior to moving to Minnesota."

The rural lifestyle appeals to her. "Everyone knows each other. Everyone is on a first-name basis." Most important of all, rural Minnesota is a good place to raise her son. But like all parents, she worries about the future that her son will face. She hopes "that he keeps his feet on the ground and stays focused-- that the world doesn't distract him." She observes that in Bricelyn, "life is good, but the real world isn't all that far away."

"It's so hard to find security and stability," Rame comments. Living with her husband and son on the farm near Bricelyn, she has found both.[22]

"Today, There's a More Casual Interpretation Of What's Right and Wrong. "

Wendy Johnson had the courage to make the decision she knew was right for her--a decision which was not applauded by all of her friends from college. She decided to take time off from a successful career in sales to be at home with her three children.

Born May 8, 1957, in Chicago, Johnson was an only child in a single-parent home. Her mother worked full-time. Johnson's grandmother helped take care of her until she was two; then, while her mother worked, she spent the days at various day-care centers. The experience of having been a latch-key child weighed heavily in her decision to stay at home with her three children.

Johnson graduated from college with a degree in accounting and business administration, worked for three years as an admissions counselor recruiting students, and then moved to Denver, where she worked for six years in sales for companies selling computer software and related equipment. She married in 1984. Her husband, who works for a telecommunications company, is also in sales. Together with their three children--sons born in 1988 and 1990 and a daughter born in 1993--they live in Englewood, Colorado, a comfortable suburb near Denver.

Staying home with her children was something she planned to do all along. She notes, "As a child, I did not feel neglected being a latch-key child. But as I got older, I came to realize that I had missed some things."

She is concerned about the impact that influences outside the home have on children. "As parents, we have control in the pre-school years and in religious training. But when they enter the public school system, peers and other influences have an impact on them. Today, there's a more casual interpretation of what's right and wrong. Children get mixed messages."

While stating that she is "not a media basher," she is concerned about the casual way in which violence is portrayed on television. "We tell our children not to hit other people. Television sends a different message. Television shows fail to reinforce what we try to teach."

As for issues of intergenerational significance, she observes that Social Security "began as a wonderful idea but needs modification." She fears that by the time she retires, "Social Security will be gone."

She favors regulation to protect the water supply and air, such as restrictions on wood-burning fireplaces, but believes it should be done on the state level, rather than on the national level.

At this point in her life, her focus is on her children and on what she can do for society. "Personally, as I'm growing older, what I can do for society is just as important as what society can do for me." Doing what she can to help make children safe is a high priority for her.

When all three of her children are in school, she plans to go back to work again. By then, she will have been out of the work force for twelve years and wonders whether she will be able to be employed at the level she was at before taking time off to spend with her children. But that's something to worry about later. For now, she is treasuring the time she is able to spend at home with her three children.[23]

"A Foundation for Family"

In the autumn of 1993, one of Janice Baugh's aunts brought to her attention a newspaper article about Habitat for Humanity, a private not-for-profit organization dedicated to making decent, affordable housing available to low-income working families. Baugh, a single mother who wants to make certain her two children have the best possible chance for successful futures, decided to check it out. The newspaper article reported that a group of volunteers had established a local affiliate of Habitat for Humanity. Baugh applied for a Habitat for Humanity home and was selected to receive the first Habitat home constructed in Davenport, Iowa. Ground-breaking for her home took place in October of 1993. The completed home was dedicated February 5, 1994.

As a Habitat home recipient, Baugh was required to contribute a minimum of five hundred hours of "sweat equity," half of which had to be completed before she was allowed to move into the house. Many, including Baugh, contribute "sweat equity" far in excess of the minimum requirement and continue working on other Habitat projects once their homes are completed.

Like other Habitat homes, Baugh's house is well-insulated, energy-efficient and solidly-constructed. To hold down construction costs, Habitat homes do not include such "extras" as air conditioning, a dishwasher, a finished basement or a garage. Most of the work on Habitat homes is done by volunteers, who spend weekday evenings and Saturdays swinging hammers (and the rest of the week giving muscles they didn't know existed time to recover).

Habitat families purchase their homes, which are sold to them for what it costs to build the homes. Mortgage payments go into the construction fund to build additional homes. Funding for construction of Habitat homes comes entirely from private contributions and the income generated by mortgage payments. No tax dollars go into the construction of Habitat homes.

Habitat for Humanity's goals go far beyond building houses. The real goal is to lend a helping hand so that economically-disadvantaged families can build a solid future for themselves. Surveys indicate, for example, that children of Habitat families do far better in school once they move into decent housing and have a better home environment.

Baugh states, "I truly believe that a house is a foundation for family. Once you have the foundation, you have security and with that security the strength to attain more secure goals."

She has not always experienced that security. Born August 19, 1962, in Davenport, Iowa, she was pregnant with her first child by the time she was a senior in high school. She stayed in school, taking evening classes so that she could graduate. Her daughter was born in 1978. Three years later, she had a second child, a son.

Baugh realized that the odds were against her and worried about "my children and myself becoming a statistic as far as being a young single black female with two children with no father in the home." She decided to do whatever she could to beat the odds and assure a future for her children and for herself.

How does the future look for Baugh and her two children? After having worked for a building materials company for four years and a bank for one year, she recently started a new job in the corporate office of a major regional retailer, where she is a credit analyst.

Her daughter has her eyes set on becoming a pediatrician. Her son is focusing his attention at the moment on being a teenager. Keenly aware that it's tough being a teenager in an urban environment, Baugh is doing everything she can to help him "survive that jungle out there." She expresses confidence that "with right guidance, he will be led to see that there are things out there to grasp hold of."[24]

"God Didn't Bring Us This Far to Leave Us"

Tyia Carrington did not hesitate at all when asked if he was willing to be interviewed for this book. He wants to open up the book to the pages on which his name appears and say to his sons and daughters, "There's your father."

Well, Tyia, here it is.

He is proud of the uniqueness of his name. "There's not another 'Tyia Carrington' in the phone book," he notes.

He was born in Braddock, Pennsylvania, March 7, 1963, the son of a food service employee at Carnegie-Mellon University and the owner of a beer garden. He had eight brothers and sisters but lost a brother in 1993 in a drowning accident.

After graduating from high school, he served in the Army for three years. He was "a Pershing missile man" while stationed in Germany. An accident involving a truck he was driving resulted in $800 being subtracted from his paycheck. The Army apparently changed its mind about who was responsible for the accident. Several months later, the Army paid him the $800 that had been withheld.

After completing his tour duty in the Army, he worked as a nurse's assistant in Pittsburgh until 1991, when he started losing control of his legs. The diagnosis was multiple sclerosis. Today, he spends most of his time confined to a wheelchair, desperately hoping that someday he will be able to walk again without having to brace himself against the wall as is necessary when, on the better days, he is able to get out of the wheelchair for brief periods of time.

"I don't want pity," he emphasizes. But he does want to walk again and, with the help of physical therapists, is working hard to regain control of his legs. "The therapy," he reports, "is going as well as it can. The doctors never ruled out that I would walk again. They just can't say when."

"I just have to take the good with the bad, because some days when I wake up, I got a good day, but when I wake up in the morning and feel bad, it's going to be a bad day. But I try to make it turn into a good day."

"Depression, stress and all that. It's rough dealing with it," he comments. "I see my boys running and playing football and stuff like that. I can't do it no more. I can just watch it. I just deal with it day to day. I'm dealing with it all right. I can't complain."

When he was discharged from the Veterans Administration hospital where he was treated, he promised the friends he had made there that he would be back to see them. He's kept his word. "There's always somebody in worse shape than I am, but I try to cheer them up, just like they try to cheer me up. They say, 'One day you're going to walk again.' I say, 'Thanks, and one day something good's going to happen for you, too, because, you know what, God didn't bring us this far to leave us. Now the picture might look bleak, but it's going to get brighter.'"

Carrington has four children. He says of his children, "I love them. I love all of them. And I'm going to be there for them, in the chair or out of the chair."

He and his wife are separated "but are still the best of friends."

Carrington's experience with multiple sclerosis has changed the way he looks at things. "I give all praise to God. If you'd known me three years ago, you wouldn't have thought I was the same person. I was bitter. When they told me I got multiple sclerosis, I asked, 'Why me?' But then I thought, there's a reason for everything. And at the same time I was asking 'Why me?' I started getting into the Bible and understanding things.

And the more I understand, I tell myself that God didn't bring me this far to leave me."[25]

Chapter 7

Generation X

(Born 1966-85)

Nomenclature is a complicated matter when it comes to the generation which follows the baby boomers. At first, there was a tendency to refer to it at the "baby bust" generation since the birth rate declined for a few years in the late 1960s. But then, in the late 1970s, the birth-rate increased again with what some demographers labeled the "baby boomlet" as baby boomers who had delayed having children became parents.[1] In addition to being demographically misleading, the "baby bust" label, as one observer notes, falsely implies that "this generation is a bust and not worth bothering with."[2]

In contrast to previous generations, there are no watershed experiences which gave form to their lives. The leading-edge members of the generation experienced their childhood years during the ill-defined and, at times, ill-willed 1970s--the decade of gasoline shortages caused by the Organization of Petroleum Exporting Countries (OPEC) flexing its muscles, the decade of Watergate and the Iran hostage crisis. They came of age just as the boom years of the 1980s started losing their glitter. Trailing-edge members have not yet come of age. Their formative experiences, whatever they might be, are yet to be experienced.

Some refer to those born during the years 1966-85 as the "post-boomer" generation, though that has the obvious disadvantage of defining the generation, not on its own merits, but in relation to the generation which preceded it. William Strauss and Neil Howe, the authors of *Generations: The History of America's Future, 1584 to 2069*, refer to the generation which followed the boomers as the "13ers," the label denoting that fact that as Strauss and Howe compute the generations, this generation is the thirteenth generation since the founding of the nation.[3] That way of identifying and labeling the generations, however, has not become common practice.

The most widely used label for the generation is "Generation X," which was popularized by Douglas Coupland in his novel of that name.[4] But even this label is problematic, for it suggests that those born during the years 1966-85 lack identity, with "X" symbolizing the unknown. Perhaps this is the reason--or perhaps it reflects the fact--that so many in this age-group are struggling with questions of identity. Though the "Generation X" label is far from satisfactory, it will be used here in keeping with what is becoming common practice.

A Much-Maligned Generation

Few generations have endured as much criticism from their elders as has Generation X. Less-than-flattering comments about Generation X abound:

> They are all completely unrealistic and don't seem to want to work hard.
>
>   Sheila James, human-resources manager.[5]

> A generation of gripers . . . .
>
>   *Psychology Today*[6]

In addition to "poor attitudes," many baby busters have poor skills and short attention spans, having been raised by a surrogate parent--a television.

The Futurist[7]

They have not learned how to read, nor do they have the expectation of delight or improvement from reading . . . . Thus, the failure to read good books both enfeebles the vision and strengthens our most fatal tendency--the belief that the here and now is all there is.

Allan Bloom, *The Closing of the American Mind*[8]

I have heard from and spoken to dozens of teachers, all of whom report that while there was once a time when a good many American high school and college students enjoyed reading, or at least were willing to do it even if they were not particularly thrilled by it, we have at present a generation whose majority has little or no interest in reading. This one factor alone would absolutely assure us a nation of dummies, even if everything else was working quite well, and we know that practically nothing is.

Steve Allen
Dumbth and 81 Ways to Make Americans Smarter[9]

They don't even seem to know how to dress, and they're almost unschooled in how to look in different settings.

Paul Hirsch, sociologist[10]

It's incredible how little they know. There's almost a total lack of knowledge.

David Warren, political scientist[11]

And so it goes, notwithstanding the fact that many Generation X members put in long hours working at fast-food restaurants, get up prior to daybreak to detassel corn (exhausting work necessary for the production of hybrid seed corn), or work late at night in college and university libraries throughout the nation writing term papers and studying for exams. Those who criticize members of Generation X seem to forget the hours of practice that go into the production of school plays and the dedication and enthusiasm with which many junior high, high school and college students participate in bands, choirs, orchestras and ensembles. Many members of Generation X are active in athletic programs, combining hard work and self-discipline with the joy of participation. An ignorant generation? Few members of older generations can navigate the information superhighway with the skill and sophistication many members of Generation X demonstrate. Indeed, it would not be surprising to hear members of Generation X say, with reference to the computer skills of older generations, "It's incredible how little they know. There's almost a total lack of knowledge."

Granted, there are some members of Generation X who lack motivation, some who are reluctant to work, some who want everything to be given to them without working for it. But any generalizations which paint all members of Generation X with such broad brush strokes do a grave injustice to the many hard-working, highly-motivated individuals who are part of Generation X.

Some Salient Characteristics

No individual is completely representative of any generation. No general description is ever completely accurate, particularly in the case of a generation such as Generation X, which encompasses a tremendous amount of diversity. But while no comprehensive description can accurately describe all who comprise the generation, it is possible to point to some salient characteristics of Generation X:

● *Diminished Earnings.* Between 1983 and 1992, the median weekly earnings of young men aged 16 to 24 who worked full-time declined by 9 percent, when adjusted for inflation, while earnings of young women in the same age-group declined by 4 percent.[12]

- *Remaining Home Longer.* Generation X members tend to remain at home longer than their predecessors in older generations, a reflection both of changing family patterns and of the economic difficulties experienced by many younger Americans.[13] There are more unmarried children under the age of thirty living with their parents than at any time since the Great Depression. A growing number are "boomerang children"-- those who have left and then returned to their parents' homes. [14]

- *Changing Family Structures.* Between 1965 and 1977--the first decade of Generation X--both the percentage of children born outside of marriage and the divorce rate in the United States doubled.[15] By 1980, only slightly more than half of dependent children lived with two married parents who had not previously been married.[16] One commentator suggests that "Generation X is helping to form a new extended American family, one that includes close friends, stepparents, adopted and half-siblings, live-in lovers, and a host of diverse relations."[17]

- *Later Marriages.* Members of Generation X tend to marry later in life than did the two generations which preceded them, delaying marriage until their education has been completed and their careers are established.[18]

- *Increased College Attendance but Little Change in Graduation Rates.* The percentage of 18-to-24-year-olds attending college in the 1990s has increased significantly from the 1980s. But the percentage earning baccalaureate degrees has increased only slightly.[19]

- *Increased Interest in the Visual Arts.* While the

proportion of young adults who read books and newspapers has declined, the proportion who go to art galleries and museums has increased in recent years.[20]

• *Higher Suicide Rates.* Members of Generation X have a higher suicide rate than did members of preceding generations at similar ages.[21]

• *Higher Rates of Incarceration.* Rates of incarceration for members of Generation X are one-third higher than those when baby boomers were similar ages (a change which, in part, reflects tougher sentencing laws for drug use and other offenses).[22]

Where Are the Jobs?

A few years ago, many believed that Generation X, the first generation in the history of this country to be smaller than the one preceding it, would be fortunate in terms of employment. Conventional wisdom held that with fewer entering the job market than was the case when baby boomers came of age, members of Generation X would have their pick of jobs, with prospective employers lining up to hire them.   Wages and salaries, it was believed, would increase substantially as prospective employers competed to hire Generation X members entering the work force.

Events proved otherwise.   The 1991-92 recession slowed down hiring for Americans of all ages just as many members of Generation X were entering the job market. The problem didn't end once economic recovery got the economy humming again. The recovery has been, as some have put it, a "jobless" recovery which has not brought with it the number of new jobs that previous recoveries generated.

What accounts for this erosion of employment opportunities? Much of it is the result of corporate downsizing, which began in the 1980s as U.S. producers, faced with stiff international competition from foreign producers, slimmed down their work forces. Computerization and improved management practices such as "just-in-time" inventory control enabled companies to get by with fewer workers. Meanwhile, the hope that new companies and other employers would pick up the slack by creating new jobs has not materialized, at least not to the extent necessary to provide the number and type of jobs that Generation X members desire. The result is that many members of Generation X have found themselves, if they are fortunate enough to be employed at all, in what Coupland has labeled "McJobs," which he defines as "a low-pay, low-prestige, low-dignity, low-benefit, no-future job in the service sector."[23]

Each year, numerous members of Generation X march across the stages of colleges and universities throughout the nation to receive their diplomas with five-figure debts to pay off but no jobs. Generation X member Steven Gibbs comments, "Perhaps the cruelest joke played on our generation is the general belief that if you went to college, you'll get a job and be upwardly mobile."[24]

A New Generation Gap

The result is anger, frustration and a new generation gap which separates Generation X from older generations. There is anger and frustration resulting from the limited job prospects in what members of Generation X had always been told was a land of opportunity. Anger and frustration resulting from the realization that they might never experience the levels of affluence attained by their parents. Anger and frustration because they might never be able to live in the types of homes their parents were able to purchase.

One Generation X member notes, "Homes in my parents' neighborhood were purchased by plumbers and electricians in the 1950s, but today it seems that only dual-income, thirtysomething professionals can afford them."[25]

Coupled with this frustration is growing resentment of the taxes paid to finance Social Security, Medicare and other programs benefiting older Americans.   For many younger workers, the amount deducted from their paychecks for Social Security and Medicare exceeds the amount they pay in income taxes.

The dismay is intensified by skepticism about the viability of Medicare and Social Security. A 1995 *New York Times/CBS News* poll indicated that 79 percent of those 18-29 years old believe that Medicare will not have the money to provide benefits for them during their retirement years.[26] Pollster Frank Luntz reports that only 28 percent of those 18-34 years old believe that Social Security will be there for them when they retire (while 46 percent believe in the existence of UFOs).[27]

Matters are made worse by the never-ending stream of criticism directed toward members of Generation X by older generations, even as members of Generation X are forced to pay the costs of problems caused by the generations preceding them. Among these problems are environmental pollution, an educational system often perceived as ineffective, a decaying infrastructure in which roads and bridges are falling apart, government incapacitated by budget deficits and political gamesmanship, and a racially-divided society that is an affront to human dignity.

Susan Mitchell, editor of *The Boomer Report*, observes, "One characteristic of young adults is already crystal clear: they resent baby boomers. In the eyes of young adults, boomers had a party and didn't clean up the mess."[28]

"I Hope to Find a Job That Will Support My Daughter the Way I Want to Support Her."

Not all that long ago, Candace Burnett, who was born February 3, 1966, in Davenport, Iowa, had a job with a trucking company. It was a good job paying a decent wage--the type of job once readily available to anyone willing to put in an honest day's work. But then, when the financial fortunes of the company for which she worked took a turn for the worse, her job ended.

So did her marriage. Her husband walked out on her and on their young child as well, failing to make good on the child support he was supposed to pay. Financial desperation drove Burnett to the welfare office to apply for public aid, an experience she painfully recalls as involving great humiliation.

With public aid keeping groceries on the table and a roof over her head, Burnett went back to school to gain the skills necessary to re-enter the work force in a productive capacity. She is anxious to complete her degree and go back to work so that she can get off public aid, which she views as nothing more than a temporary measure to help her get back on her feet.

"When I complete my degree," she notes, "I hope to find a job that will support my daughter the way I want to support her." With the job market tight, she worries that she might not be able to find such a job. Ideally, Burnett would like a job with a trucking company, perhaps as an office manager or in some other administrative position. She likes the trucking business, but will take a job wherever she can find one.

Her voice fills with anger and dismay when she speaks of the abuses she has observed among others on public aid. She tells of rent receipts that are falsified and phony claims about looking for work. "There are those," she reports, "who have no intention of finding a job. They are just trying to live off the system--and they are getting away with it."

The dismay and anger reflected in the tone of her voice intensify when she speaks of the stigma tagged on all welfare recipients as a result of the abuses perpetrated by those "ripping off the system." She is very distressed by "the ridicule I have to endure because of what other people do."

Being blamed for something others do is never pleasant. Being stigmatized because of the dishonesty and irresponsibility of others is infuriating. But she realizes that reforming the welfare system is not within her power, though she hopes others will do something about it. At the moment, her attention is focused on her studies, for she knows that getting off public aid and providing a better life for her daughter will help tip the odds in favor of her daughter having a bright future. She hopes very much that her daughter won't experience what she has gone through.[29]

"My Generation Could No Longer Afford To Be Idealistic."

A common denominator which cuts across all generations is that the United States is a nation of immigrants. One does not have to go back many generations in most families to find someone who was born in another country. And every generation includes some who are themselves immigrants. Among those in Generation X who are foreign-born is Karin Swann, born May 8, 1967, in East Moseley, England, just a short distance from London.

Swann's father, who was born in a small English farm town, spent his childhood years in one of the less prosperous parts of London. With the help of some scholarship assistance, he attended Cambridge, where he earned a Ph.D. in physics prior to joining the faculty of the Royal School of Mines in London. Swann's mother, who speaks six languages, was born in Turkey.

The Swann family came to this country in 1977, the move occasioned by her father's decision to leave academia to pursue business interests in the Pittsburgh area. Three years later, her parents divorced. Her father now lives in the Caribbean. Her mother, who went back to school and remarried, continues to live in the Pittsburgh area.

After graduating from Sewickley Academy in Pittsburgh, Swann attended the University of California at Berkeley, graduating in 1990 with a degree in interdisciplinary studies and psychology. Elected to Phi Beta Kappa, she was invited to be one of the student speakers at commencement.

Berkeley was a formative experience for her. "While I was there," she recalls, "I got radicalized." She became a strongly-committed feminist and "passionately political in a non-main-stream sense."

Much of what happened at Berkeley when she was there was set against the backdrop of the student activism of the 1960s. Swann suggests that the 1960s--especially as they are remembered today--somehow stole something from her generation. "My generation could no longer afford to be idealistic. Many would-be idealistic youth were instead plagued by a sense of hopelessness and alienation. Student activists responded with both political and personal anger as if our desire for change could only get channelled through contempt."

Issues had also become more complicated with various advocacy groups pursuing deeply fragmented political agendas. "There were tremendous identity battles which divided young people," Swann recalls. She left Berkeley frustrated by and disillusioned with the factionalism which typified student politics.

Hoping to gain a perspective that was broader than that offered by the bitterly divisive factionalism at Berkeley, she spent a year in Washington, D.C., working with *The MacNeil-Lehrer Newshour*. She was hired to assist with coverage of the Gulf War. Her job involved research, monitoring tapes, logging tapes and script preparation.

Her sense of what happened in the Persian Gulf is that "we went in way too soon" before diplomatic options and other means of resolving the crisis had been exhausted. While *The MacNeil-Lehrer Newshour* showed a greater willingness to ask tough questions than did others in the media, she was surprised by how passive the media were, accepting with regularity the rules and parameters for coverage set down by the Pentagon.

After the Gulf War, Swann spent several months working for the International Women's Media Foundation in Alexandria, Virginia, where she designed an extensive database for international networking and coordinated a conference in Prague,

Czechoslovakia. The spring of 1992 found her at the Center for History in the Media, Washington, D.C., where she did research for a PBS documentary on the Mississippi Blues.

Then it was back to the classroom again, this time at the University of Wisconsin, Madison, where she completed a master's degree in political science in 1993. Though pleased with the program there, she decided to enroll in an interdisciplinary Ph.D. program at the University of California at San Diego, where she is working in the area of communications. A particular interest is youth rights, which accounts for her involvement in the San Diego Youth Congress, a program designed to make certain that youth in the San Diego area have a chance to be heard.

Like many members of Generation X, she views the future with considerable apprehension. "Our generation has come of age in a complicated time. It often seems as if we have become more divided from one another, rather than united by anything. Women's vastly increased participation in the work force, changing family structure and the divorce rate have called conventional values into question. The question 'Who am I?' takes on an extra burden in light of these and other changes."

As an out lesbian since her years at Berkeley, Swann suggests that questions of identity and gender-roles are particularly relevant to her generation. She concludes that her generation is challenged by the responsibility to establish new values based on difference. "In the interest of making more humane, sensible provisions for the future, we need to integrate what we can use from the past with what we--with all our differences-- experience in the present."[30]

"I Want to Help My People"

A member of the Ácoma Pueblo Tribe, Sharlya Sanchez was born July 1, 1975 in Albuquerque, New Mexico. Today, she makes pottery, which she sells at the Ácoma Pueblo visitor center, as she works to support her daughter, who was born June 10, 1994, and to save money to continue her education. She hopes to go to New Mexico State University to get a degree in nursing and then return to the Ácoma Pueblo. "I want to help my people," she explains.

In the meantime, she is gaining proficiency in making pottery, one of the traditional crafts of the Ácoma Pueblo. The clay used to make Ácoma pottery comes from a source accessible only by foot, the exact location of which remains a tribal secret. The fine-grained, gray clay enables making pottery with exceptionally thin walls. The pottery Sanchez makes is black-on-white with black geometrical patterns painted on a white slip. Nature provides the inspiration for the patterns she paints. Traditionally, Ácoma potters have used slender, fine-tipped brushes made from the spines or leaves of the yucca plant to paint their pottery.

Ácoma, dating back a thousand years, is believed to be the oldest continuously inhabited community in what is now the United States. The village is located on a massive sandstone mesa which rises 367 feet above the valley floor, reaching an elevation of 7,000 feet. The three-story stair-stepped adobe buildings which occupy the 70-acre flat top of the mesa face south so that each level can be warmed by the winter sun. Rising above the residences is the chapel of the San Esteban del Rey Mission, construction between 1629 and 1640. Men of the Ácoma Pueblo, laboring under the direction of Fray Juan Ramirez, carried the massive beams for the roof of the chapel from a mountain more than twenty miles away without, according to tradition, letting the huge beams touch the ground.

Today, about fifty Ácoma live in the pueblo on a permanent basis. Others, preferring the modern conveniences of electricity and running water, live in nearby villages on the reservation but maintain homes in the pueblo, where they spend part of the summer and important feast days. Sanchez' mother recently inherited a home in the pueblo. Among the Ácoma, the family home is passed on to the youngest surviving daughter.

When a Spanish expedition under the command of Francisco

Vásquez de Coronado entered what is now New Mexico in 1540, they encountered villages inhabited by people who derived their support from a highly-sophisticated system of agriculture. Using the Spanish word for "village," the Spaniards referred to the inhabitants of these villages as the "Pueblo." As a result, the term applies both to the villages and to the people who inhabit them.

Upon seeing Ácoma for the first time, a Spanish soldier described it as "a rock out of reach, having steep sides in every direction, and so high that it was a very good musket that could throw a ball so high."[31] But by the end of the century, the Spanish invaders had climbed the heights and levied heavy demands on the Ácoma for food and other supplies. The Ácoma defied the Spanish invaders, who subjected Ácoma to a bloody siege in 1599 in which eleven Spaniards and several hundred Ácoma were killed. Once the Spaniards had suppressed the uprising, they dealt harshly with the survivors.

In New Mexico today, there are nineteen remaining inhabited pueblos. Ácoma is one of the seven pueblos where the Keresan dialect is spoken. Notwithstanding the Spanish surnames which are a legacy of the Spanish invaders, very few Ácoma speak Spanish--a reflection of the bitter feelings about the brutality of the Spanish conquest. Sanchez speaks fluent English and a few words in Spanish. She is working to become fluent in the Keresan dialect.

Jobs on the reservation are scarce. Sanchez' father works in Alaska, returning home occasionally for a few weeks. Her mother, who also makes pottery, drives a school bus.

Sanchez, in keeping with the extended family structure prevalent among the Ácoma, was raised "mainly by my grandmother." With assistance from the Southwestern Indian Foundation, she attended a private parochial school. When she entered high school at the nearby Laguna Pueblo, she was far more advanced than those coming from other schools, which she attributes to the quality of the education she received in the parochial school. Like many Ácoma, she combines traditional Ácoma religious practices with the Roman Catholicism brought to the area by Spanish missionaries.

When Sanchez' daughter was born, one of her grandfathers made for her a cradle board. Ácoma tradition holds that the frame of the cradle board should be built of wood from a tree that has been struck by lightning. This, according to tradition, will impart strength to the child.

Sanchez thinks a lot about her daughter and about her daughter's future. Along with saving money for her own college education, she is putting aside some money for her daughter-- difficult to do in the economically-depressed environment of the reservation.

The past, the present and the future intersect in her life. Even as she plans for the future, she devotes considerable time and energy to helping preserve the Ácoma Pueblo traditions so that her daughter will experience both a bright future and the richness of the Ácoma Pueblo traditions.[32]

"We Are Going to Have to Spend Our Whole Lives Supporting Baby Boomers When They Grow Old"

While in high school, Winnie Dunbar was recruited to work on Prevention Power, a project initiated as part of an effort to reduce the incidence of teenage pregnancy. She helped design a questionnaire to be used in a survey to identify the factors which contribute to the high incidence of teenage pregnancy.

Dunbar has her own views on the matter. She sees the media as part of the problem. "If you look at the TV programs that are popular among teenagers, there are sex and drugs all over the place."

Drugs and alcohol, she suggests, often result in injudicious decisions. "People feel that if they don't get high on something, the weekend is a bore. And when they get high, they let down their guard and spend the night with someone they meet." She adds, "It's kind of scary as to how it is. Some girls have lists of guys they have slept with, which they compare."

Also contributing to the high incidence of teenage pregnancy, she believes, is degeneration of the family unit. She notes that many girls "feel unloved and want someone to love them." This loneliness results in deliberate decisions to have babies. Dunbar suggests that it is erroneous to assume that all teenage pregnancies are accidental.

Unlike many in her age-group, Dunbar has had the good fortune to come from a strong family that is very supportive of her. Her father is a chemist who has held management positions in several different companies. Her mother is a music teacher.

Dunbar was born March 1, 1977, in Marlton, New Jersey. She has an older brother and a younger sister. The family has moved six times, never staying in any place more than five years. Their moves have taken them to Des Peres, Missouri, Boxford, Massachusetts, Bettendorf, Iowa, Grand Rapids, Michigan, and back to Bettendorf, Iowa. Dunbar currently spends most of the year in Chicago, where she is a student at Loyola University preparing for a career as a mid-wife or as a neonatal nurse.

Dunbar worries about what is happening to the environment. Particular concerns include nuclear waste disposal, injudicious use of fossil fuels, depletion of the ozone layer and destruction of tropical rain forests.

She also worries about what will happen when baby boomers start retiring. "There are such a great number of them," she notes, "and we're going to have to spend our whole lives supporting them when they grow old." She doubts that Social Security will be there when her generation retires. She also notes that job prospects for her generation are limited because "baby boomers hold so many of the jobs." She adds that "the significance of a college degree isn't as great as it used to be for finding a job."

She believes that the generation gap between her generation and older generations also involves technology. "Boomers," she suggests, "won't open their eyes to Internet" and other technological developments.

While having many concerns about the future, Dunbar

believes there is reason for optimism. She is looking forward to what computers will enable in the years to come and sees prospects for great progress in medicine in areas such as gene-splicing. And she is very excited about the work that is being done with AIDS. She is hopeful that a cure will be discovered.

Dunbar reflects many of the concerns that are widespread among members of Generation X. At the same time, like many of her peers, she demonstrates resilience and optimism about the future.[33]

"There Will Be a Revolution If Things Do Not Change!"

Like many others his age, Brian Benda, born January 25, 1979, in Richmond, Virginia, and now living in Chattanooga, Tennessee, intensely dislikes the "Generation X" label. He emphatically states, "I *hate* the word and the connotation I receive from its meaning!" He characterizes the label as "a name without a name--a blind man without a vision." He adds, "Are we really that worthless as a generation to be given no formidable title whatsoever?"

He fears that when he is an adult, Social Security, Medicare and Medicaid will all experience bankruptcy. And he worries that his generation, which will be in positions of leadership by that time, will be blamed for the demise of these programs even though it is the short-sightedness of today's leaders that is causing the problems. "[Today's leaders] are the ones who are pulling our nation farther and farther into an uncontrollable debt. They are the ones who are corrupting our governmental structure. They are the ones who are acting and passing laws that will benefit the middle-aged and elderly generations of today, leaving younger generations stranded in the dark."

Benda warns that the failure of older generations to pay attention to the concerns of younger generations will result in "one of the greatest rebellions of all time." He states, "There *will* be a revolution if things do not change! This revolution will not only bring down the power and world dominance of the United States of America, but will create a global society that lives with hostility towards everyone. Nations will divide. Cultures, races, and the people will divide."

He adds that he himself is not advocating revolution. He believes that better communication can prevent such a disaster. But he fears that if there is not communication that transcends generational lines, we are headed for such an uprising.

Benda's father is a mechanical engineer, his mother a diagnostic speech and language therapist. He has a younger sister and a younger brother. An avid soccer player, Benda plays on a team that is ranked in the top ten nationally in his age-group. At school, he is active in student government.

He plans to go to college and become a criminal defense lawyer. Though planning to become a defense lawyer, he has little sympathy for juveniles who break the law. He is supportive of legislation to try as adults juveniles accused of serious crimes. "There are a lot of juveniles murdering innocent individuals and getting away with totally devastating the lives of others," he states.

And what of the future? Even though he warns that there might be an uprising of younger generations and fears what might happen if this occurs, he still finds room for optimism. "It all goes back to communication," he suggests. "I'm not a pessimist. I believe the future is going to be good, but we're going to have to work at it."[34]

"If He Could See Us Now, Tears Would Drop from His Eyes"

At the 1995 Martin Luther King Day celebration in Rock Island, Illinois, Corey Desadier, who was born February 26, 1982, in Rock Island, was awarded a prize for an essay he wrote. "As I walk down the street this day," his essay begins, "my heart fills with sorrow." The essay speaks of how Martin Luther King fought hard for freedom "always nonviolent no matter what, and we finally got the freedom." But, Desadier states, "we abuse it." He continues:

> We kids take guns to school and
> Skip it to smoke drugs.
>
> When I go to bed at night,
> I think, did he die for nothing?
> If he could see us now
> Tears would drop from his eyes.

Like many children living in urban areas, Desadier lives in almost constant fear of violence. From the playground of the elementary school he attended prior to moving on to junior high, he could see drug dealers plying their trade. When leaving school to go home, he feared that he "might be hit by a speeding car or get caught up in the middle of a drug drop."

"I try to keep my head straight," he notes as he describes the way he carefully looks each situation over to see which side of the street might be the safest and carefully plans where to walk and what to do to reduce the risk of becoming a victim of violence. Whenever possible, he stays inside because that is safer than being out on the street.

A boy three years younger than Desadier--a boy he knows from the elementary school he attended--was recently arrested and charged with attempted first-degree murder and aggravated battery. The boy is accused of driving a kitchen knife into the back of his mother's live-in boyfriend during a domestic squabble. The boy lived five blocks from where Desadier lives.[35]

Desadier lives with his mother; his parents split up several years ago. "I love both of them equally," he states. He has two older sisters and three nieces who are frequent visitors.

When Desadier was five, he was diagnosed as having diabetes. Because of the diabetes, he has to watch his diet carefully. Like many others on diets, he confesses, "I slip sometimes."

Desadier believes that movies and television are part of the problem because "kids see violence all the time on TV and in movies." He states, "Mothers and fathers need to give kids something positive to think about. Parents need to think about their kids--that is what really matters."

Desadier's prize-winning essay concludes with a poem:

> "Keep to the march! Keep to the song!"
> Keep on resisting where there is wrong.
> "Fight to be equal! Fight to be free!"
> But only fight NONVIOLENTLY!
>
> "I HAVE A DREAM," said the man with no gun,
> Of equality for everyone,
> Of an end to war and poverty.
> The poor are a mighty family.
> Brothers and sisters, join with me.[36]

Chapter 8

The Twenty-First Century Generation

(Born after 1985)

The pressing issues of the day which dominate the front pages of newspapers are not of immediate concern to the youngest generation comprising the current U.S. population-- those born after 1985, who, if fate is kind, will live the major portion of their lives in the twenty-first century. While adults are preoccupied with distant matters, such as the budget battles in Washington, and more immediate matters, such as trying to balance the family budget, children have deeply serious conversations about puppies and kittens, Power Rangers and My Little Ponies, chocolate chip cookies and brownies with chocolate frosting. Adults can't hold a candle to children when it comes to having deeply serious conversations. With youthful exuberance, children play hopscotch on sidewalks marked with colored chalk, make paper airplanes that fly in unpredictable ways, and use brightly-colored crayons to add a personal touch to coloring books, all the while giggling and laughing as only children can do. Such are the delights of childhood.

Childhood Poverty

But while the years of childhood might seem idyllic to the outside observer, such is not always the case. Growing numbers of children in the United States--the richest nation in the world-- live in poverty. The percentage of children living in poverty in

*Figure 8-1: Poverty Rates for Children
And Older Americans*

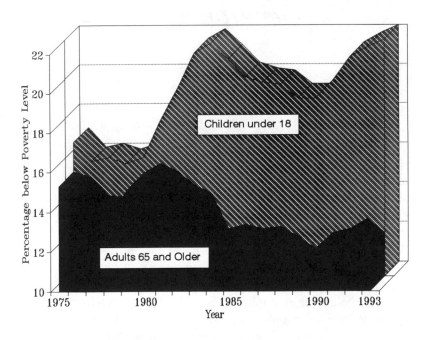

Based on U.S. Bureau of the Census data included in various editions of Statistical Abstract of the United States. *The poverty index is based on money income and does not take into account noncash benefits such as food stamps, Medicaid and subsidized public housing.*

the United States increased from 16.5 percent in 1975 to 22 percent in 1993.[1] (During the same period, the percentage of Americans age sixty-five and older living in poverty decreased from 15.3 percent to 12.2 percent.[2])

While no one wants to be poor in a society which strongly emphasizes affluence, poverty is not invariably disastrous for those who experience it. Many older Americans, including some profiled in previous chapters in this volume, experienced childhood poverty but rose above it to secure a better life for themselves and for their families. Some were strengthened by the hardship they endured. Others viewed it as irrelevant as they found good jobs at decent wages after graduating from high school or as they worked their way through college and entered the salaried work force.

As we approach the end of the twentieth century, however, good jobs at decent wages are no longer readily available upon graduation from high school. Nor does a college diploma guarantee financial comfort. There is a growing gap between the haves and the have-nots, with educational success (or lack thereof) and marketable skills (or lack thereof) determining who is on which side of the gap. Some experience levels of affluence exceeding that of their parents. Others, including some with college degrees, struggle to survive economically.

Peter B. Goldberg, president and chief executive officer of Family Service America in Milwaukee, notes that in recent years, "the traditional avenues by which families might escape poverty narrowed. The tone of our time-honored messages to poor kids--get an education, stay out of trouble, develop a work ethic--became increasingly hollow . . . ."[3]

U.S. Senator Daniel Patrick Moynihan observes:

> The U.S. today may be the first society in history where children are much worse off than adults. It is time we realized we have a problem of significant social change unlike anything we have experienced in the past. [And] we are completely ignoring it.[4]

A substantial amount of data indicates that children who experience poverty perform less adequately in school and are less likely to stay in school, thereby placing them several steps behind in the educational sweepstakes so pivotal for future success.[5] In an editorial in *Social Work*, Patricia L. Ewalt notes that since children living in poverty often have less parental supervision, they miss more days of school, are less likely to complete high school and are less likely to go to college than are those from more affluent backgrounds.[6] In the United States, approximately 500,000 children drop out of school each year.[7]

Child psychologists Eric F. Dubow and Maria F. Ippolito of Bowling Green State University report that research they have done indicates that poverty "during the toddler and preschool years explained a significant proportion of the variance in changes in academic achievement during the elementary school years."[8] Similar conclusions are reached by Greg J. Duncan of the University of Michigan and Jeanne Brooks-Gunn and Pamela Kato Klebanov of Columbia University, who report that their data "are consistent with the hypothesis that family income and poverty status are powerful determinants of the cognitive development and behavior of children, even after we account for other differences . . . between low- and high-income families."[9]

The trend-lines are unmistakable: childhood poverty foreshadows a troubled future for many members of the Twenty-First Century Generation.

Changes in Family Structure

Several factors have contributed to the growth of childhood poverty in recent years. Among them are the diminished earnings of younger Americans (a number of whom are parents) and the tendency of our political system to favor older Americans when making funding decisions.[10] The greatest contributing factor, however, is the deterioration of the family structure. William Galston, a domestic policy advisor in the Clinton administration, observes:

> Changes in family structure over the past generation are strongly correlated with rising rates of poverty among children . . . . [C]hild poverty rates today would be one-third lower if family structure had not changed so dramatically since 1960. Fifty-one percent of the increase in child poverty observed during the 1980s is attributable to changes in family structure during that period.[11]

Economic Costs of Divorce

Though the rate of divorce has declined slightly in recent years, nearly one of every two marriages ends in divorce.[12]   In about 30 percent of these cases, the marriage is dissolved before the oldest child reaches the age of sixteen.   Two-thirds of the children of divorced parents experience their parents' marital breakup prior to starting school.[13]

While ending an unhappy marriage is sometimes the lesser of evils, divorce often imposes significant economic costs on children. In theory, child-support payments by the noncustodial parent provide for the financial needs of the children of divorced parents.   But in practice, the current system of child support leaves huge gaps.   Under the best of circumstances, court-ordered child-support payments often cover only a portion of the costs of raising a child. The descent to poverty is accelerated by the fact that in a significant number of cases (estimates range as high as 50 percent), noncustodial parents fail to pay the entire amount of court-ordered child support payments--if, indeed, they pay anything at all.[14]

Needs unmet by child-support payments are only part of the problem. Divorced women, many of whom are the custodial parent, often find themselves in a disadvantageous financial situation after divorce. Though average compensation levels for women have been rising, they continue to be significantly lower than those for men. As a result, women are more likely than men to experience poverty following divorce. When lower earnings levels of divorced women are coupled with the failure of their former husbands to pay child-support, the results can be devastating. S. Wayne Duncan of the University of Washington observes:

> As marriages have been increasingly likely to end in divorce, the number and percentage of children spending part of their childhoods in single-parent families has notably increased. The economic consequences for many children and . . . their mothers are generally serious and at times so severe that they lead them into poverty. Meanwhile, fathers' incomes rise, but only about half pay their full court-ordered child support.[15]

Births to Unmarried Women

Even more significant in terms of economic impact on children is the huge increase in the number of births to unmarried women, many of whom are teenagers:

• In 1970, 10.7 percent of all babies born in the United States were born to unmarried women. By 1992, the percentage had nearly tripled to 30.1 percent.[16]

• Among whites, the percentage of babies born to unmarried women increased by a factor of four from 1970 to 1992--from 5.7 percent to 22.6 percent. Among African Americans, the percentage more than doubled from 1970 to 1992--from 37.6 percent to 68.1 percent.[17] (Though the data are incomplete, there is some indication that the birthrate among unmarried African American women is now declining while the birthrate among unmarried white women continues to rise sharply.[18])

• In the past two decades, the number of teenage pregnancies has nearly doubled.[19] Births to teenage mothers, most of whom are unmarried, account for nearly 15 percent of all babies born in the United States.[20]

• Sixty-six percent of all children under the age of six who live only with their mother live in poverty (compared to 12 percent of children under the age of six living with married parents).[21]

Figure 8-2: Births to Unmarried Women

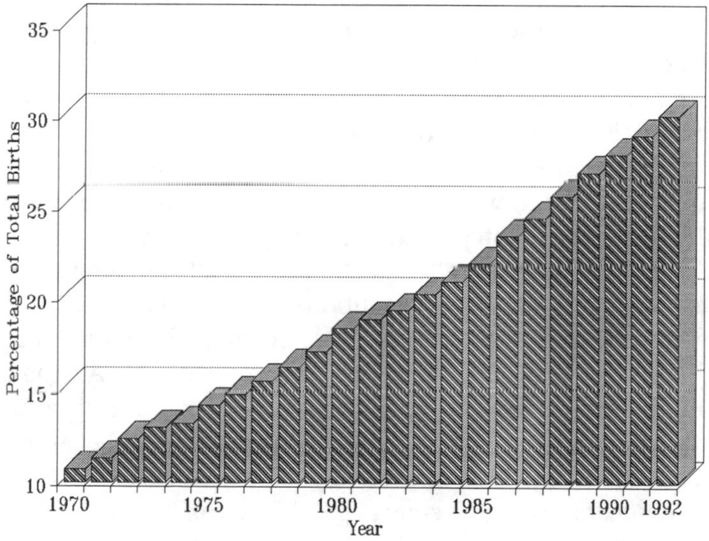

Based on data from the U.S. National Center for Health Statistics included in various editions of Statistical Abstract of the United States.

• Many unmarried teenage mothers end up on welfare. Douglas Besharov of the American Enterprise Institute observes, "The increase in welfare dependency is among those unwed mothers who first go on welfare as teens."[22]

● Estimated costs to taxpayers for teenage pregnancy total $32 billion annually.[23]

As noted in the previous chapter, many members of Generation X believe they are being shortchanged by older generations--and there are plausible arguments to support this view. The irony is that the members of Generation X--men and women alike--who fail to practice reproductive responsibility are significantly shortchanging those who follow them.

"Born to Pay"

While the childhood poverty rate is alarmingly high and the number of babies born to unmarried women has increased substantially in recent years, it is not the case, of course, that all children live in poverty or that the majority of all babies are born to unmarried women. Seven of every ten babies in this country are born to women who are married. Four of every five children in this country live above the poverty level.

But even those more fortunate face a challenging future. As Philip Longman put it in the title of a book published shortly after the first of the Twenty-First Century Generation began arriving on the scene, they are "born to pay."[24] As today's children grow older, they will be asked to shoulder a significant portion of the costs of Social Security and other benefits for older Americans, costs which will increase substantially when baby boomers reach retirement age. They will bear a disproportionate share of the costs of our $5 trillion national debt, both in terms of paying the taxes necessary to cover interest on the national debt and in terms of opportunity lost as a result of the drag on the economy resulting from the heavy borrowing necessary to finance the national debt. They will pay a substantial share of health-care costs for older Americans without any realistic hope of receiving comparable benefits themselves when they reach retirement age. To these matters we now turn.

Part III
The Challenge of Justice

Chapter 9

Deficits and Budget Battles

The nation was more than two centuries old when, in 1981, the debt run up by the federal government exceeded $1 trillion for the first time.[1] During those two centuries, the nation endured the Great Depression and numerous lesser depressions, built railroads and highways spanning the continent, and fought nine major wars--the American Revolution, the War of 1812, the Mexican-American War, the Civil War, the Spanish-American War, World War I, World War II, the Korean War, and the War in Vietnam. It took only five years for the second trillion dollars of debt to accumulate and another four years for the third. The fourth trillion dollars of debt was run up in little more in two years.[2] Today, the federal government is in the hole more than $5 trillion--that's a five with twelve zeros after it.

The $5 trillion in debt breaks down to almost $20,000 for each person currently comprising the U.S. population--$100,000 for a family of five, more than the net assets of most families. Such is the legacy of a century of deficits as our government has failed to exercise the fiscal discipline necessary to produce a balanced budget.

Figure 9-1: Growth of the National Debt 1920-95

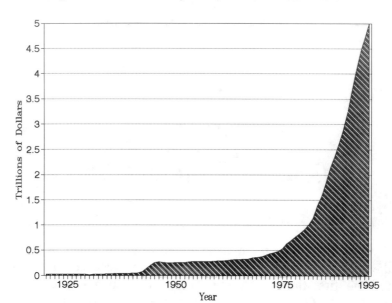

Based on data included in various editions of Statistical Abstract of the United States and in Historical Statistics of the United States.

Do Deficits Matter?

It is always tempting to try to explain away unpleasant facts by suggesting that they are in some way insignificant. Thus, it is not surprising that there are various rationales for ignoring the $5 trillion of unpleasantness that is our national debt. "Don't we just owe this money to ourselves?" "Can't the federal government just print more money?" "Won't growth of the economy get rid of the debt?" Such are the rhetorical questions raised by those who would like to believe that rhetoric can solve problems.

Unfortunately, economic realities can't be changed by rhetoric. The suggestion that we just owe the money to ourselves misses the boat by the width of the Pacific Ocean. A considerable portion of our national debt (including 20 percent of recently-issued debt[3]) is held by foreign investors--investors who could dump the government bonds they have purchased just as quickly as they bought them. It is startling to realize that our credit markets are, in substantial measure, at the mercy of foreign investors who don't necessarily view our well-being as their top priority.

Even the portion of our national debt that is held by U.S. citizens can't be ignored. Those who have purchased savings bonds to put aside money for their children's education or for their retirement expect to be repaid when the bonds mature--and have every right to have this expectation met. To fail to do so would be a huge breach of faith and a grave injustice.

The suggestion that the federal government could just "print more money" to cover deficit spending comes with its own set of problems. The unpleasant fact of life is that expanding the money supply brings with it inflation, including, in extreme cases, hyperinflation such as Germany experienced in the 1920s and many South American countries experienced in the 1970s and 1980s. Even relatively modest rates of inflation take a substantial bite out of savings and other available resources when projected over a number of years. For example, suppose the rate of inflation remains at about 2.5 percent. Fifty years down the road, when the last Generation X members will be nearing retirement, a new car costing $20,000 today would cost nearly $69,000--an amount which, though unwieldy, might be manageable if personal income grows over the intervening five decades. But now suppose that as a result of the government injudiciously expanding the money supply, inflation kicks up to 10 percent and stays there for the next five decades. If this were to happen, the Generation X member approaching retirement would have to pay $2.3 million for a car which today costs $20,000. It is difficult to imagine how personal income can grow at a rate sufficient to make a $2.3 million car affordable.

The contention that our economy can grow its way out of the national debt is also problematic. The national debt, of course, will continue to get larger as long as the federal government continues to run budget deficits. So the real question is whether economic growth, which increases the amount the government collects in taxes by expanding taxable income, can get rid of budget deficits and replace them with budget surpluses large enough to pay off the national debt. Paying off the current national debt, it should be noted, would require budget surpluses of $100 billion a year over a period of fifty years. That's how deep the hole is that we have dug for ourselves.

If the real interest rates (actual interest rates minus the rate of inflation) paid to finance the national debt were less than the growth rate of the economy, and if increases in spending in all areas other than interest on the national debt did not exceed the growth rate of the economy, the federal budget deficit would diminish. In time, deficits would disappear and be replaced by budget surpluses.

There are two problems, however, with this rather rosy scenario. One problem is that real interest rates often exceed the growth rate of the economy. When this happens, the budget deficit increases, rather than decreases, unless there are other factors such as spending cuts which offset the larger bite taken by interest on the national debt. There are also demographic factors which come into play. Chief among these is the fact that the aging of the U.S. population increases substantially the cost of programs such as Medicare which benefit the elderly.

Realistically speaking, our $5 trillion national debt will probably never be paid off. Not even Speaker of the House Newt Gingrich and other hard-line Republican budget-cutters propose generating budget surpluses large enough to retire the national debt. Like it or not, our huge national debt, in all probability, is here to stay.

That does not mean, however, that the national debt can just be ignored or that budget deficits which add to the national debt are a matter of indifference after all. There are several reasons for being concerned about budget deficits and the national debt. First of all, the carrying costs of the national debt--the interest which must be paid on the money borrowed to finance it-- siphons off money that could be used for other purposes. For example, suppose that interest rates paid on the money borrowed to finance our $5 trillion national debt average 6 percent this coming year. The amount paid in interest will add up to $300 billion--money that could be spent on education, health care and other programs or rebated to taxpayers in the form of lower taxes. Were it not for the interest which must be paid on the money borrowed to finance the national debt, there would be no federal budget deficits. And there would be money left over to spend on other things. Such is the impact of our national debt!

The national debt takes a bite out of people's pockets in other ways as well. Because in the credit markets, money, in effect, is a commodity which is bid up or down depending on supply and demand, greater demand for money in the form of increased borrowing pushes up interest rates. When the federal government enters the credit markets to finance the national debt by auctioning off treasury bills, the government, in effect, is competing with private individuals applying for mortgages to buy new homes, corporations taking out loans to finance new factories, students taking out loans to pay for their college educations and farmers borrowing money to buy new tractors and combines. When there is competition for the money that is available to be lent, those who have money to lend can ask for and receive higher interest rates on the money they lend.

Small changes in interest rates add up to huge amounts when applied to large debts, such as our national debt. For example, suppose that the average interest paid to finance our $5 trillion national debt this coming year ends up being 7 percent, rather than 6 percent. That's an additional $50 billion that has to be taken from other programs or otherwise covered.

Small changes in interest rates also make huge differences when projected over a number of years. A couple taking out a thirty-year fixed-rate $70,000 mortgage to finance a new home at 7 percent interest will have a monthly payment of $465.71. Over the thirty-year life of the mortgage, they will pay a total of $167,655.60--the $70,000 financed plus $97,655.60 in interest. What happens if they end up paying 8 percent interest? Their monthly payments are now $513.64; over the life of the mortgage, they will pay more than $17,000 in additional interest. And what if the interest rate is 9 percent? Their monthly payments would then be $563.23 a month and they would end up paying more than $35,000 in additional interest, compared to the 7 percent mortgage.

The changes in interest payments go the other way as well. If reducing the federal budget deficit resulted in thirty-year fixed mortgage rates dropping by two points, the couple buying the house would save more than $35,000 over the life of the mortgage. Political rhetoric aside, the best "tax cut" for most middle-class Americans is getting interest rates down. A $600 per year tax credit for children under eighteen adds up to far less than a typical middle-class family would save on interest if mortgage rates and interest rates for car loans were to go down just one point. And a drop in interest rates that would enable financing our $5 trillion national debt at 5 percent, rather than 6 percent, would reduce by $50 billion a year the spending cuts necessary to achieve a balanced budget while a two-point drop in interest rates would result in annual savings of $100 billion.

There are other costs as well. Since a substantial portion of the private sector operates, at least in part, on borrowed money, higher interest rates make it more difficult for business enterprises to modernize plants and buy new equipment, expand their training programs, make greater commitments to research and development and do the other things that contribute to productivity. It is only with increased productivity that higher wages and salaries are possible in a changing world economy. And increased productivity is essential if domestic producers are to survive in the face of stiff foreign competition.

In 1992, investment banker Peter G. Peterson and former Senators Paul Tsongas and Warren Rudman founded The Concord Coalition, a nonpartisan advocacy group that supports policies and proposals that would help achieve a balanced budget. The coalition notes that from 1946 to 1973, what Americans produced for each hour of work increased 2.9 percent each year while from 1974 to 1994, the increase was only 1.1 percent each year. They estimate that if productivity had increased as much from 1974 to 1994 as in the previous three decades, the median annual family income today would be $15,500 higher today than is the case.[4]

There are, to be sure, a wide variety of factors that adversely affect productivity. Among these are a decline in the work ethic, the decay of roads and other parts of our infrastructure, and the deterioration of our educational system, resulting in entry-level workers who are not adequately prepared to do what is required of them in jobs which are technologically demanding. But even when other factors are taken into account, it is difficult to avoid concluding that growth of productivity is inhibited by higher interest rates that make it more difficult for employers to invest in training, new equipment and the other things that contribute to growth of productivity.

What will happen if we ignore the problems posed by our mushrooming national debt? The Concord Coalition warns:

> If we ignore our mounting debt, if we just wish it would go away and do nothing about it, it will grow and grow like a cancer that will eventually overwhelm our economy and our society . . . . Our productivity growth will remain stagnant; more of our workers will have to settle for low-paying jobs; and our economy will continue its anemic growth. America will decline as a world power . . . . Working people will be required to pay an ever larger share of their earnings to support a growing retired population and to pay the exploding interest on the debt that the older generation accumulated. Eventually, working people will refuse to submit to the crushing burden forced upon them by their elders. They will vote for leaders who will slash entitlement programs, even on the truly needy, rather than raise taxes still further. Millions of elderly people who thought that they could count on their retirement benefits will find that the resources are not there to meet their needs. There will be a generational conflict pitting American against American, child against parent, in a way that our nation has not seen before.[5]

Jefferson and Madison

In a letter to James Madison dated September 6, 1789, (though not delivered until the first month of the next year), Thomas Jefferson asserted that no generation ought to "contract debts greater than may be paid during the course of its own existence." Making reference to the new French constitution being written while he was in Paris (Jefferson wrote the letter while in France but didn't deliver it until returning to this country), the letter suggests that "with respect to future debts, would it not be wise and just for that nation to declare, in the constitution they are forming, that neither the legislature, nor the nation itself, can validly contract more debt than they may pay within their own age, or within the term of nineteen years?"[6] (Jefferson computes the duration of a generation to be nineteen years.)

In a reply dated February 4, 1790, Madison disagrees with Jefferson's argument:

> Debts may be incurred for purposes which interest the unborn, as well as the living: such are debts for repelling a conquest, the evils of which descend through many generations. Debts may even be incurred principally for the benefit of posterity . . . . The term of nineteen years might not be sufficient for discharging the debts in either of these cases."[7]

As Madison correctly notes, the benefits of debts incurred to repel an invader might last for generations, as might the benefits of debts incurred to build roads and schools. But, for the most part, investment in the future is not what accounts for our massive federal budget deficits today. Rather, they are, in large part, the result of money spent on current consumption for a host of programs ranging from Medicare to farm subsidies. Younger generations and those yet to be born will bear many of the costs of these programs while enjoying few of their benefits. Younger generations and those yet to be born will have to make do with less help from government because the government is broke. They are the ones who will have to pay higher interest rates on their home mortgages than would be the case if financing the national debt did not push up interest rates. They are the ones who will find employment opportunities limited because of sluggish economic growth resulting from interest rates which inhibit investment.

In a thoughtful and thought-provoking book entitled *Facing Up: How to Rescue the Economy from Crushing Debt and Restore the American Dream*, Peter G. Peterson states:

> We seem to have forgotten what Jefferson understood so clearly at the dawn of democracy in the modern world: To encumber the next generation with debt is to deny them the full measure of their freedom. To place the weight of these trillions upon trillions of dollars upon unborn children is to rob them of what Jefferson and the founding fathers promised us: life, liberty, and the pursuit of happiness.[8]

The Contract with America

A promise to balance the federal budget in seven years is at the heart of The Contract with America crafted by Newt Gingrich, a platform on which many Republicans ran in 1994. With the election of Republican majorities in both houses of Congress, the GOP Contract with America became the engine driving much of the legislative agenda in the first few months of the 104th Congress.

While many aspects of the Contract with America remain controversial, Gingrich and other Congressional Republicans deserve credit for insisting that balancing the budget be part of the legislative agenda, even after the proposed balanced budget amendment failed in the Senate. Previous Congresses would have simply paid lip service to balancing the budget and then continued their free-spending ways. The 104th Congress is serious about balancing the budget.

Congressional Republicans are to be commended for insisting that realistic numbers be used when making budget projections. There is a long history of using unrealistically optimistic assumptions to estimate revenue levels and program costs, the result being that deficits have often ended up being much larger than projected. There is much to be said for honesty in budgetary matters (and elsewhere).

Gingrich and other Congressional Republicans also deserve credit for having the courage to place on the table popular entitlement programs such as Medicare, Medicaid, veterans' benefits and farm subsidies. As dedicated budget watchers are keenly aware, it is the mushrooming costs of entitlement programs that are driving up federal spending and that, in large part, account for the huge budget deficits that have been run up. At present, entitlements account for 61 percent of the federal budget; if no changes are made, entitlements are expected to comprise 80 percent of federal expenditures ten years down the road.[9] Some projections suggest that by the year 2013, entitlements and net interest on the national debt will consume the entire federal budget.[10] In practice, of course, that will not happen; something will have to give way before entitlements and net interest devour the entire federal budget. What projections such as these make clear, however, is a very basic fact of life: the rapid growth of entitlement programs cannot continue indefinitely.

Entitlement programs were established with the best of intentions. As their proponents are quick to note, they help millions of Americans by ensuring a degree of financial security many would not otherwise have. But unless spending on these programs is brought under control, they will result in fiscal disaster for the nation. The unsettling irony in all of this is that good and decent programs which help millions of Americans today threaten the well-being of our children and grandchildren by undercutting the economic foundations essential for a bright future.

While Congressional Republicans deserve the gratitude of future generations for putting budget-balancing proposals on the table, the Republican plan, like all political documents, is flawed. One flaw is that the plan does not distinguish between programs such as farm subsidies and Medicaid financed by general revenues and programs such as Social Security and the Hospital Insurance portion of Medicare (Part A) financed by earmarked taxes channeled through designated trust funds. Several of the trust funds, at least at the moment, are building up substantial surpluses. For example, during the current year, the revenues generated by the Social Security payroll tax are expected to exceed benefit costs by nearly $60 billion. During the next seven years, the temporary surplus in the Social Security trust fund is expected to grow by nearly $600 billion.[11] Including Social Security in budget calculations makes the current federal budget deficit appear to be $60 billion less than would be the case if the general revenue shortfall were viewed in isolation.

The political advantage of including the trust fund surpluses in budget calculations is that it is possible to reach a balanced budget on paper without making as many spending cuts as would be necessary if only programs funded by general revenues were considered. (There is also an economic argument for including the trust funds since trust fund surpluses are lent to the federal government to help fund current operations, thus lessening the pressure on credit markets.) The practical problem, however, is that there will be the devil to pay down the road when the temporary trust fund surpluses are needed for the purposes for which they are intended. Once baby boomers start retiring and drawing down the temporary surpluses in the Social Security trust fund, at which time benefit costs will exceed revenues generated by the payroll tax, the budget will once again be out of balance. Drastic adjustments will have to be made to bring the budget back into balance.

Wisdom is on the side of leaving designated trust funds out of deficit calculations and instead coming up with a plan for bringing the costs for programs which are supposed to be financed by general revenues into balance with general revenues. If more than seven years are required for this, so be it. It is important that our nation's fiscal house be put in order in a way that will be workable for future generations, rather than simply opting for a short-term fix that will cause other problems down the road. The time framework for accomplishing this objective is secondary to the urgency of getting the job done the right way.

There are also other problems with the GOP plan. For political reasons, the bulk of the program cuts would come in the later years of the seven-year plan while the tax cuts would be front-loaded in the early years. In fact, over half the cuts in programs in the GOP proposals (as well as in proposals submitted by President Clinton) would not go into effect until after the year 2000--that is, not until after the next three elections.[12] It will take a tremendous amount of political willpower to stay the course in the first two years of the new century when the impact of the proposed budget cuts, if adopted, will become quite pronounced.

As often happens, the long term has been sacrificed to minimize political costs in the short term. Legislatively, the current Congress cannot bind future Congresses. Unless a constitutional amendment mandates balancing the budget, no multi-year balanced budget plan will be successful if future Congresses lack the willpower to implement it. Wisdom would be on the side of saving the tax cuts as a reward for restraining the growth of expenditures, rather than front-loading the tax cuts in the early years while pushing off the bulk of the spending cuts until later.

Another problem is that the Republican budget plan allows little room for flexibility in the event of a recession. Balancing the budget is best done on the strength of a recovery. If a recession, comparable to the ones that have occurred periodically in the post-World War II years, slows down the economy just as the more drastic budget cuts are going into effect in the year 2000, the public clamor for scrapping the balanced budget plan might well drown out voices of fiscal conservatism.

Finally, as often happens in the political arena, the costs of balancing the budget aren't allocated equally. Much of the controversy about Republican budget proposals has centered around proposed changes in Medicare intended to restrain the growth of spending in this area. Overlooked in this high-octane debate is the fact that proposed funding reductions for programs such as Head Start and Medicaid that benefit children are far more severe than the restraints that would be placed on the growth of funding for Medicare.

As noted in Chapter 1, senior citizens pack political clout disproportionate to their numbers. The political reality is that younger generations and those yet to be born often end up holding the short end of the stick. Budget issues involve questions of intergenerational justice both with respect to (a) the costs imposed on our children and grandchildren resulting from further growth of the national debt and (b) the relative funding levels for programs of significance for different age-groups. Perfect justice would entail minimizing the debt load on future generations while equitably distributing available resources (and necessary costs such as taxes) among existing generations. Achieving a balanced budget by allocating available resources and necessary costs among existing generations in an inequitable manner would be only half a loaf insofar as intergenerational justice is concerned.

The Ten-Percent Solution

Is there a better way of balancing the budget? The answer is to be found in the "ten-percent solution." This approach would separate programs that are supposed to be funded by general revenues from programs such as Social Security and the Hospital Insurance part of Medicare (Part A) funded by ear-marked taxes channeled through designated trust funds. Questions of solvency pertaining to the trust funds must be addressed on a case-by-case basis, rather than as part of the overall budget. The ten-percent solution would reduce the gap between general revenues and the costs of programs that are supposed to be funded by these revenues by 10 percent the first year and by an additional 10 percent each subsequent year (20 percent the second year, 30 percent the third year, etc.), excluding any year in which the economy was in recession. After ten years, plus however many years the economy was in recession, the budget would be balanced.

Table 9-1: The Ten-Percent Solution[13]

Year	Beginning Deficit (Billions)	Percent Reduced	Amount Reduced (Billions)	Year-End Deficit (Billions)
1	$250.0	10	$25.0	$225.0
2	225.0	20	45.0	180.0
3	180.0	30	54.0	126.0
4	126.0	40	50.4	75.6
5	75.6	50	37.8	37.8
6	37.8	60	22.7	15.1
7	15.1	70	10.6	4.5
8	4.5	80	3.6	0.9
9	0.9	90	0.8	0.1
10	0.1	100	0.1	none

The ten-percent solution would have the advantage of effecting the major portion of deficit reduction during the first five years of the program. Unlike proposals that would delay the heavier cuts until later, the ten-percent solution, if started on the strength of a recovery, would reduce the risk that major budget cuts would go into effect just as the economy was losing steam. Tax cuts in the later years could reward the American public for the sacrifices necessary to make deficit reduction a reality. The ten-percent solution would also have the advantage of identifying a goal to be realized each year, which would more firmly fix in the public mind what needed to be done and would provide useful reference points for measuring progress.

Welfare for the Well-Off

General strategies for deficit reduction are only part of the picture insofar as intergenerational justice is concerned. As already noted, the way that deficit reduction is realized is also of significance.

In the debate about welfare reform, many assume that low-income individuals are the only recipients of government largesse. Actually, most spending for entitlement programs goes to those above the poverty line. Peterson estimates that only about one out of every eight dollars spent by the federal government on social programs goes to families below the poverty line.[14] He writes, "Looking back over the random, mindless history of upward benefit expansion over FDR's original vision of a benefit floor, a true safety net for the poor, I am reminded not of a safety net but of a well-padded hammock for the rest of us."[15]

The Supplemental Medical Insurance portion of Medicare (Part B) is an example of this. Because those covered by Medicare who do not opt out of the Supplemental Medical Insurance Program (it can be declined) have a monthly premium subtracted from their Social Security checks, it is often assumed that Part B beneficiaries are just getting what they pay for. In reality, the premiums paid by Part B beneficiaries cover only 31.5 percent of benefit costs. (Part of the debate about Medicare is whether premiums should remain at 31.5 percent of benefit costs or should be allowed, as current law provides, to drop to 25 percent of benefit costs.) Part B benefit costs not financed by premiums are covered by general revenues--or somewhat more accurately, by a combination of general revenues and borrowing to finance the budget deficit. This subsidy of nearly 70 cents on the dollar goes to the wealthy, as well as to those below the poverty line.   If Part B of Medicare were a self-financing program, allowing everyone to share equally in the benefits would not be problematic.   But with a significant portion of benefit costs pushed off on our children and grandchildren as a result of deficit spending, subsidizing the well-off is ethically unacceptable.

The subsidized portion of Medicare is but one example of welfare for the well-off.   Other examples include subsidies for wealthy farmers, special tax breaks for designated industries, federally-owned range land rented to ranchers at rates below prevailing market levels, and much more.   In an editorial dripping with sarcasm, *Business Week,* a periodical not noted for political liberalism, harshly criticizes the Republican majorities in Congress for wanting to slash spending on welfare mothers and the working poor while maintaining subsidies for others:

> Congress wants to end social welfare because it is morally bad and financially irresponsible, but maintaining corporate welfare for oil drillers, ethanol producers, cotton growers, rural utility electricity suppliers, shipbuilders, and commercial broadcasters is just fine.[16]

The reality is that all federal subsidies must be on the table with those benefiting the well-off targeted for reduction or elimination. Making reference to a well-known cartoon character, Peterson observes, "The real enemy, as Pogo put it, is us: the great American middle-class majority, whose non-means-tested entitlement subsidies far outweigh the benefits we direct at the poor."[17]

The Concord Coalition's Zero Deficit Plan

In 1993, The Concord Coalition released its Zero Deficit Plan (ZDP), a blueprint for balancing the federal budget by 2000 through a combination of spending cuts and carefully-targeted tax increases. In 1995, the coalition issued a revised Zero Deficit Plan, calling for elimination of the federal budget deficit by the year 2002. The 1995 plan includes the following proposals (many of which were also included in the 1993 plan):[18]

• *Reduce Defense Spending.* The ZDP would make slightly greater reductions in defense spending than currently projected, resulting in defense spending in 2002 which is 19 percent less than the 1995 level.

• *Reduce Foreign Aid.* The Concord Coalition argues that "helping other countries must take a subordinate position to restoring our own economic health."

• *Means-Test All Entitlements.* In what The Concord Coalition characterizes as "the centerpiece" of its proposal, the ZDP calls for reducing benefit checks for all entitlements, including Social Security, by 10 percent for each $10,000 in income over $40,000. Thus, those making $40,000 or less would receive the full amount while those making $40,000 to $50,000 would have their benefit checks reduced by 10 percent, those making $50,000 to $60,000 by 20 percent, etc.

• *Increase Medicare Supplemental Medical Insurance (Part B) Payments by Beneficiaries.* The ZDP proposes increasing the deductible paid by Medicare Part B beneficiaries, introducing a 20 percent copayment requirement for clinical services and home health visits, and increasing the premiums paid by Medicare Part B beneficiaries.

• *Accelerate the Rise in the Social Security Retirement Age.* The ZDP calls for increasing the age for full-benefit retirement to 68 by the year 2007.

- *Federal Retirement Reform.* The ZDP calls for changing the guidelines for retirement benefits for federal employees to make them more comparable to those in the private sector.

- *Agriculture Program Reforms.* The ZDP would further reduce agricultural subsidies.

- *Welfare and Work Reforms.* The ZDP includes several welfare reform proposals intended to reduce welfare costs by promoting the transition to paid employment.

- *Increase Gasoline Tax.* The ZDP calls for increasing the federal tax on gasoline by 25 cents a gallon over a period of five years.

- *Tax Above-Average Employer-Paid Health Insurance.* The ZDP proposes treating as taxable income the value of employer-paid health insurance above the average cost of employer-paid health insurance.

- *Increase Alcohol and Tobacco Taxes.* The ZDP calls for increasing the federal cigarette tax to $1 per pack (from the current $.25 per pack) and the tax on distilled spirits to $16 per proof gallon.

- *Limit Home Mortgage Interest Deduction.* The ZDP proposes phasing in limitations on home mortgage interest deductions so that by the year 2002, deductions would be limited to $12,000 for single taxpayers and $20,000 for couples.

All of the specific proposals made by The Concord Coalition are debatable; many are very controversial. And, like GOP budget proposals (as well as those of President Clinton), the

Concord plan does not separate Social Security and other programs funded by earmarked taxes channeled through trust funds from programs that are supposed to be funded by general revenues. (This is not to suggest there are no problems with Social Security; long-term funding problems related to Social Security will be discussed in Chapter 11.)

Whatever the merits of the particular proposals, however, The Concord Coalition deserves a substantial measure of credit for mapping out a no-nonsense approach to a very serious problem that few have been willing to address in an honest, straightforward manner.

A Long and Difficult Road

As this volume goes to press, the budget battles in Washington continue, with philosophical differences about the role and function of government exacerbating the differences of opinion about appropriate funding levels. The debate is likely to be a lengthy one.

There are, however, some basic realities we would all be well-advised to acknowledge. When it comes to restraining the growth of federal spending, we must all be willing to take a hit. In particular, we must be prepared to make do with scaled-back federal subsidies, especially those directed toward current consumption and those benefitting the more affluent.

At the same time, wisdom is on the side of making certain there is adequate funding for research and development, education, building our infrastructure and other areas that represent an investment in our future and that of our children and grandchildren. Doing what needs to be done to make certain that this country will be competitive in a rapidly-changing world economy is a shared responsibility of the private and public sectors.

When budget crunches occur, it is often tempting to preserve subsidies for current consumption at the expense of investment in research and development and other areas that are of significance for the future. The pain of reductions in subsidies for current consumption is always immediate and often severe. The benefits to be gained by investing in the future often seem remote. Thus it is not surprising that the short term often takes priority over the long term, a form of myopia which imposes severe costs on future generations. Eating our seed corn is both short-sighted and exceedingly detrimental to efforts to ensure a greater measure of intergenerational justice for all generations.

Realism suggests that because of the influence that special interest groups and high-paid lobbyists have on the political processes, completely eliminating welfare for the well-off is probably not going to happen. However, whatever can be accomplished in terms of scaling back subsidies for the well-off, both direct subsidies and indirect subsidies in the form of special tax breaks, would be a step in the right direction.

Realism also suggests that whatever is accomplished in Washington is not likely to be a complete resolution of our budgetary problems. Rather, what we face is a constant struggle day after day and year after year as we travel down a long and difficult road that stretches ahead of us as far as the eye can see. Long and difficult though the road might be, however, it is a path we must take, a struggle in which we must engage, if a greater measure of intergenerational justice is to become a reality.

In the final analysis, it is not simply a matter--or even primarily a matter--of what Congress and the president are willing to support. In a democracy, what we the people are willing to support and commit ourselves to doing is of paramount significance. We the people give shape to the character of the nation. We the people define the terrain across which future generations must travel and the measure of justice of which they will partake.

Chapter 10

Medicare and Health Reform

Much of the heated rhetoric in the bitter budget debates in Washington has swirled around Medicare. Democrats charge Republicans with wanting to slash Medicare to finance tax cuts for the wealthy while Republicans insist that they are merely trying to save Medicare from impending fiscal collapse. As is almost always the case, the reality is far more complex than the political rhetoric suggests.

Contrary to what many assume, Medicare is not a single program. Rather, Medicare is comprised of two different programs with different sets of problems. Part A of Medicare (Hospital Insurance Program), which is financed by a payroll tax on current workers, is the part of Medicare facing bankruptcy. Part B of Medicare (Supplemental Medical Insurance Program), which helps pay for physicians' fees, ambulance service and other costs not covered by Part A, has a different funding mechanism and a different set of problems. Medicare beneficiaries who elect to receive Part B coverage (it can be declined) have a monthly premium deducted from their Social Security checks. As noted in the previous chapter, these monthly premiums pay 31.5 percent of Part B benefit costs with the remainder coming from general revenues--or, to be more precise, from a combination of general revenues and the borrowing that the federal government must do to cover the federal budget deficit.

The problems related to Part B are twofold in nature. One is that with benefit costs growing more than three times as fast as the economy, Part B places a good deal of stress on the federal budget and adds significantly to the budget deficit. The second involves considerations of equity. As stated in the previous chapter, it is unconscionable to subsidize the well-off to the tune of nearly 70 cents on the dollar while piling up a mountain of debt that will have a devastating impact on the future of our children and grandchildren. At the same time, paying premiums equal to 31.5 percent of average benefit costs strains the budgets of many low-income families and individuals.

The solution to both problems is to use a sliding fee scale so that those with high incomes would pay premiums equal to 100 percent of average benefit costs while those below the poverty line would receive a 100 percent subsidy. Those in between would pay part of average benefit costs with the percentage varying according to income level. If properly constructed, a sliding fee scale could help reduce the federal budget deficit by scaling back the subsidies to those with higher incomes. As will be noted in the pages that follow, there are compelling reasons to explore alternatives to Medicare. But as long as Part B of Medicare remains in operation, equity is on the side of using a sliding fee scale for premiums.

Impending Bankruptcy

Revenues from the payroll tax used to finance Medicare Part A benefits are channeled through the Hospital Insurance Trust Fund. Each year, the trust fund's board of trustees is required by law to issue a report detailing the revenues and expenditures for that year and indicating whether the fund is on an actuarially sound basis for financing anticipated benefit costs in the years to come. It is with respect to the latter that the trust fund has run into trouble. The 1995 report of the board of trustees projects that the trust fund will be exhausted shortly after the turn of the century if present trends continue. The report contains three sets of projections based on differing economic and demographic assumptions. The most optimistic projection suggests that the Hospital Insurance Trust Fund will be exhausted in the year 2006. The pessimistic projection points to 2001 as the year the trust fund will be exhausted while the intermediate projection suggests this will happen in 2002.[1] Recent reports indicating that the balance in the trust fund began declining during the 1995 fiscal year--two years earlier than expected--suggest that the pessimistic projection might be closest to being accurate.[2]

When the trust fund is depleted, payroll taxes, if continued at currently projected levels, will not provide sufficient revenue to pay for the benefits promised under Part A. When this happens, there will be three options: (1) increase payroll taxes to generate more revenue, (2) slash Medicare benefits, or (3) come up with a new program to replace Medicare.

Even though Republican proposals for Medicare are phrased in terms of "saving" Medicare, the reality is that Part A of Medicare, in all probability, cannot be maintained on a long-term basis. When baby boomers retire and place immense cost pressures on the system, it is very unlikely that Part A of Medicare, as currently structured and financed, can survive. All that can be accomplished by reform proposals, such as those drafted by Congressional Republicans, is to buy a few more years to allow more time to develop an alternative to Medicare that will provide adequate financing for the health-care needs of baby boomers when they reach retirement age.

That's not to suggest that Part A of Medicare should not be reformed. Since developing an alternative to Medicare is going to take a good deal of work and much discussion, there is something to be said for taking measures to delay for a few years the impending bankruptcy of the trust fund. But a temporary fix will not solve the long-term problem.

An Alternative to Medicare

Any workable alternative to Medicare must assure basic health coverage, must be financed adequately and must be consistent with plausible standards of intergenerational equity. Intergenerational equity can be served by developing (a) an alternative to the current intergenerational transfer system of financing Medicare Part A benefits for the elderly by a payroll tax on current workers, and (b) a system of health-care financing that extends coverage to all age-groups (which would also address problems related to Medicaid).

What might a workable, equitable alternative to Medicare entail--one that would assure universal coverage for all Americans? Two key elements should be the core of this new approach: (1) expanded publicly-funded preventive medicine programs such as vaccinations and prenatal care that help keep people healthy and hold down health-care costs by preventing serious illness, and (2) a national voucher system that would assure that every U.S. citizen could purchase health insurance, with back-up insurance provided by the federal government for those unable or not inclined to exercise their voucher option.[3]

How would a national voucher system operate? Each year a specified number of dollars generated by tax revenues would be earmarked by the federal government for the purchase of health insurance by each U.S. citizen. The voucher amount would increase with age since those who are older often have greater health-care needs than those who are younger. Special provisions would be made for those who are disabled or who have chronic illnesses requiring more extensive care. U.S. citizens could then use their vouchers to purchase the type of health insurance they preferred. For those qualifying for group plans, be they employment-related group plans or regional group plans set up to accommodate the voucher system, the vouchers could be used to purchase coverage via a group plan. Or, if preferred, coverage could be purchased on an individual basis.

What about those who find the world of health insurance too confusing to deal with or who are incapacitated and thus unable to exercise their voucher option? In such cases, the government would provide back-up insurance purchased from the private sector at competitive market rates, thereby making certain that all U.S. citizens would have access to basic health care.

Such an approach would have two major advantages over our current patchwork system of financing health care. It would ensure that Americans of all ages would be treated equally. (As noted in Chapter 2, allocating greater benefits to those who are older does not constitute unequal treatment if it is reasonable for others to expect similar treatment when they are older; the system here being proposed would provide such an assurance, unlike the current Medicare system.) Second, in an era of limited resources, a voucher system would give each individual the opportunity to establish priorities with respect to the funding of his or her own health care.

The latter merits more detailed comment. With health-care expenditures currently 14 percent of our gross domestic product (GDP) and projected to grow to 18 percent of GDP in ten years if current practices are continued,[4] covering everything would either require a tax hike no one would tolerate or accelerate the slide down the slippery slope of budget deficits leading to fiscal doom. If not everything is to be covered, who should decide what is covered and what is not? A voucher system would allow each individual the opportunity to establish priorities for himself or herself, while at the same time assuring access to basic health care. Some, for example, might give dental care priority over nursing-home care while others might give priority to nursing-home care and other forms of extended care.

Financing Health Reform

How should a national voucher system providing universal coverage be financed? It is essential that such a system (or any other form of health reform) be financed by something other than a payroll tax on current workers. In this country, a disproportionate share of health-care costs is built into payroll, placing U.S. producers at a competitive disadvantage in comparison to foreign producers. U.S. producers cover benefits for employees, the payroll tax to finance Medicare Part A benefits, and indirect subsidies to those who are uninsured (as a result of the cost-shifting that occurs when hospitals and other health-care providers charge those with insurance more than the actual cost of providing the services and then use the net revenues to subsidize care for those who lack insurance).

Comparison with the way Japan finances health care is instructive. Japan has two health insurance programs which together provide coverage for the entire population--Health Insurance for Employees (HIE) and National Health Insurance (NHI). HIE covers the majority of workers and their dependents while NHI covers retirees, the unemployed, those who are disabled and workers not covered by HIE. Private sector Japanese employers and employees covered by HIE contribute payroll taxes which average about 4.5 percent for both employer and employee. Administrative and claims handling costs are covered by the Japanese government. In the case of NHI, half of the funding comes from national and local taxes with the remaining half coming from income-adjusted premiums paid by those covered.[5]

The practice of financing a substantial portion of health care through payroll in this country is, in substantial measure, a historical accident. In the years immediately following World War II, wage-and-price controls stood in the way of increasing wages and salaries. They did not extend, however, to fringe benefits, which made the addition of health insurance a way of increasing compensation while living within the letter of the law. When Medicare came on the scene in the 1960s, the United States still had the dominant world economy. With the United States in the driver's seat economically speaking, U.S. producers could pretty much do anything they wished, as long as other domestic producers did the same. It was easy for U.S. producers to pass increased costs on to consumers in the form of higher prices. Thus, the use of a payroll tax to finance Part A of Medicare was a convenient way of getting the job done.

But times have changed. Stiff competition from foreign producers limits what U.S. producers can do. The time has come to rethink the way that health care is financed--a necessity that dovetails with the need to find a workable alternative to Medicare (and to Medicaid).

How might a national voucher system such as the one outlined above be financed? The best way would be via an earmarked national sales tax, excluding food and medicine, supplemented by increased taxes on tobacco, liquor and other products detrimental to good health. A national sales tax levied on imported Hondas, Toyotas and Volkswagens, as well as on domestically-produced Fords, Chevrolets and Chryslers, would have the advantage of shifting at least part of the cost of health care out of payroll, thereby helping level the playing field for U.S. producers. As an alternative to a national sales tax, an earmarked income tax surcharge might also be considered, though that would not deal with the problem of competitive disadvantage as effectively as would a national sales tax.

In the current political climate, any discussion of new taxes is about as popular as root canal surgery. And for good reason. There is a long history of tax increases that have been accompanied by even greater increases in federal expenditures, the result being that the federal government has dug deeper into taxpayers' pockets even as it has added huge sums to the national debt. With this type of history, any suggestion that taxes should be increased ought to be viewed with great caution and considerable skepticism.

What is being proposed here, however, is essentially changing the accounts through which health care is financed. A national sales tax to finance health care for all Americans would be accompanied by repeal of the Medicare payroll tax used to finance Medicare Part A benefits and the premiums that Medicare beneficiaries now pay to cover part of the cost of Medicare Part B benefits. Shifting a major portion of the cost of health care for employees out of payroll would place U.S. producers in a stronger competitive position, enabling them to reduce prices for their products, increase compensation levels for workers, invest more in research and development, or some combination of all of the above. Price reductions would offset, at least in part, the earmarked national sales tax or income tax surcharge. Price reductions for U.S. products would stimulate sales, resulting in more jobs for U.S. workers as factories geared up to respond to increased consumer demand. Both U.S. consumers and U.S. workers would end up being winners.

Defined Contributions and Defined Benefits

A perennial problem with publicly-funded social programs--including Part A of Medicare--is that the benefits promised often exceed available revenue. Defined-contribution pension programs suggest a solution to this problem. In defined-contribution pension programs, a specified amount is set aside and invested each year to provide for each employee's pension when he or she retires. The level of benefits received upon retirement depends on the amount of money in the pension fund which has been invested on behalf of that person. Larger pension contributions and more astute investments result in larger pensions. (In contrast, defined-benefit pension programs specify the level of benefits to be received--and hope that there is enough money in the pension fund to cover the benefits.)

If the U.S. is to opt for publicly-funded universal health insurance, there is much to be said for assuring solvency of such a program by taking a defined-contribution approach, rather than a defined-benefit approach. The voucher system here being proposed would lend itself to such an approach. The earmarked source of revenue would set the funding level for the program, which in turn would enable determining the amount to spend for health insurance for each person. For those exercising the voucher option, the competitive pressures of the marketplace, with various insurers competing for customers, would determine benefit levels.   For those staying with the back-up insurance purchased for them by the government, competitive bidding by national and regional insurers would determine benefit levels. Individuals, of course, would be free to purchase additional insurance to the extent that their private resources allow.

If an earmarked source of revenue were used to finance such a program, wisdom would be on the side of holding back a portion of the revenue when the economy was booming to supplement the revenue collected during times of recession. Otherwise, the level of benefits would bounce up and down depending on how the economy was doing in any given year.

In all cases, a combination of the amount of funding committed to health insurance and market conditions would determine benefit levels.   Insurance companies that effectively used cost-containment measures such as health maintenance organizations (HMOs) and other forms of managed care would gain market share.

Some degree of government intervention in the marketplace would be necessary to prevent consumer fraud and to assure quality. For example, truth-in-advertising standards would have to be maintained to prevent unscrupulous insurance companies from exploiting unwitting consumers. Insurance reform is also needed to eliminate risk rating (the practice of identifying those individuals who either have or might develop potentially serious health problems and excluding them from coverage).[6] Specifying appropriate standards of medical practice as a precondition for reimbursement would also be necessary to prevent cost-cutting detrimental to the health and well-being of patients. But these are all manageable problems.

Health Care and Intergenerational Justice

Bold thinking and new ideas are required to solve the problems facing us and to ensure a greater measure in inter-generational justice. A defined-contribution national voucher system financed by a non-payroll tax has much to recommend it:

> ● *A national voucher system such as the one proposed here would be inclusive.* If we are to take seriously that notion that everyone is our neighbor, any publicly-funded system of financing health care ought to include in its coverage everyone who is a citizen of the political entity using its taxing authority to finance the system.

> ● *A national voucher system offering universal coverage would eliminate the injustice of current workers being taxed to finance levels of benefits for older Americans which are not likely to be available in future years, if the current system is not changed.* The present way of financing Part A of Medicare (Hospital Insurance Program) imposes a grave injustice on younger generations. A system which offers universal coverage to Americans of all ages would diminish this injustice. Financing universal health insurance from revenue sources such as a sales tax toward which those of all ages would contribute would ensure a greater measure of justice among generations.

> ● *A national voucher system covering all U.S. citizens would give all Americans access to the same type of health care.* Proposals to shift Medicare beneficiaries to health maintenance organizations (HMOs) and other forms of managed care have evoked considerable controversy. Many of the workers taxed to finance Part A of Medicare have their health care provided by HMOs and other forms of managed care--if, indeed, they are fortunate enough to have health benefits. Why should they be taxed to provide types of care to others to which they themselves do not have access? A national voucher system providing universal coverage would put everyone on the same basis.

• *A defined-contribution approach would guarantee fiscal responsibility.* A defined-contribution program in which benefit levels are determined by market factors, rather than legislatively, would avoid the problem of cost overruns. Unlike Part A of Medicare, there would be no possibility of the program going broke. Unlike the subsidized portion of Part B of Medicare, a defined-contribution program would not add to the mountain of debt towering over our children and grandchildren. The only question remaining would be what the level of taxation should be. Once market surveys determined what benefit levels would be enabled by various levels of taxation, the level would be determined by democratic processes, as are other matters of taxation.

• *In an era in which choice in health care is becoming an endangered species, a voucher system would maximize individual choice.* Realism suggests that unlimited coverage is not in the cards. A voucher system would enable each individual to establish funding priorities with respect to his or her own health care and a choice of participation in the broadest possible range of health systems.

• *As noted above, financing a national voucher system by a non-payroll tax such as an earmarked national sales tax would help level the playing field for U.S. producers.* Continuing to have a disproportionate share of health care costs built into the costs of production, which is what happens when health care is financed via payroll, is neither in the interests of U.S. workers nor helpful to the cause of justice.

• *Financing a voucher system by an earmarked national sales tax would mean that everyone would help finance health care.* Since everyone is a consumer, a national sales tax would mean that everyone would pay some-thing to help finance the national voucher system.

• *Financing a voucher system by an earmarked national sales tax which excluded food and medicine would result in greater contributions by those who are more affluent.* Since those who are more affluent tend to spend more on consumer goods ranging from new dishwashers to new automobiles than do those who are less affluent, a greater portion of the tax burden of financing such a system would be born by those with greater levels of disposable income.

• *Getting a national voucher system in place prior to the collapse of Part A of Medicare would avert the cata-strophic disruption that would result from such a collapse.* Wisdom is always on the side of solving problems before they become crises. As noted above, Medicare is not likely to survive on a long-term basis. The only question is whether we have the foresight and willpower to develop a workable alternative to Medicare before the situation becomes catastrophic.

No approach to anything as complex as health insurance is without its limitations. The downside of a national voucher system is that some individuals might make choices when purchasing health insurance that they would later regret. But is not living with the consequences of the decisions we make part of life? Is it not part of the process of learning what responsibil-ity entails? With appropriate consumer education, the incidence of injudicious decisions could be minimized.

The advantages of a defined contribution national voucher system financed by a non-payroll tax outweigh any inherent disadvantages by a huge margin. No other system of financing health care would ensure a greater measure of justice. No other way of financing health would provide a more practical solution to the problems we face. No other approach offers greater hope for averting the catastrophe that will overwhelm us if we fail to take corrective action.

Going back to the drawing board and designing an entirely new system for financing health care requires willingness to embrace bold new approaches. Change is always stressful. But sometimes it is necessary. In the case of health care, the crisis we face is so great that anything less than complete restructuring of the way health care is financed would be to fail to address the problem.

Chapter 11

Social Security: Will the Promise Be Kept?

President Franklin Delano Roosevelt was dismayed that the Social Security Act, which was awaiting his signature after both houses of Congress had passed it, was not getting the publicity he believed it deserved. On August 14, 1935, he summoned photographers to the Cabinet Room in the White House to record the signing of a piece of legislation he characterized as "the cornerstone in a structure which is being built but is by no means complete."[1]

There was other news that day. Mussolini was threatening to invade Ethiopia. A former British Chancellor of the Exchequer warned that Europe was on the brink of a world war "too terrible to contemplate." In this country, Democratic political strategists were taking soundings of public opinion to see if there was support for a constitutional amendment that would broaden the powers of the federal government. At Ebbets Field in Brooklyn, the Dodgers, known in those days more for losing than for winning, defeated the Chicago Cubs twice, taking both ends of a double header by scores of 9-5 and 3-2.

But President Roosevelt's publicity ploy worked.   The

signing ceremony, in which he used several pens to write each letter of his name, dominated the news that day.[2] And many would say appropriately so, for the enactment of Social Security was a watershed in the social and political landscape of this country.

No government program has been as enthusiastically received as Social Security. In the half-century Social Security has been in operation, the program has maintained a floor of economic decency for millions of older Americans who would otherwise have been destitute. It has enabled millions of older Americans to maintain their independence, rather than be forced to live with younger members of their families as was common in the days prior to Social Security.

Social Security has also been popular with younger generations. Prior to Social Security, younger generations were expected to care for their parents and other family members who were no longer able to provide for themselves. Social Security has enabled a greater degree of independence and freedom for younger generations, as well as for older generations.

But wonderful though the program has been in its half-century of existence, Social Security faces a difficult future--not in the next decade or so, but thirty to forty years down the road. Secretary of Labor Robert B. Reich bluntly warns that Social Security "will be broke three decades into the next century."[3]

From Retirement Savings To Transfer Payments

Four years after signing the Social Security Act of 1935, President Roosevelt signed another Social Security Act, this time without the hoopla that surrounded the signing of the first bill.[4] Though the signing of the Social Security Act of 1939 was not as high profile as the signing of the 1935 bill, in many respects it was more significant for it substantially transformed the nature of Social Security.

The retirement portion of the 1935 bill (it also included provisions pertaining to unemployment compensation and other matters) provided that each qualified worker retiring at the age of sixty-five, starting January 1, 1942, would receive a pension, varying from $10 to $85 a month depending on the total amount of wages earned by the beneficiary after December 31, 1936. The 1935 act also provided that if a qualified employee died prior to collecting benefits, survivors would receive a lump sum payment calculated on the basis of the amount the worker had paid in, plus interest. The program was to be financed by a 1 percent payroll tax on employers and a 1 percent tax on employees' wages and salaries up to $3,000, starting January 1, 1937, with the tax on each to increase by a half-percent every third year until it reached 3 percent.[5]

The amendments enacted in 1939 froze the earmarked tax on employers and employees at 1 percent for 1940, 1941 and 1942. They also liberalized benefits by moving up by two years (to January 1, 1940) the time that qualified retirees could first start drawing benefits, by increasing benefit levels for qualified retirees and by adding benefits for widows and dependent children. Both houses of Congress passed the 1939 amendments by lopsided margins. Only four senators--all of them Democrats--voted against the amendments.[6] *The New York Times* characterized the new law as "decidedly superior to the law it supplants," adding that "it moves away from the private insurance concepts that marred the former law, and substitutes a much closer approach to true social insurance."[7]

Whether the new law in fact was superior was--and still is--a matter for debate. What is clear, though, is that the 1939 amendments significantly changed Social Security. As originally envisioned, Social Security was a mandatory savings program for retirement. The 1939 amendments made Social Security a European-style social welfare program in which government uses the power to tax to transfer wealth from those currently employed to those currently retired, offset by a vague promise to current workers that when they retire, those working at that time will return the favor.

Yet the imagery of the original law persists, even though no one ever received a benefit check under the system envisioned by those who drafted the 1935 law. With few exceptions, the millions who have received Social Security checks in the last five decades characterize the benefits they have received as simply "getting back what they have paid in."

"From New Deal to Raw Deal"

Until recently, Social Security, enacted as part of Roosevelt's New Deal, has been a very good deal for those drawing Social Security checks. While many believe that they are just getting back what they have paid in, plus interest, in reality most have received far more. It is estimated that a middle-income worker who retired in 1985 can anticipate, if he or she lives a normal life expectancy, receiving $1.60 for every dollar paid in-- after adjusting for inflation and accounting for the interest that could have been earned if the money had been invested elsewhere. Because benefit rates are tilted in favor of low-income workers, someone who retired at the lower end of the wage scale in 1985 can expect to get back $2.50 for every dollar put in, once again after accounting for inflation and computing interest on the money paid in. Even the wealthy have profited from Social Security. A high-income individual who retired in 1985 can expect to get back $1.40 for every dollar put in--not a bad return on investment.[8]

But the days of government largesse are fast becoming history. A middle-income worker retiring in the year 2000 should expect to do no better than break even while a middle-income worker retiring in the year 2010 is likely to get back only 80 cents on the dollar. This turn of fortune prompted a headline writer for *Business Week* to characterize Social Security as going "From New Deal to Raw Deal."[9]

Suggesting that Social Security has become a raw deal might overstate things a bit. Nevertheless, it is clear that younger generations, compared with those currently retired, will (a) pay more in Social Security taxes and (b) get less in return. Quite obviously, there are some significant issues of justice among generations at stake here.

Granted, there are always disparities among generations. Some come of age during wartime and pay with their lives. Others live their youthful years during peacetime and never serve in the military. Some live in times of prosperity. Others experience hard times.

The differences among generations with respect to Social Security, however, are not just the result of the luck of the draw. The disparities, in substantial measure, result from the way the Social Security system is structured and from various policy decisions that have been made, beginning with the 1939 decision to change Social Security from a mandatory savings program to a "pay-as-you-go" program in which taxes on current workers are used to finance the benefits for those currently retired.

An irate reader, responding to a newspaper article noting that younger generations are unlikely to get back what they pay into Social Security, commented:

> Anybody that goes around saying that the '70s generation is going to have to accept 80 cents on the dollar is cracked in the proverbial head. For one thing, I expect 100 cents on the dollar plus interest, or I want my money back. And if I can't get my money back, then I'll have to go into a bank and take it back.[10]

The reader, whose comments appear to have been edited a bit to conform to standards of public decency, falsely assumes that the money paid into Social Security is sitting in a bank somewhere and could be refunded. Would that were true! Unfortunately, as noted in subsequent pages, the money has already been spent. More on that later.

There are two basic issues of intergenerational justice that arise with respect to Social Security. One involves the long-term viability of the program, which, as will be noted in subsequent sections, is not assured. The collapse of Social Security would obviously be a huge injustice to younger generations, many of whom have already made contributions to the system via the payroll tax. Any plausible standard of intergenerational equity mandates doing what is necessary to maintain the viability of Social Security.

The second issue of intergenerational justice involves the allocation of costs and benefits among generations. The mere survival of Social Security will not ensure a full measure of intergenerational equity. The distressing fact of life about the mess we are in is that disproportionate costs are going to be imposed on younger generations to make up for the largesse the federal government has bestowed on older generations. Put in slightly different words, since what has been done in previous years can't be undone, younger generations are stuck with injustice. The only question which remains is whether these costs will be allocated as equally as possible in the years to come or imposed disproportionately on some generations.

Increased Benefits and a Declining Ratio Of Workers to Beneficiaries

In 1950, the average monthly benefit received by a retired worker was $43.56.[11] By 1994, the average monthly benefit had grown to $860.17[12]--a hefty increase even when adjusted for inflation. While the substantial increase in benefit levels has been a very welcome development for those receiving benefits, it has had the practical impact of significantly increasing the cost of operating the system, as has the increased number of individuals receiving benefits--37.6 million in 1995, up from 2.9 million in 1950.[13]

This would not be problematic if the number of employed workers with taxable earnings were growing fast enough to offset the increased number of beneficiaries or if wages and salaries were growing fast enough to offset the increased level of benefits.   Neither has happened.   In 1950, there were 16.5 workers with taxable earnings for each person receiving benefits. By 1994, the ratio had dropped to 3.3 to 1.   In the next forty years, the ratio is expected to drop to 2 to 1.[14]

Figure 11-1:   Number of Workers Per Beneficiary

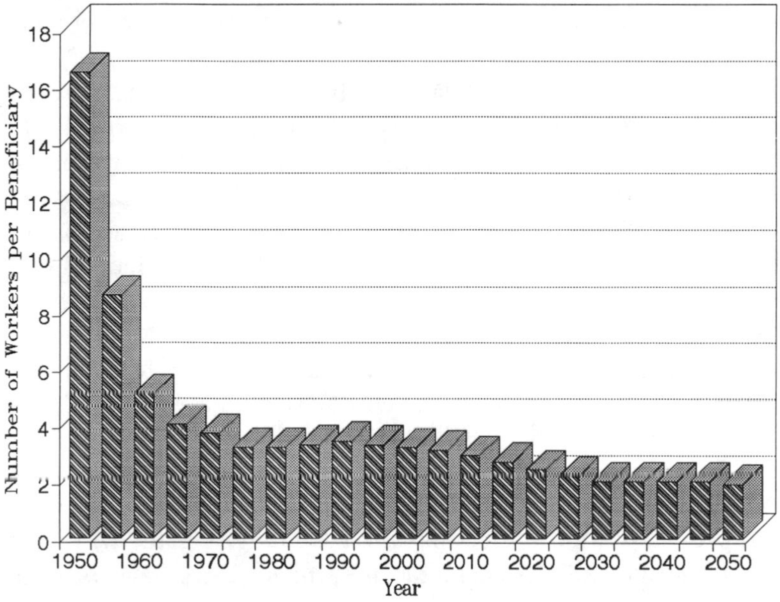

Based on historical data 1950-1994 and projections for 1995-2050 included in the 1995 Annual Report of the Board of Trustees of the Federal Old-Age and Survivors Insurance Trust Fund. *Projections reflect the intermediate range of demographic and economic assumptions.*

There are factors that could change the projected decline in the ratio.   For example, robust economic growth could significantly increase the number who are employed.   During the boom years of the 1980s, which saw the creation of nearly 20 million new jobs, the number of workers per beneficiary actually increased slightly.[15]   Another factor that could slow down the projected decline in the number of workers per beneficiary would be a substantial increase in immigration. Few immigrants have parents who qualify for Social Security benefits. As long as the newcomers find employment, immigration increases the number of workers paying the Social Security tax without, at least in the short term, increasing the number of retirees drawing benefits. But even taking into account factors such as these, a continued decline in the number of workers per beneficiary is probable--a trend likely to be accelerated once baby boomers start retiring.

The long-term financial viability of Social Security, of course, does not depend solely on the ratio of workers to beneficiaries. In the final analysis, it is the total amount of taxable income generated by all workers subject to the payroll tax that is the key factor. If this country experiences a substantial, sustained increase in productivity enabling huge increases in wages and salaries, the funding crunch down the road might be averted, or at least diminished. Investing in education and in computers and other technologies that increase productivity, thereby enabling higher wages and salaries, is a way of helping protect Social Security for future generations.

But while productivity gains in the last couple of years have been encouraging, the track record of the last twenty years does not provide reason for optimism. Productivity gains will have to be substantially greater than they historically have been in order to generate the additional wealth necessary to make possible wage and salary increases sufficiently large to sustain Social Security in its present form without tax increases.[16]

The competitive pressures of a changing world economy, it might be added, make it far more difficult to translate productivity gains into wage and salary increases. Whenever international competition is a factor, any comparative advantage resulting from productivity gains must be measured in relation to productivity gains and other factors affecting costs of production in other countries. In short, productivity gains typically enable wage and salary increases only if they are greater than productivity gains in other countries that produce products that compete with domestically-produced products.

The Trust Fund Report

In practice, the revenues generated by the Social Security taxes levied on workers and employers don't go directly to Social Security beneficiaries. Instead, they are deposited in a special trust fund, which is the account on which checks issued to beneficiaries are drawn. Each year, the board of trustees of the Social Security trust fund, which is officially known as the Federal Old-Age and Survivors Insurance (OASI) Trust Fund, is required by law to issue a report indicating the status of the fund and making projections of future expenditures in relation to anticipated revenues. The projections must include both short-range actuarial estimates covering the next ten years and long-range actuarial estimates covering the next seventy-five years. The short-range projections in recent reports indicate that the OASI Trust Fund is in solid financial shape for the next ten years or so. It's the long-range projections which give cause for concern and lead Secretary of Labor Reich, who is one of the trustees of the OASI Trust Fund, to warn that Social Security will be broke three decades into the next century.

The technicians who put together the report take into account both economic and demographic factors. Economic factors include increases in wages and salaries after inflation, the unemployment rate and interest rates. Demographic factors include the birth rate, life expectancy and immigration. Since no one can predict with complete accuracy how these factors will sort out in the years to come, the annual OASI Trust Fund Report, like the Hospital Insurance Trust Fund Report, includes three sets of projections. Alternative I is the most optimistic, Alternative III is the most pessimistic, and Alternative II falls somewhere in between.

Compared with the other two projections, Alternative I assumes a greater increase in wages and salaries adjusted for inflation, lower unemployment rates, lower interest rates, higher birth rates, lower life expectancy and higher net immigration.[17]

(It might seem odd that the most optimistic projection assumes lower life expectancy than the more pessimistic projections, but we need to keep in mind the fact that government bureaucrats don't always think the same way the rest of us do.)

Because the projections in previous annual reports were criticized for being excessively optimistic, the 1994 and 1995 reports make more conservative economic and demographic assumptions. For example, the intermediate (Alternative II) projection in the 1994 and 1995 reports assume that after adjusting for inflation, the average annual wage increase will be 1.0 percent, compared with estimates of 1.1 percent in the 1992 and 1993 reports.[18] Though adjustments of that magnitude might seem minor, they make a significant difference when compounded over a number of years. As a result, the projections included in the 1994 and 1995 report are somewhat more pessimistic than those included in previous reports.

The 1995 OASI board of trustees report states that if the intermediate set of assumptions (Alternative II) proves accurate, the OASI Trust Fund will be exhausted in the year 2031 (compared to 2036 in the 1994 report). Should the more pessimist assumptions represented by Alternative III prove accurate, the fund will be depleted in the year 2020. (The board of trustees, which also oversees the Disability Insurance [DI] Trust Fund, recommends combining the OASI and DI trust funds in view of the fact that the DI Trust Fund is nearly exhausted; the projected years of exhaustion for the combined funds are 2030 under the intermediate assumptions and 2016 under the more pessimistic set of assumptions.)[19]

What will happen when the temporary surplus in the OASI trust fund is exhausted, be it in the year 2031 or some other year? There will still be money coming in from the Social Security payroll tax, but it won't be sufficient to pay for the benefits promised to those qualifying for Social Security.

If nothing is done until the trust fund experiences bankruptcy, the options for dealing with this problem will be limited. None of them will be pleasant. They will include the following:

- slash benefits so that outlays for benefits would not exceed revenues from the Social Security tax on workers;

- increase the Social Security tax on those working at that time to generate additional revenue to finance the levels of benefits future retirees anticipate;

- borrow money to make up the difference between revenue coming in and outlays for benefits (a course of action that would push the nation closer to bankruptcy and impose additional costs on future generations);

- divert funds from non-payroll tax revenues (which, unless non-payroll taxes were increased, would also add to the national debt).

A Paper Surplus

There's another complicating factor as far as future Social Security recipients are concerned. The federal government has borrowed the temporary multi-billion OASI Trust Fund surplus to help finance our astronomical federal budget deficits, leaving nothing but a huge pile of I.O.U.s in the trust fund. While the 1995 trust fund report assures us that these I.O.U.s "are backed by the full faith and credit of the U.S. government, the same as other public-debt obligations of the U.S. government,"[20] these I.O.U.s are not securities that can be sold on the open market when the trust fund needs the money. In order for the trust fund to get the money back when it is needed to cover benefit costs, the Department of Treasury must transfer to the trust fund money obtained from other sources, such as income taxes or additional borrowing.

The use of the temporary surplus in the OASI Trust Fund to pay for current expenditures itself poses a question of intergenerational justice. As noted in Chapter 9, a substantial portion of current government spending is for entitlement programs, which are weighted heavily toward older generations. Borrowing the Social Security funds to finance current consumption in effect allocates the cost of current consumption to the future taxpayers who will have to come up with the money when it is needed to pay benefits for future retirees. According to the most recent intermediate projection, the Social Security program will need to start drawing upon the surplus in the year 2019.[21]

The Social Security amendments enacted in 1977 and 1983 adjusted tax rates and benefit levels to avert bankruptcy of the system at an earlier date. The amendments have resulted in the temporary surplus in the OASI Trust Fund (at least on paper), leading some to suggest that Social Security is currently, in part, "advance funded" rather than simply funded on a "pay-as-you-go" basis. That, however, is misleading. With the temporary surplus being borrowed by the federal government to finance current consumption, Social Security, for all practical purposes, is still operating on a "pay-as-you-go" basis. Social Security taxes paid by current workers are used to finance benefits for current retirees plus, as a result of the temporary surplus being borrowed by the federal government, other forms of current consumption. When current workers retire, their benefits will be financed by a combination of the Social Security taxes paid by those working at that time and the additional taxes future taxpayers will have to pay to replace the money borrowed from the OASI Trust Fund. When all things are considered, it makes little difference through which account money is channeled. Whenever tax revenues are used for current consumption, government is operating on a "pay-as-you-go" basis. The temporary surplus in the OASI Trust Fund is nothing more than a paper surplus consisting of a huge pile of unmarketable I.O.U.s left by the federal government as it has borrowed the money to finance other programs.

An Implicit Promise

Implicit in the "pay-as-you-go" approach is a promise to current workers: if you pay for the benefits for those who are currently retired, those working when you retire will pay for your retirement benefits. However well-intended this implicit promise might be, it poses ethical and practical problems.

A promise is normally understood as a commitment made by the one doing the promising. How can anyone make a commitment on behalf of others without at least touching base with those who will be asked to make good on the commitment? If Smith, without discussing the matter with his brother, promises his next-door neighbors that his brother will paint their garage, is Smith's brother in any way obligated to paint the garage? Can the government in any meaningful way promise that my grandchildren and others not yet born will pay for my retirement benefits when I retire several years down the road? In *Facing Up: How to Rescue the Economy from Crushing Debt & Restore the American Dream,* Peter G. Peterson writes:

> As I recall (from a college course in commercial law), one fundamental requirement of a valid contract is a "meeting of the minds" of the parties to that contract: between those who pay and those who receive. But no such meeting of the minds exists. I'm not aware that anyone has consulted my grandson, Peter Cary, now aged three, about the staggering tax rates that honoring our current entitlement "contracts" will require him to pay when he enters the workforce.[22]

To what extent, if at all, can one Congress and president make promises that are binding on future Congresses and presidents? Are there any moral claims to be made that go beyond simply saying that there is a moral obligation to respond to expectations that have been raised--a moral obligation stemming from the desirability of minimizing the disappointment that might otherwise be experienced by those led to believe that they have been promised something?

There is also a potential political problem. The level of benefits those of us not yet retired will receive when we retire will be determined, not by what current government officials promise, but by the allocation decisions made by future Congresses and future presidents elected by a plurality of future voters. It is within the range of the possible that younger taxpayers at some point in the future might brush aside the expectations of those retired at that time and refuse to pay the higher taxes that will be necessary to pay projected levels of benefits--taxes that, according to the Social Security Administration's intermediate set of projections, would consume more than 17 percent of taxable payroll by 2040.[23] Adding in Medicare (if Medicare has not been replaced with an alternate system of financing health care) would bring the payroll tax to 26 percent of taxable payroll.[24] Income taxes and other federal, state and local taxes would take additional bites out of what would be left of workers' paychecks. If disgruntled members of younger generations constitute a majority of voters at some point in the future, the ground rules governing Social Security could be changed substantially. For that matter, the entire system could be abolished.

Fears and Anxieties

Since the Social Security funding crisis is not likely to become severe until a couple decades into the next century, it is tempting to ignore the problem as long as possible. The emotions surrounding Social Security are so intense that any discussion of reform immediately places one in a hot seat with sparks flying all over the place. Politicians who have favored revamping Social Security have had a tendency to become former politicians.

But ignoring the issues of justice pertaining to Social Security will only make the disparities among generations worse, setting the stage for a war between generations. For reasons of self-interest as well as reasons of equity, older generations and younger generations alike would be well advised to come to grips with the issues of intergenerational justice surrounding Social Security. When measured in terms of quality of life, reconciliation between generations with a renewed sense of community is surely preferable to intergenerational conflict.

Any discussion of justice among generations must begin with recognition of the fears and anxieties experienced by various age-groups. Members of younger generations must try to gain a sense of how precarious life often seems to those experiencing the more advanced years of life. Those retired and nearing retirement often experience considerable anxiety when they realize that unlike those who are younger, it is no longer possible for them to secure additional income by entering the labor market. Fear that inflation might eat up the money they have saved adds to their insecurity, as do concerns about health and worries about paying for nursing home care and other forms of care not covered by Medicare or other health plans.

Many older Americans are widows who came of age before the women's rights movement opened career opportunities and affirmed a more assertive role for women. They spent the major portion of their adult years dependent on their husbands, both financially and emotionally. Mortality patterns that favor women took their husbands from them, leaving them alone and forcing them to cope with things they never had to worry about before. For these women, as well as for millions of other older Americans, Social Security has become a lifeline offering a modicum of security in a world that often seems very threatening.

Those on Social Security must try to understand how things look to younger generations. In the 1950s and 1960s--the prime productive years for most who are now retired--it was possible for a family with a single wage-earner to buy a home. Today, with rare exception, it takes two incomes to pay the mortgage. Many now retired enjoy higher levels of affluence than their parents, a form of upward mobility that came to be equated with the American Dream. Today, as many as 80 percent of younger

Americans have to make do with lower levels of affluence than those enjoyed by their parents.[25]

Younger generations worry a lot about the future. "Do you think we'll get anything out of Social Security?" is a question many ask. And when they see the sizable deductions for Social Security and other taxes taken out of their paychecks, which even without deductions would not in many cases be large enough to pay the mortgage for the type of home their parents purchased, anger starts building up deep inside.

There probably will have to be benefit reductions beyond those already scheduled. (Beginning in the year 2000, the age at which full Social Security retirement benefits will first be available will gradually be raised until it reaches sixty-seven by the year 2022.[26]) But there is another point that needs to be stressed here as well. If there is to be reduction of benefits--or at least restraint in the increase of benefits--such discussions ought not occur apart from discussions of ways that communities can be responsive to the needs of older Americans. Churches and synagogues need to rediscover what it means to be caring communities, responsive to those in need. We must develop new ways of responding to the fears and anxieties that are so prevalent today. Innovation is essential. For example, some communities have experimented with volunteer banks in which participants of all ages swap volunteer hours to help each other do the things one isn't well equipped to take care of oneself.[27] Such efforts can reduce the vulnerability so many older Americans experience and can help mitigate any adjustments that might be made in Social Security benefit levels. Rediscovering what it is to be a neighbor is essential if any changes in Social Security are to be made.

Should Social Security Be Partially Privatized?

Senators Bob Kerrey (D-NE) and Alan Simpson (R-WY) have proposed partially privatizing Social Security by allowing covered workers to divert a portion of the payroll taxes they pay for Social Security into personal investment plans (PIPs) modeled after the Thrift Savings Plan available to federal employees and the independent retirement accounts (IRAs) available to many other employees. The benefit formula for those electing to put part of what they pay in payroll taxes into PIPs would be adjusted downward so that their Social Security benefits, when they retire, would reflect the fact that they contributed less to the Social Security trust fund. This would be offset, however, by the benefits derived from the PIP.[28] Senator Kerrey argues that the proposal would provide "a glimmer of hope for tens of millions of American families who today have little chance of accumulating wealth. With just 2 percent of wages, 137 million workers would accumulate hundreds of billions of dollars in new savings over the next nine years."[29]

Is the Kerrey-Simpson proposal a good idea? Putting a portion of the payroll tax into IRA-type accounts would probably generate a higher rate of return on those funds than is generated by the interest paid by the federal government on the trust fund balances. However, as will be noted later in this chapter, that objective could be realized without privatization.

Robert J. Myers, an actuary who served in various capacities in the Social Security Administration and its predecessor agencies from 1934 to 1970, has reservations about partial privatization:

> Proposals that would privatize Social Security by permitting individuals to elect to withdraw from it, either completely or partially, have the problem that those who would do so would, in general, be the low-cost cases (e.g., young, high-paid persons with no dependents). On the other hand, the high-cost cases (e.g., older, low-paid persons with dependents) would remain in the Social Security program, and its relative costs would soar, quite likely necessitating large costs to the general fund of the Treasury.[30]

He further warns that "privatization proposals that involve only partial transfer of the Social Security contribution rate (such as

2 percent) have the problem of very high administrative expenses with regard to low earners." He adds that "such persons will need supplementation by public assistance, whose cost, coming from general revenues, will be met by the high earners, who thought that they were doing so much better through the privatization procedure."[31]

The strongest argument in favor of privatization is that it might be reassuring to younger Americans to know that there was a retirement fund for each individual with his or her name on it that would guarantee that he or she would get at least something back from Social Security. This is reason enough to give serious consideration to partial privatization.

As for maintaining the solvency of the system, however, privatization would not accomplish anything that could not be achieved in other ways. And by increasing administrative costs, partial privatization could make maintaining solvency more difficult.

Restraining the Growth of Benefit Costs

While there are measures such as devising a better investment strategy for the temporary surplus in the Social Security trust fund which can delay the exhaustion of the fund by a few years, it is not likely that the solvency of the fund can be ensured on a long-term basis without (a) raising the payroll tax, (b) restraining the growth of benefit costs, or (c) some combination of both. Since younger Americans aren't likely to get a return on their contributions to Social Security that is as generous as that which older Americans are receiving, exacerbating this inequity by increasing the payroll taxes on younger workers is out of the picture. Accordingly, attention must be focused on restraining the growth of benefit costs as a means of maintaining the long-term viability of Social Security while ensuring a greater measure of intergenerational equity.

How might this be accomplished? Proposals for restraining

the growth of benefit costs include the following:

● *Increase the age of eligibility for benefits.* The Concord Coalition proposes replacing the current law, which calls for gradually raising to sixty-seven the age at which full benefits can be received, with a new guideline that would raise the age for full benefits to sixty-eight by the year 2007 and the age at which partial benefits can be claimed to sixty-five by the same year.[32] Legislation introduced by Senators Kerrey and Simpson would accelerate the current schedule for raising the retirement age and then further increase the retirement age to seventy for persons presently under the age of twenty-nine.[33] These proposals take into account the fact that people are living longer today than when Social Security was established. In 1940, when the first benefit check was issued, a sixty-five-year-old, on the average, lived about thirteen more years; today, the life expectancy of a sixty-five-year-old is seventeen more years.[34] But while accelerating the schedule for raising the age at which benefits can be drawn would restrain the growth of benefit costs, such proposals are problematic in two respects. First of all, raising the retirement age often creates difficulties for those in areas such as construction that are physically demanding; working until the age of seventy is not a realistic possibility in many cases. Second, delaying the retirement age could cause problems for members of younger generations trying to find jobs. Increasing the age of retirement might mean, at least for a transitional period, that there would be fewer positions to be filled (if job growth were insufficient to generate the number of new positions needed to accommodate younger workers).

● *Change the way that inflation is measured and cost-of-living adjustments are computed.* A number of economists today believe that the current consumer price index (CPI) used to measure inflation overstates inflation by as much as 1.5 percentage points. Since annual increases in Social Security benefits are linked to changes in the CPI, adjusting the way that the CPI is computed would change benefit levels. Caution is in order, however, when tinkering around with the formula for computing cost of living adjustments. While it might be true that the current method of computing CPI overstates inflation by failing to take into account changes in the "market basket" of goods and services purchased or for product improvement, such as the addition of air bags and anti-lock brakes to automobiles, it is not a foregone conclusion that the CPI overstates cost increases for older Americans. The cost of medicine, for example, has been going up at a rate far higher than the general rate of inflation. Any changes in the formula for measuring inflation should take into account the "market basket" of goods and services typically purchased by those of various ages. If this were done, the revised CPI might indicate that the cost of living is increasing faster for older Americans than for those who are younger because older Americans often spend more on prescription drugs and other forms of health care than do younger Americans.

● *Change the formula for computing benefit levels.* Social Security benefits are computed as follows:

● 90 percent of average indexed monthly earnings (AIME) in the first bracket (which includes all AIME up to a level that in bureaucratic jargon is called the first "bend point"), plus

● 32 percent of AIME in the second bracket (AIME between the first and second "bend points"), plus

- 15 percent of AIME in the third bracket (AIME above the second bend point).[35]

Growth of benefit costs could be restrained by adjusting downward the percentages used to compute benefit levels. This could be done either across the boards by reducing the

Figure 11-2: Current Formula for Computing Social Security Benefits

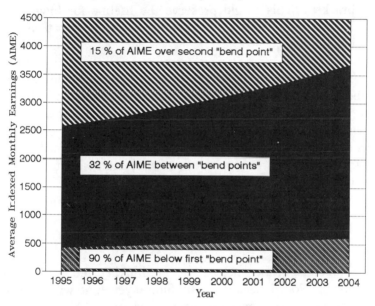

Based on data included in the 1995 Annual Report of the Board of Trustees of the Federal Old-Age and Survivors Insurance Trust Fund. *Average Indexed Monthly Earnings (AIME) are computed for each beneficiary based on his or her historical earnings data, adjusted for inflation. To compute monthly benefits, AIME are separated into three levels, separated by two "bend points." The basic monthly benefit (Primary Insurance Amount or "PIA") is the total of 90 percent of AIME up to the first "bend point," 32 percent of AIME between the first and second "bend points," and 15 percent of AIME above the second "bend point." "Bend points" are adjusted each year to reflect changes in average wages. Figure 11-2 shows both current and projected "bend points."*

percentage used in each bracket or selectively by reducing one or two of the percentages while leaving the other one or two unchanged. Reducing the percentage in each bracket would be particularly hard on low-income individuals, for whom Social Security is a vital lifeline. For this reason, it would be preferable to restrain the growth of benefit costs by scaling back the percentages used to compute benefits in the top two brackets with the largest reduction coming in the top bracket. This would preserve the lifeline for lower-income individuals while slowing down the growth of benefit costs.

There is room for debate as to what changes should be made in the funding formula for Social Security benefits and whether some other approach is preferable. This much, however, is beyond dispute: without restraint in the increase of Social Security benefit costs, the problems of intergenerational justice confronting us will become more severe, increasing the risk of war between generations.

Rethinking Social Security

Economic reality necessitates rethinking the nature and function of Social Security. In future years, it will have to function less like a pension system and more like a form of antipoverty insurance that exists to make certain that no older Americans will go hungry or lack shelter. To a greater extent than is the case today, retirement needs beyond the bare essentials will have to be provided in other ways--by pension systems of various types and by IRAs and other savings for retirement.

At some point in the future, it might make sense to base the benefit levels on the average cost of a basic, healthy diet, decent housing and other bare essentials, rather than on the recipient's earning record. If this approach were taken, it would mean that, in return for contributing a certain percentage of income each year while working, every American would be guaranteed that he or she wouldn't go hungry or lack shelter during the retirement years. Everyone would contribute the same percentage of income in order to receive this guarantee. Everyone would receive the same level of benefits upon reaching the age of eligibility.

Any changes in the formula for computing benefits, it might be added, should be accompanied by repeal of the limitation on earnings for those receiving benefits. Those who receive Social Security benefits should be free to earn as much as they want, including continuing to work full-time, should they so choose. Even under present circumstances, the limitation on earnings makes little sense. If Social Security increasingly assumes the function of antipoverty insurance, rather than a pension system, it will make no sense at all to limit in any way possibilities for augmenting income by continuing to work. For some, continuing to work might be a matter of personal preference simply because they enjoy their jobs. For others, it might be a financial necessity if they are to experience the standard of living they desire. For all, continuing to work without being penalized ought to be an option. In a country which claims to emphasize the importance of work and of freedom of choice, limiting the earnings of those receiving Social Security benefits is a strange anomaly.

Marketable Securities

The short-term impact of restraint in the increase of benefit levels for Social Security would be an increase in the temporary surplus in the Social Security trust fund. Down the road a few years, the trust fund would still be drawn down once baby boomers start retiring. But it wouldn't be drawn down as fast. And most important of all, the trust fund wouldn't be exhausted, if appropriate adjustments were made.

If the federal government continues using the surplus in the Social Security trust fund to help finance the federal budget deficit, little will be gained by restraining the growth of Social Security benefits. Those not yet retired will not come out ahead by simply having a larger pile of unmarketable I.O.U.s in the trust fund, which will be worthless if younger generations decide not to pay them. Any savings should be invested in marketable securities that can be sold when the money is needed, as should all new money coming into the trust fund that is not immediately needed for benefits.

There is also a psychological factor that comes into play. Those on Social Security are more likely to be amenable to restraint in the growth of benefits if the money saved is set aside for future retirees in an identifiable, visible manner, rather than simply disappearing in to the bottomless pit of the federal budget deficit. Making the Social Security trust fund, at least in part, a pension fund with marketable securities would give necessary visibility to savings resulting from changing the benefit formula.

Investing in marketable securities offers the prospect of a greater rate of return than the federal government is currently paying on money borrowed from the fund. In recent years, the effective annual rate of interest earned by assets in the OASI Trust Fund has averaged 8 percent;[36] in the last fifty years, the average return on Treasury bonds has been 5.5 percent, compared with 11.8 percent for stocks.[37] The Social Security trust fund exists to help Social Security beneficiaries, both present and future, not to assist the federal government in the financing of deficits in other areas.

Granted, there are potential problems that could arise if a branch of the federal government got involved in the market in a major way. It might not be appropriate to have the federal government buy stock in General Motors Corporation in preference to stock in Chrysler Corporation or stock in Motorola, Inc., in preference to stock in Texas Instruments, Inc. But as do many pension fund managers, the managers of the Social Security trust fund could take an indexed approach to investment by purchasing on a proportional basis stocks and bonds issued by companies included in a broadly-based index such as the Russell 3000, which includes both large and small companies. The indexed approach would avoid the political controversies likely to result from an active management approach that would involve choosing some stocks and bonds in preference to others.

As for the appropriateness of a branch of the federal government getting involved in stock and bond markets, so doing would consistent with what pension funds do on the state level, apart from the magnitude of the potential investments. An indexed approach to investment would diminish any problems resulting from the magnitude of the investment of Social Security funds. Special provisions limiting the amount of stocks and bonds that the managers of the Social Security trust fund could buy or sell on any given day or in any given week could put a damper on market swings resulting from large-scale sales or purchases of stock and bonds.

Another way of minimizing the impact of large-scale government involvement in securities markets would be to divide for investment purposes the temporary surplus in the Social Security trust fund into smaller investment funds--perhaps even as many as several hundred--and then contract with private fund managers, who would actively manage the various investment funds. All returns from the smaller investment funds would be channeled into the Social Security trust fund, from which benefits would continue to be paid.

Social Security and Budget Deficits

On various occasions, senior citizen lobbying groups have strenuously opposed proposed balanced budget amendments, arguing that cuts in Social Security ought not be used to balance the federal budget. Those who make this argument have a point. As noted in Chapter 9, the current federal budget deficit isn't the result of Social Security. It has come about because the cost of programs which are supposed to be funded by general revenues far exceed the general revenues available. Government officials have found it convenient to include Social Security in budget calculations because with the paper surplus in the Social Security trust fund temporarily increasing, adding Social Security to the calculations masks the true magnitude of deficits in other areas. Any balanced budget amendment worth its salt must exempt Social Security and other programs financed by earmarked taxes from its requirements. Any adjustments made in Social Security benefits must be made to maintain the long-term viability of the program, not to make the federal budget deficit in other areas appear smaller than it really is.

A related point needs to be stressed. Any adjustments made to assure the long-term viability of Social Security must be accompanied by restraint in spending in other federal programs. If Social Security savings were eaten up by larger deficits in other areas, future taxpayers would gain nothing. They would simply be forced to pay out of the other pocket to cover the cost of current consumption.

It might be added that actually reducing the federal budget deficit by slowing down the increases in spending in other areas, thereby allowing revenues to catch up with expenditures as the economy continues to grow, would benefit Social Security. Diminishing the role of the federal government in credit markets would ease the pressure on interest rates. Lower interest rates would encourage investment in new computer technologies, new machinery for factories and other productivity-enhancing measures. Improved productivity could enable higher wages and salaries, which in turn would generate more revenue via the payroll tax to finance Social Security benefits for present and future retirees.

Some Concluding Considerations

There are no tidy solutions to the problems of intergenerational justice relating to Social Security--or to any other problems of intergenerational justice, for that matter. All we can do is work through these matters as best we can.

As we wrestle with the difficult issues related to Social Security, some basic facts of life are worth keeping in mind:

● *The past is history; it is only the future that we can do something about.* Because of the demographic and economic changes that have occurred, the very generous returns that previous retirees have gotten on what they paid into Social Security cannot be duplicated for future retirees. What is important as far as justice among generations is concerned is that future benefit levels and tax levels be as equitable as possible.

● *Problems, when ignored, almost always get worse.* Taking immediate action to assure the long-term viability of Social Security would involve relatively modest adjustments. On the other hand, waiting until the trust fund is exhausted will necessitate greater benefit reductions or larger tax increases. For example, if nothing is done until the year 2030 (the projected date of exhaustion for the combined OASI and DI trust funds, using the intermediate demographic and economic assumptions), benefits would have to be reduced by nearly 25 percent in order to bring them in line with projected income.[38] As the mechanic in a television commercial advertising oil filters reminds us, "You can pay me now or you can pay me later." Paying now would cost relatively little. Paying later will necessitate an expensive overhaul.

● *Any adjustments in benefit levels should be gradual, rather than precipitous.* Because planning for retirement involves long-term considerations, any adjustments in benefit levels should be phased in over a number of years, rather than implemented immediately. As much stability as possible is essential in a program of such vital importance to so many people.

Wisdom is on the side of dealing with the problems related to Social Security within the context of a caring community in which there is sensitivity to the concerns and well-being of members of all generations. If we are all willing to give a bit and be responsive to the needs and concerns of others, Social Security both can be and will continue to be the cornerstone of old-age security for generations to come. And a greater measure of justice among generations will be ensured.

Chapter 12

From Conflict to Community

Some prominent themes emerge from the portraits of generations that comprise Part II of this volume:

- Those who are too young to remember the Great Depression and World War II have little awareness as to how terrible those experiences were.

- Many members of older generations had relatively low expectations but have experienced levels of affluence that have far exceeded their expectations.

- Many members of younger generations have relatively high expectations and are frustrated by the difficulty of realizing them in a changing economic environment.

- Members of older generations who came of age when good jobs with decent wages were readily available have little understanding of the job anxiety and economic insecurity experienced by many who are younger.

• Many members of all generations falsely assume that their experiences either have been or can be duplicated by members of other generations.

• Many members of younger generations have high anger levels related to the taxes they pay to finance benefits for older generations.

• The tendency to find fault with other generations is common to all generations.

A Crisis of Values

When my wife worked at a senior citizen center in the late 1960s, some of the people who visited the center were not comfortable receiving Social Security checks, believing that the money should go to those with greater needs. Today, it is rare to find anyone who views Social Security or any other publicly-funded entitlement program in such a manner. Entitlements have become a way of life. Politicians who are demagogues rather than statesmen--and there seem to be far more of the former than the latter--eagerly tell voters that they deserve everything they get, and more. Whenever there is discussion of restraining the growth of entitlement programs, demagoguery crescendos to a deafening roar as politicians preoccupied with being reelected represent themselves as defenders of the entitlement programs that have become a national addiction.

This addiction results in tremendous costs extending far beyond the costs of the programs themselves. *Newsweek* columnist Robert J. Samuelson observes:

> The promise of entitlement was not only false but ultimately disruptive. It subtly subverted personal and institutional responsibility. There was a growing tendency for everyone to look somewhere else for solutions to their largest problems.[1]

Few Americans today seem to remember--and even fewer seem to heed--the ringing words of an idealistic young president who, on a wintery day scarcely more than three decades ago, inspired the nation with an eloquent inaugural address in which he stated, "And so, my fellow Americans: ask not what your country can do for you--ask what you can do for your country."[2] Instead, the prevailing philosophy for many suggests, "Ask not what you can do for your country--ask what it can do for you."

While many entitlement programs benefit those who are older, self-centeredness is not unique to older Americans. An entire generation of younger Americans has grown up believing that in the beginning, God created the heavens, the earth, CD players and designer jeans--and that we are entitled to the whole works. "I want what I want and I want it now" is the creed by which many live as they worship at the altar of self-gratification. Career advancement and the acquisition of material possessions are what count above all else in the lives of many.[3]

We are not likely to realize a greater measure of intergenerational equity unless we break out of the entitlement mentality and discover what loving our neighbors as ourselves entails. We must transcend self-interest and give recognition to the humanity of those whose lives intersect with ours--our families and our neighbors, both those who are near and those who are distant. In the final analysis, many of the problems we face are not simply political or economic in nature. Rather, they involve basic ethical values with which we must come to grips if we are to resolve these problems. This is true of the budget crisis facing the country and the difficult issues surrounding Medicare and Social Security, as well as environmental concerns and other issues that have not been discussed in detail in this volume.

Seeing the Person Behind the Faults

One of the most insightful (and least noted) Biblical passages tells of Jesus having dinner with tax collectors and other sinners:

> And as he sat at dinner in the house, many tax collectors
> and sinners came and were sitting with him and his disciples.
> When the Pharisees saw this, they said to his disciples, "Why
> does your teacher eat with tax collectors and sinners?" But
> when he heard this, he said, "Those who are well have no
> need of a physician, but those who are sick. Go and learn
> what this means, 'I desire mercy, not sacrifice.' For I have
> come to call not the righteous but sinners." Matthew 9.10-13
> (RSV)

The tax collectors of Jesus' day were notorious crooks who cheated taxpayers by charging them more than they owed and cheated the government by skimming off part of the take. Yet, here was Jesus having dinner with them! The religious types were aghast! Didn't Jesus realize what he was doing?

Jesus was able to see something most of us fail to see--the person behind the faults. Jesus realized that even crooked tax collectors are human beings worthy of our compassion and understanding, while in no way condoning cheating or any of the other terrible things the crooked tax collectors were doing.

The people most of us meet in day-to-day life have flaws of character of far lesser magnitude than the crooked tax collectors of Jesus' time. Yet we often magnify the things they do, making mountains of mole hills, and, in the process, block out any possibility of seeing their humanity. When we start criticizing other people for this and that, for wrongs that we perceive or imagine, it is very easy to overlook the fact that those with whom we share earthly existence are real people who, like ourselves, have hopes and fears, moments of joy and moments of sorrow, times of success and times of failure.

When addressing intergenerational issues, it is very easy to focus only on the differences between generations and on the faults of other generations, some of them real, some of them imagined. This, however, does nothing to resolve intergenerational conflict. Focusing on the faults of others results in bitterness and divisiveness, pushing us toward the chasm of a war between generations. It is only if we are able to see the person behind the faults--if we are aware of their fears and anxieties--that the groundwork can be laid for bridging the gaps between generations. Compassion and understanding must replace anger and bitterness.

"For It Is in Giving That We Receive"

A few years ago, a student stopped by my office bubbling with enthusiasm about an experience she had with Generations, a program introduced by campus ministry to encourage students to spend time with folks in different age groups. As part of this program, she was regularly visiting a resident in an area nursing home.

"I thought I was helping Margaret," the student exclaimed, "but it's amazing how much she has been helping me!"

She had discovered the nature of charity.

When we hear the word "charity," we often think about giving money to those who are less fortunate--for example, donating money to the local food pantry or to the Salvation Army. Helping those who are less fortunate is an important part of charity. But it is only a small part of what charity, when fully understood, entails. Charity, in its fullest sense, is living in and experiencing community. It is discovering the humanity of others--and our own humanity in the process. It is understanding others and being understood.

The English word "charity" comes from the Old French word *charité*, which carried with it the notions of fondness, affection and valuing greatly--connotations that are today often associated with the English word "cherish." Also of etymological significance is the Latin word *caritas*, which was often used to translate the Greek word *agápē*, found both in the love commandment ("You shall love your neighbor as yourself") and in Paul's reference to faith, hope and love in I Corinthians 13. *Caritas* was often defined as "dearness, love founded on esteem."[4] The Greek verb from which *agápē* is derived is customarily defined as "to treat with affection" and "to regard with brotherly love" as when treating a stranger as if he or she were a member of the family. Ancient Greeks, by the way, did not use the term *agápē* to refer to giving money to those less fortunate; rather, they used the term *eleēmosynē*, from which the English word "alms" is derived. *Eleēmosynē* involved pity, which *agápē* did not.[5]

We all both need and desire charity. This is not to suggest, of course, that everyone should be getting food stamps, regardless of income level. Rather, it is to suggest that we all have a need to be taken seriously, to be treated with respect and esteem, and to be understood--in short, to be treated in a charitable manner. "They just don't get it" is the recurring lament of frustrated teenagers, alienated spouses and others pained by the brokenness of relationships of various sorts. "They just don't get it" is the signpost marking the chasms separating generations.

Charity involves more than simply being charitable in our relations with others. As the student involved in Generations discovered, when we take time to listen to others and give recognition to their humanity, our own lives are enriched in the process. There is a good deal of wisdom to be found in a beautiful old prayer attributed to St. Francis of Assisi that reads, in part:

> Lord, make us instruments of your peace . . . .
> Grant that we may not so much seek
>   to be consoled as to console;
>   to be understood as to understand;
>   to be loved as to love.
> For it is in giving that we receive . . . . [6]

In many cases, when we seek understanding just for the sake of being understood, love just for the sake of being loved, and consolation just for the sake of being consoled, the result is failure and frustration. As the insightful centuries-old prayer reminds us, it is as we extend understanding to others that, in many cases, others come to better understand us. And similarly with being loved and consoled, for "it is in giving that we receive." When this happens, we experience healing and reconciliation. In "The Excursion," first published in 1814, a year in which war-ravaged Europe enjoyed a brief respite from the Napoleonic wars, the English poet William Wordsworth observes:

> The charities that soothe, and heal, and bless,
> Are scattered at the feet of Man--like flowers.
> The generous inclination, the just rule,
> Kind wishes, and good actions, and pure thoughts--
> No mystery is here![7]

Building Bridges

Building bridges to span the chasms separating generations is as simple as taking the time to listen to the concerns of those in other age-groups. It is as simple as gaining a better understanding of where others are coming from by taking note of the experiences which have been formative for them and the crises which they have endured. It is as simple as being less inclined to judge and more willing to understand. It is as simple as blocking out time to spend with family members and friends in other age-groups.

How might this be accomplished? Possibilities include the following:

● Invite a grandchild to help carve pumpkins for Halloween.

● Invite a grandparent to help fly a kite on a windy day--you might be surprised how much grandparents know about flying kites.

● Whether one is thirteen or thirty, ask a grandparent or an older neighbor to teach one how to knit, how to bake bread, how to play the harmonica, how to tie flies, how to make model airplanes or whatever is of interest that the grandparent or neighbor knows how to do.

● Plan at least three family outings each year involving at least three generations; better yet, involve at least three generations of three different families.

● Ask students in writing classes to interview members of different generations and write a report based on the interviews.

● Take freshly-baked brownies to a nursing home and share them with the residents when they gather for coffee.

● Volunteer to help a neighbor rake leaves.

Sometimes intergenerational bridge-building is simply done on an *ad hoc*, spontaneous basis. Sometimes bridge-building is the result of special programs sponsored by public or private agencies or organizations. Examples include the following:

● *Clearview Nursing Home Programs.* Clearview Nursing Home in Juneau, Wisconsin, hosts an annual Halloween party for children in the area. Clearview also has a day-care center on its premises; originally established as a service to employees, the day-care center provides an opportunity for Clearview residents to interact with children.[8]

● *Academy of Senior Professionals at Eckerd College (ASPEC).* Eckerd College in St. Petersburg, Florida, has established the Academy of Senior Professionals at Eckerd College (ASPEC), an intergenerational learning experience drawing upon the insights of retired professionals with a wealth of experience in a wide variety of disciplines. Students welcome the opportunity to meet with ASPEC members, in many cases forming friendships which extend beyond the college years.[9]

• *Illinois READS.* The Illinois Department on Aging sponsors Illinois READS (Retirees Educating and Assisting in the Development of Students). This state-sponsored program involves volunteers in reading programs and other activities designed to help elementary school-age children.[10]

• *CASTLE (Calling All Students/Seniors To Learning Exchange).* Pittsburgh Public Schools and Pittsburgh Citiparks have teamed up with Generations Together, the intergenerational studies program at the University of Pittsburgh, to establish CASTLE (Calling All Students/Seniors To Learning Exchange), an intergenerational mentoring program designed to help students through the critical transition from middle school to high school.[11]

• *Umoja-Unity Across Generations.* Generations Together has also played a major role in establishing Umoja-Unity Across Generations, an intergenerational mentoring program based in Pittsburgh's African American community. Intergenerational teams comprised of older adults (over age fifty) and teachers foster the development of self-confidence, self-respect and a sense of cultural identity by working with elementary school-age children in a variety of in-school and out-of-school programs and activities.[12]

• *Project EASE (Exploring Aging through Shared Experiences).* Developed by the cooperative extension service at Cornell University, Project EASE is designed to bring together senior citizens and children ages 9-13 for meaningful, goal-oriented interaction. Three types of projects have been designed for use with Project EASE: (1) service projects in which youth groups join with groups of senior citizens to plan and carry out community service projects, (2) shared group activities in which youth groups and senior citizens engage in activities of mutual interest such as gardening or dramatic activities, and (3) one-on-one matching, whereby youth group members and senior citizens are paired up and then get together for shared activities and other events.[13]

● *Grandfriends: An Intergenerational Volunteer Program.* Sponsored by Skokie School District 73.5 in Skokie, Illinois, Grandfriends is designed to foster the development of reading skills and enhance intergenerational understanding by involving children and older adults in reading programs that involve reading aloud. To facilitate programs of this sort, the school district has developed an intergenerational bibliography of children's literature.[14]

Dividends

Intergenerational experiences pay significant dividends. Sally Newman, executive director of Generations Together, notes that successful intergenerational programs benefit participants of all ages. Benefits to older adults include:

- greater self-esteem
- greater satisfaction in life
- higher levels of cognitive function
- improved social life
- greater interest in the community

- greater overall happiness
- new friends and a new social network

Benefits to children, Newman observes, are equally significant. Among them are the following:

- improved academic performance
- more positive peer interactions
- improved self-esteem and sense of self-worth
- better school attendance
- more positive social behavior

Newman notes there other benefits as well. She reports that teachers and other professional staff often experience improved motivation and greater work satisfaction. More positive relations across generational lines are often reflected in other aspects of community life, such as intergenerational conversations in the local supermarket and elsewhere in the community. And when school referendums are on the ballot, older adults who have participated in intergenerational programs are more inclined to support them.[15]

One of the older adults participating in Cornell's Project EASE observed, "You hear so many bad things about kids nowadays--it was good to see a group of nice ones." One of the youth participants commented, "I was surprised to meet a 94-year-old woman who has a lot of energy and loves activities like sports and pumpkin painting."[16] Such are the dividends provided by intergenerational programs and activities.

Rediscovering and Renewing the American Dream

In an insightful essay entitled "How Our American Dream Unraveled," Robert J. Samuelson observes, "After World War II, we believed that prosperity would create the ultimate Good Society. We were wrong."[17]

Contrary to what the nonstop television commercials with which we are bombarded would have us believe, we cannot consume our way to happiness. While poverty is not a state of affairs to be idealized, greater levels of affluence do not necessarily correlate with greater quality of life or greater happiness. It is interesting to note that many who experienced the Great Depression in the 1930s and World War II in the 1940s do not remember the prosperous post-war years as the best years of their lives. That is not to suggest, of course, that we should attempt to recreate the Great Depression so that more people could have the opportunity to experience it. The Great Depression and World War II were terrible experiences that no one who endured them wants to relive. Yet there is a depth of experience given expression in a greater sense of community and a heightened sense of purpose that is often present in times of difficulty but lacking in times of comfort and prosperity.

The comparative emptiness of the post-war years serves to remind us that there is far more to life than the acquisition of material possessions. This is not to suggest that there is anything wrong with enjoying a new car, new dining room furniture or the latest CD. Creature comforts, however, are not of primary significance when it comes to determining quality of life. Far more important is the quality of the interpersonal relationships we experience. It is deeply ironic that as levels of affluence have increased in this country, so also has the divorce rate and other forms of brokenness in interpersonal relations.

A related point is worth noting. Toning down the high levels of anger, which are so widespread today, is highly desirable. Anger contributes nothing to the quality of life. Anger makes life unpleasant for other people and adds immensely to the unhappiness of those who are angry. While there is a time and a place for anger, it has gotten out of hand in contemporary American society.

We would all be better off if, instead of being preoccupied with what we don't have and wrongs that we believe have been done to us, we took note of what we do have. During the Great Depression and other times of hardship, people were deeply appreciative of what they had. In the times of prosperity which, with brief interruption, have prevailed in the half-century following World War II, there has often been a tendency to overlook what we have as we angrily demand more. The result is greater unhappiness.

As the examples noted on previous pages illustrate, breaking down the barriers of age-segregation that stand in the way of enhanced interpersonal relations can pay rich dividends in terms of quality of life for young and old alike. Breaking down age-segregation can also set the stage for dealing with intergenerational issues, ranging from Social Security to adequately funding education, in a manner that is equitable to all generations--an approach that involves taking everyone's well-being into account and maintaining appropriate balance. Rediscovering what it is to be a neighbor is the key to ensuring a greater measure of intergenerational equity and experiencing the greatest quality of life possible. Isn't ensuring justice and the opportunity to experience the greatest possible quality of life what the American Dream ought to be about?

Notes

Introduction

1. John Rawls, *A Theory of Justice* (Cambridge, Mass.: The Belknap Press of Harvard University Press, 1971), 284.

2. Julián Marías, *Generations: A Historical Method*, tr. Harold C. Raley (University, Alabama: The University of Alabama Press, 1970), 155. Marías suggests that "the duration of a generation must be very close to fifteen years, because it is at about the age of fifteen that we leave childhood, and about the age of thirty that we begin our participation in historical events" (pp. 164-65). The life stages of contemporary Americans, however, correlate more closely to a twenty-year life-stage framework, which is what has been used in this volume. Using a twenty-year framework, the life stages break down as follows:

Age	Life Stage
birth-20	years of growth and preparation
21-40	years spent getting established
41-60	prime career years
61-80	vigorous years of maturity and retirement
81-	advanced years

Not everyone, of course, fits neatly into these parameters. More than one frustrated parent has a son or daughter in his or her thirties still at home, still trying to figure out what to do. On the other hand, some are very successful in business or other endeavors long before they reach the age of thirty and everything from there on is downhill. Similarly, there are some in their eighties who haven't slowed down a bit while others become incapacitated in the middle years of life. But even though the twenty-year framework is only a rough approximation, it provides useful reference points for identifying stages of the life cycle and sorting out the generations in contemporary American society.

3. These six generations were mapped out by defining the highly-publicized and much-discussed Baby-Boom Generation as those born in the twenty years following World War II and then mapping out twenty-year periods both before and after the Baby-Boom Generation to identify the time parameters for the other generations.

4. Karl Barth, *Church Dogmatics*, vol. 3, part 4, *The Doctrine of Creation*, tr. A.T. MacKay *et al* (Edinburgh: T. & T. Clark, 1961), 466.

Chapter 1: Conflict and Justice

1. Scott Schmidt, "My G-G-Generation," *The Chicago Sun-Times*, 4 August 1995.

2. Reinhold Niebuhr, *The Nature and Destiny of Man*, vol. 2, *Human Destiny* (New York: Charles Scribner's Sons, 1964), 255.

3. Reinhold Niebuhr, *Moral Man and Immoral Society* (New York: Charles Scribner's Sons, 1960), xv.

4. Niebuhr broke sharply with the Social Gospel movement (with which he at one time identified), contending that Walter Rauschenbusch and the other leaders of the Social Gospel movement were naive about the prospects for perfecting human nature. See, e.g., Reinhold Niebuhr, *An Interpretation of Christian Ethics* (New York: Harper & Brothers Publishers, 1935), 169-98.

5. See, e.g., "The Ethics of Jesus and the Social Problem," "Religion and the Class War in Kentucky," "Ideology and the Social Struggle" and "Inflation and Group Consciousness" in D.B. Robertson, ed., *Love and Justice: Selections from the Shorter Writings of Reinhold Niebuhr* (Philadelphia: The Westminster Press, 1957), 29-40, 108-13, 115-17, 117-19.

6. U.S. Department of Commerce, *Statistical Abstract of the United States: 1993*, 113th ed. (Washington, D.C., 1993), 454.

Chapter 2: A Matter of Balance

1. Matthew 22.35-39. Luke 10.27. See also Matthew 22.39, Mark 12.31, Luke 10.27, Matthew 19.19, Romans 13.9, Galatians 5.14 and James 2.8. Unless otherwise noted, all Biblical quotations are from *The New Oxford Annotated Bible with the Apocrypha (Revised*

Standard Version), ed. Herbert G. May and Bruce M. Metzger (New York: Oxford University Press, 1977).

2. Luke 10.29-35.

3. Luke 10.36-37.

4. Søren Kierkegaard, *Works of Love,* tr. Howard and Edna Hong (New York: Harper and Brothers, 1962), 142.

5. Barth, *Church Dogmatics*, 3,4:285-323.

6. As for why we should identify the love commandment as the ultimate ethical norm rather than, say, self-interest or nationalism, when all things are considered we can do no more than affirm it as an article of faith. In the final analysis, any discussion of ethical norms must be prefaced with the simple statement, "This I believe." For a more detailed discussion of these matters, see Daniel E. Lee, *Hope Is Where We Least Expect to Find It* (Lanham, Maryland: University Press of America, Inc., 1993), 9-26.

7. R. Jebb. Quoted in *The Oxford English Dictionary* (Oxford: Clarendon Press, 1989), 3:42.

8. Sometimes the person we have the most difficulty affirming and recognizing as a person is oneself. For a discussion of these matters, see "Rediscovering the Person in Oneself" in Lee, *Hope Is Where We Least Expect to Find It*, 37-43.

9. See, e.g., Richard T. DeGeorge, "Do We Owe the Future Anything?" and James P. Sterba, "The Welfare Rights of Distant Peoples and Future Generations" in James P. Sterba, ed., *Morality in Practice,* 2nd ed. (Belmont, Calif.: Wadsworth Publishing Company, 1988), 108-15, 115-27.

10. George F. Will, "Too Much of a Good Thing?" *Newsweek*, 23 September 1991, 68. Will is commenting on some arguments made by Mary Ann Glendon in *Rights Talk: The Impoverishment of Political Discourse* (New York: The Free Press, 1991).

11. Robert D. Putnam, "Raising Generation of Loners," *The Dispatch*, 2 January 1996, sec. A.

12. *The Ethics of Aristotle: The Nicomachean Ethics Translated,* tr. J.A.K Thomson (Baltimore: Penguin Books, 1953), 147.

13. *Ibid.*

14. *Ibid.*, 145-46.

15. Norman Daniels, *Am I My Parents' Keeper? An Essay on Justice between the Young and the Old* (New York: Oxford University Press, 1988), 41.

16. See, e.g., Niebuhr, *Moral Man and Immoral Society*, ix, xi. The title of this widely-read volume calls attention to this theme.

Chapter 3: The World War I Generation

1. Woodrow Wilson, *A History of the American People*, vol. 5 (New York: Wm. H. Wise & Co., 1931), 300.

2. Thomas A. Bailey, *The American Pageant: A History of the Republic*, 2nd ed. (Boston: D.C. Heath and Company, 1961), 744.

3. "McKinley's War Message" in Henry Steele Commager, ed., *Documents of American History*, 7th ed., vol. 2 (New York: Appleton-Century-Crofts, 1963), 1-4.

4. Theodore Roosevelt, *The Rough Riders* (New York: Charles Scribner's Sons, 1923), 139.

5. David F. Trask, *The War with Spain in 1898* (New York: Macmillan Publishing Co., Inc., 1981), 421. Cable communications with Hong Kong had not yet been restored, which contributed to the delay in getting word of the protocol calling for cessation of hostilities to American forces in the Philippines.

6. In his laboratory notebook, Bell recounted the momentous event of March 10, 1876 as follows: "I then shouted into the M[outhpiece] the following sentence: 'Mr. Watson--come here--I want to see you.' To my delight he came and declared that he had heard and understood what I said." Quoted by Robert V. Bruce in *Bell: Alexander Graham Bell and the Conquest of Solitude* (Boston: Little, Brown and Company, 1973), 181.

7. Wyn Wachhorst, *Thomas Alva Edison: An American Myth* (Cambridge, Mass.: The MIT Press, 1981), 5.

8. Bailey, *American Pageant*, 812-13.

9. U.S. Department of Commerce, *Statistical Abstract of the United States: 1995*, 115th ed. (Washington, D.C., 1995), 632.

10. Fred Howard, *Wilbur and Orville: A Biography of the Wright Brothers* (New York: Alfred A. Knopf, 1988), 136-39.

11. Elizabeth Cady Stanton, Susan B. Anthony and Matilda Josly Gage, eds., *History of Woman Suffrage*, vol. 1 (New York: Source Book Press, 1889), 71.

12. Alma Lutz, *Susan B. Anthony: Rebel, Crusader, Humanitarian* (Boston: Beacon Press, 1959), 198-202, 209-13.

13. Inez Haynes Irwin, *The Story of Alice Paul and the National*

Women's Party (Fairfax, Virginia: Denlinger's Publishers, Ltd., 1977), 30.

14. Quoted by Irwin in *ibid.*, 97.

15. *Ibid.*, 198-203.

16. *Ibid.*, 255-56, 292-93.

17. Bailey, *The American Pageant*, 664-65.

18. Commager, ed., *Documents of American History* 1:148.

19. Ida Husted Harper, ed., *The History of Woman Suffrage*, vol. 5 (New York: Source Book Press, 1922), 649-55.

20. "Negro Problem Solved: North Carolina's Governor So Asserts at Banquet," *The New York Times*, 19 December 1903. Unless otherwise noted, all references to *The New York Times* are to the late city edition, when there are multiple editions.

21. Stephen B. Oates, *Let the Trumpet Sound: The Life of Martin Luther King, Jr.* (New York: Harper & Row, 1982), 16.

22. Martin Luther King, Jr., "I Have a Dream," in James Melvin Washington, ed., *A Testament of Hope: The Essential Writings of Martin Luther King, Jr.* (San Francisco: Harper & Row, 1986), 217-20.

23. Mark 10.31.

24. Bailey, *American Pageant*, 515-16.

25. U. S. Bureau of the Census, *Historical Statistics of the United States: Colonial Times to 1970* (Washington, D.C., 1975), 1:10.

26. *Statistical Abstract of the United States: 1995*, 8.

27. *Historical Statistics of the United States* 1:386.

28. *Statistical Abstract of the United States: 1994*, 128.

29. Bailey, *American Pageant*, 554.

30. *Statistical Abstract of the United States: 1995*, 193.

31. Bailey, *American Pageant*, 559.

32. *Statistical Abstract of the United States: 1995*, 105.

33. *Historical Statistics of the United States* 1:213.

34. *Ibid.*, 1:166; *Statistical Abstract of the United States: 1995*, 426. Hourly wages in manufacturing, adjusted for inflation, hit their peak in 1985 and then began declining.

35. *Historical Statistics of the United States* 1:15.

36. *Statistical Abstract of the United States: 1995*, 16.

37. *Historical Statistics of the United States* 1:55.

38. Elizabeth Frost and Kathryn Cullen-DuPont, *Women's Suffrage in America: An Eyewitness History* (New York: Facts on File,

1992). See also Harper, ed., *The History of Woman Suffrage* 5:632.

39. Interviewed 31 August 1995. The quotations about voting in the first election are cited by Rebecca Morris in "102-Year-Old Aledo Woman Remembers," *The Dispatch* (Moline, Illinois), 26 August 1995.

40. *The New York Times*, 3 December 1895.

41. *Historical Statistics of the United States* 1:386.

42. Interviewed 11 April 1993. The profile also draws upon Conrad Bergendoff, "Augustana--A People in Transition," in J. Iverne Dowie and Ernest M. Espelie, eds., *The Swedish Immigrant Community In Transition: Essays in Honor of Dr. Conrad Bergendoff* (Rock Island, Illinois: Augustana Historical Society, 1963). Recollections from Bergendoff's Middletown days are based on both sources; his views on issues of day were expressed in the interview with author.

43. John Bach McMaster, *The United States in the World War (1918-20)*, New York: D. Appleton-Century Co., 1936), 85-86.

44. "Wilson's Speech for Declaration of War against Germany," in Commager, ed., *Documents of American History* 2:131.

45. *The Times History of the War,* vol.21 (London: The Times, 1920), 66-67.

46. *The Times History of the War* 21:72.

47. Interviewed 28 July 1995.

48. Interviewed 6 September 1995.

49. Will, Woltman, Shellpfeffer and Voss were interviewed 5 August 1995.

Chapter 4: The World War II Generation

1. Quoted by Jonathan Daniels in *The Time Between the Wars: Armistice to Pearl Harbor* (Garden City, New York: Doubleday & Company, Inc., 1966), 117.

2. Quoted by Bailey in *American Pageant*, 786.

3. Quoted in *ibid*.

4. Kal Wagenheim, *Babe Ruth: His Life and Legend* (New York: Praeger Publishers, 1974), 168-69.

5. Leonard Mosley, *Lindbergh: A Biography* (Garden City, New York: Doubleday & Company, Inc., 1976), 101-12.

6. *Ibid*, 115-16.

7. Bailey, *American Pageant*, 816.

8. Herbert Hoover, "The Philosophy of Rugged Individualism."

Included in Commager, ed., *Documents of American History* 2:222-25.

9. Quoted by Daniels in *The Time Between the Wars*, 181.

10. John Kenneth Galbraith, *The Great Crash--1929* (Boston: Houghton Mifflin Company, 1961), 116.

11. Bailey, *American Pageant*, 819.

12. *Ibid*, 825-26.

13. Quoted by Walter S. Ross in *The Last Hero: Charles A. Lindbergh* (New York: Harper & Row, 1968), 310.

14. Quoted by Mosley in *Lindbergh*, 288.

15. Reinhold Niebuhr, "To Prevent the Triumph of an Intolerable Tyranny." Included in Robertson, ed., *Love and Justice*, 272-28.

16. Bailey, *American Pageant*, 873-74.

17. Terry Hughes and John Costello, *The Battle of the Atlantic* (New York: The Dial Press, 1977), 187-88; Samuel I. Rosenman, ed., *The Public Papers and Addresses of Franklin D. Roosevelt: 1941 Volume* (New York: Harper & Brothers, 1950), 532.

18. Rosenman, ed., *Papers of Roosevelt: 1941*, 515.

19. *Ibid.*, 522.

20. Samuel Eliot Morison, *The Battle of the Atlantic: September 1939-May 1943* (Boston: Little, Brown and Company, 1947), 125-35. See also Hughes and Costello, *The Battle of the Atlantic*, 190-207.

22. *Ibid.*

22. Interviewed 14 August 1995.

23. Photograph and caption included in Walter Lord, *Day of Infamy* (New York: Henry Holt and Company, 1957), 54-55.

24. Interviewed 26 July 1995.

25. John W. F. Dulles, *Yesterday in Mexico: A Chronicle of the Revolution, 1919-1936* (Austin, Texas: University of Texas Press, 1961), 11-13.

26. Lisa Mohr, "Memories of Mexican Immigrants to the Q-C," *The Dispatch and the Rock Island Argus*, 10 September, 1995, sec. G.

27. Interviewed 29 July 1995.

28. Interviewed 25 July 1995.

29. Interviewed 9 September 1995.

30. Interviewed 15 September 1994.

Chapter 5: The Silent Generation

1. Quoted by Herbert Feis in *From Trust to Terror: The Onset of*

the Cold War, 1945-50 (New York: W.W. Norton & Company, Inc., 1970), 77.

2. *Ibid.*, 338-346.

3. Wilfried Loth, *The Division of the World: 1941-55* (New York: St. Martin's Press, 1988), 212-13.

4. Volumes providing a more detailed discussion of the events of the Korean War include Clay Blair, *The Forgotten War: America in Korea 1950-53* (New York: Times Books, 1987) and Max Hasting, *The Korean War* (New York: Simon and Schuster, 1987). The latter volume includes a very useful chronology of events.

5. David Halberstam, *The Fifties* (New York: Villard Books, 1993), 49.

6. *Ibid.*, 53-54.

7. Quoted by Cabell Phillips in *The Truman Presidency: The History of a Triumphant Succession* (New York: The MacMillan Company, 1966), 387.

8. Quoted in *ibid.* 389.

9. Blanch Wiesen Cook, *The Declassified Eisenhower: A Divided Legacy* (New York: Doubleday & Company, Inc., 1981), 158.

10. Halberstam, *The Fifties*, 252-53.

11. Quoted by Bailey in *The American Pageant*, 944.

12. Halberstam, *The Fifties*, 196-200.

13. *Ibid*, 508-13.

14. *Ibid*, 567-69.

15. *Ibid.*

16. *Ibid*, 155-64.

17. *Ibid*, 539-43.

18. Quoted by Oates in *Let the Trumpet Sound*, 66.

19. Quoted by Halberstam in *The Fifties*, 562.

20. *Ibid.*, 567.

21. *Ibid.*, 570-71.

22. *Ibid.*, 570-76.

23. *Ibid.*, 462-66.

24. *Ibid.*, 457-59.

25. Albert Goldman, *Elvis* (New York: McGraw-Hill Book Company, 1981), 118-19.

26. Quoted by Halberstam in *The Fifties*, 456.

27. Wade Greene. Quoted by William Strauss and Neil Howe in *Generations: The History of America's Future, 1584 to 2069* (New

York: Quill, 1991), 281.

28. Interviewed 8 June 1995. Risdal is the author's uncle.

29. Interviewed 4 October 1994.

30. Interviewed 14 September 1995.

31. Interviewed 25 July 1995. The quote on sustainable agriculture appeared in *Leopold Letter: A Newsletter of the Leopold Center for Sustainable Agriculture* 7 (Summer 1995): 2.

32. Interviewed 20 June 1995.

33. Interviewed 20 October 1995. The author attended the Martin Luther King Day celebration on January 16, 1995, when Jenkins delivered the keynote address.

34. Interviewed 8 October 1994.

35. Interviewed 25 June 1995.

Chapter 6: The Baby Boom Generation

1. "Vietcong attack 7 Cities; Allies Call off Tet Truce," *The New York Times*, 30 January 1968; "Foe Invades U.S. Saigon Embassy; Raiders Wiped out after 6 Hours; Vietcong Widen Attack on Cities," *The New York Times*, 31 January 1968.

2. For two highly-readable accounts of the battle of Trenton, see Burke Davis, *George Washington and the American Revolution* (New York: Random House, 1975), 160-76, and James Thomas Flexner, *Washington in the American Revolution (1775-1783)* (Boston: Little, Brown and Company, 1968), 171-90.

3. James J. Wirtz, *The Tet Offensive: Intelligence Failure in War* (Ithaca, New York: Cornell University Press, 1991), 1-2.

4. "Up Tight at Khe Sanh," *Newsweek*, 12 February 1968, 30-31.

5. "Johnson Says He Won't Run; Halts North Vietnam Raids; Bids Hanoi Join Peace Moves," *The New York Times*, 1 April 1968.

6. Quoted in *ibid.*

7. "Martin Luther King Is Slain in Memphis; A White Is Suspected; Johnson Urges Calm," *The New York Times*, 5 April 1968.

8. "Siege of Khe Sanh Declared Lifted; Troops Hunt Foe," *The New York Times*, 6 April 1968.

9. "Kennedy Shot and Gravely Wounded after Winning California Primary; Suspect Seized in Los Angeles Hotel," *The New York Times*, 5 June 1968.

10. "Kennedy Is Dead, Victim of Assassin; Suspect, Arab Im-

migrant, Arraigned; Johnson Appoints Panel on Violence," *The New York Times*, 6 June 1968.

11. "Decision to Abandon Khe Sanh Explained in Saigon," *The New York Times*, 28 June 1968.

12. "Billions of Boomers," *American Demographics* 14 (March 1992): 6.

13. Leon F. Bouvier and Carol J. De Vita, "The Baby Boom-- Entering Midlife," *Population Bulletin* 46 (November, 1991): 4-5.

14. *Ibid.*, 4-6.

15. Interviewed 8 August 1995.

16. Interviewed 14 July 1995.

17. See also the discussion of the love commandment in Chapters 2 and 12.

18. Interviewed 28 June 1995.

19. For a useful historical and anthropological account of the Quiché Mayas, see Robert M. Carmack, *Quiché Mayas of Utatlán: The Evolution of a Highland Guatamala Kingdom* (Norman, Oklahoma: University of Oklahoma Press, 1981). A moving personal story of a Quiché woman is to be found in Elisabeth Burgos-Debray, ed., *I, Rigoberta Menchú*, tr. Ann Wright (London: Verso Editions, 1984).

20. Interviewed 8 June 1995.

21. Interviewed 9 October 1994.

22. Interviewed 26 June 1995. Biographical information is also based on an article by Rame in *The Minnesota Hunter & Jumper Association Newsletter* 24 (October-December 1993): 1.

23. Interviewed 28 June 1995.

24. Interviewed 10 July 1995.

25. Interviewed 9 October 1994.

Chapter 7: Generation X

1. Susan Mitchell, "How to Talk to Young Adults," *American Demographics* 15 (April 1993): 50.

2. *Ibid.*, 51.

3. Strauss and Howe, *Generations*, 317-34.

4. Douglas Coupland, *Generation X: Tales for an Accelerated Culture* (New York: St. Martin's Press, 1991).

5. Quoted in "Twentysomethings: A Generation of Gripers and How they Grew," *Psychology Today* 25 (May-June 1992): 11.

6. *Ibid.*

7. "Baby Busters Enter the Work Force," *The Futurist* 26 (May-June 1992): 53.

8. Allan Bloom, *The Closing of the American Mind* (New York: Simon and Schuster, 1987), 62-64.

9. Steve Allen, *Dumbth and 81 Ways to Make Americans Smarter* (Buffalo, N.Y.: Prometheus Books, 1989), 23.

10. Quoted by Neil Howe and Bill Strauss in *13th Gen: Abort, Retry, Ignore, Fail?* (New York: Vintage Books, 1993), 23.

11. Quoted in *Ibid.*, 25.

12. Nicholas Zill and John Robinson, "The Generation X Difference," *American Demographics* 17 (April 1995): 26. See also "Generation X-onomics," *The Economist* 330 (March 19, 1994): 27.

13. Karen Ritchie, "Marketing to Generation X," *American Demographics* 17 (April 1995): 36.

14. Howe and Strauss, *13th Gen*, 105.

15. Zill and Robinson, "The Generation X Difference," 28.

16. Strauss and Howe, *Generations*, 325.

17. Ritchie, "Marketing to Generation X," 36.

18. *Ibid.*, 37. See also Zill and Robinson, "The Generation X Difference," 29

19. *Ibid.*, 26.

20. *Ibid.*

21. John L. McIntosh, "Generational Analyses of Suicide: Baby Boomers and 13ers," *Suicide and Life-Threatening Behavior* 24 (Winter 1994): 334-42.

22. Strauss and Howe, *Generations*, 326.

23. Coupland, *Generation X*, 5.

24. Quoted by Howe and Strauss in *13th Gen*, 94.

25. Quoted in *ibid.*, 96.

26. Robin Toner, "Generational Push Has Not Come to Shove," *The New York Times*, 31 December 1995, sec. 4.

27. *Ibid.*

28. Mitchell, "How to Talk to Young Adults," 51.

29. Interviewed 15 September 1995. See also Dan Lee, "Welfare: Mother's Story," *The Dispatch*, 2 April 1995, sec. A.

30. Interviewed 17 August 1995.

31. Quoted by Alfonso Ortiz in *The Pueblo* (New York: Chelsea House Publishers, 1994), 34.

32. Interviewed 4 October 1994.

33. Interviewed 1 December 1995.

34. Interviewed 7 October 1995. Some of the quotations come, with Benda's permission, from E-mail messages he has sent to members of the "Kid/Teen Rights Discussion Group" on Internet.

35. Charles Keeshan, "Small Boy, Big Trouble: 9-Year-Old R.I. Child Accused of Attempted Murder," *The Dispatch*, 29 December 1995.

36. Interviewed 3 January 1996. Quotations from Desadier's essay are used with his permission and the permission of his mother.

Chapter 8: The Twenty-First Century Generation

1. *Statistical Abstract of the United States, 1995*, 480.

2. *Ibid.*, 481.

3. Peter B. Goldberg, "Poverty and Nutrition: If Steinbeck Were Alive Today," *Families in Society: The Journal of Contemporary Human Services* 76 (1995): 46.

4. Quoted in *ibid.*, 47.

5. For a useful summary of some of the literature in this area, see Eric F. Dubow and Maria F. Ippolito, "Effects of Poverty and Quality of the Home Environment on Changes in the Academic and Behavioral Adjustment of Elementary School-Age Children," *Journal of Clinical Child Psychology* 23 (1994): 402.

6. Patricia L. Ewalt, "Who Cares for the Children?" *Social Work* 40 (March 1995): 149.

7. Dubow and Ippolito, "Effects of Poverty," 408.

8. *Ibid.*, 409.

9. Greg J. Duncan, Jeanne Brooks-Gunn, and Pamela Kato Klebanov, "Economic Deprivation and Early Childhood Development," *Child Development* 65 (1994): 315.

10. Noted on pp. 4-8 and 24 above. See also Aletha C. Huston, Vonnie C. McLoyd and Cynthia Garcia Coll, "Children and Poverty: Issues in Contemporary Research," *Child Development* 65 (1994): 276.

11. Quoted by William J. Bennett in *The Index of Leading Cultural Indicators* 1 (March 1993), 6.

12. *Ibid.*, 13; *Statistical Abstract of the United States, 1995*, 73.

13. S. Wayne Duncan, "Economic Impact of Divorce on Children's Development: Current Findings and Policy Implications,"

Journal of Clinical Child Psychology 23 (1994): 446.

14. *Ibid.*, 447-48.

15. *Ibid.*, 449.

16. *Statistical Abstract of the United States, 1995*, 77.

17. *Ibid.*

18. "A Milestone for Black Families: Fewer out-of-wedlock Births," *Business Week*, 8 January 1996, 26. See also "Single Motherhood; Stereotypes vs. Statistics," *The New York Times*, 11 February 1996, sec. 4, national edition.

19. Bennett, *Index of Leading Cultural Indicators*, 8.

20. "Teen Pregnancy: Epidemic Should Get Attention in 1996," *The Star-Tribune*, 27 December 1995, sec. A.

21. Bennett, *Index of Leading Cultural Indicators.*, 6.

22. Quoted in "Teen Pregnancy."

23. *Ibid.*

24. Philip Longman, *Born to Pay: The New Politics of Aging in America* (Boston: Houghton Mifflin Company, 1987).

Chapter 9: Deficits and Budget Battles

1. *Statistical Abstract of the United States, 1994*, 330.

2. *Ibid.* For a useful overview of various milestones in the path which has resulted in our $5 trillion debt, see "U.S. Budget Milestones," *The Concord Courier* 3 (Fall 1995): 6-7.

3. Concord Coalition, *The Zero Deficit Plan: A Plan for Eliminating the Federal Budget Deficit by the Year 2002* (May 1995), 5.

4. *Ibid.*, 6.

5. *Ibid.*, 9.

6. James Morton Smith, ed., *The Republic of Letters: The Correspondence between Thomas Jefferson and James Madison 1776-1826*, vol. 1 (New York: W.W. Norton & Company, 1995): 632-34.

7. *Ibid*, 651.

8. Peter G. Peterson, *Facing Up: How to Rescue the Economy from Crushing Debt & Restore the American Dream* (New York: Simon & Schuster, 1993), 44.

9. "The De-Entitling of America," *Business Week*, 20 November 1995, 182.

10. See, e.g., Robert Kerrey, "Should Congress Pass Legislation to Partially Privatize the Social Security System? Pro," *Congressional*

Digest 74 (October 1995): 238. In 1994, Senator Kerrey chaired the Bipartisan Commission on Entitlements and Tax Reform, a commission unable to reach consensus with respect to entitlement reform.

11. *1995 Annual Report of the Board of Trustees of the Federal Old-Age and Survivors Insurance and Disability Insurance Trust Funds* (April 3, 1995), 76.

12. See, e.g., "Facing Facts: The Truth about Entitlements and the Budget," *Fax Alert from The Concord Coalition* (19 December 1995).

13. The federal budget deficit for the fiscal year which ended September 30, 1995, was officially reported to be $163.8 billion. If adjusted to exclude the trust fund surpluses, the deficit would be nearly $100 billion higher.

14. Peterson, *Facing Up*, 104.

15. *Ibid.*, 105.

16. "Hypocrisy Was Left Untouched," *Business Week*, 6 November 1995, 184.

17. Peterson, *Facing Up*, 97.

18. Concord Coalition, *The Zero Deficit Plan* (1995), 19-44.

Chapter 10: Medicare and Health Reform

1. *The 1995 Annual Report of the Board of Trustees of the Federal Hospital Insurance Trust Fund*, 3.

2. Robert Pear, "Shortfall Posted by Medicare Fund Two Years Early," *The New York Times*, 5 February 1996, national ed.

3. This proposal is an expanded version of a blueprint for health-care reform outlined in a paper presented by the author at The Third International Conference on Health Law and Ethics held in Toronto July 19-23, 1992. See also Daniel E. Lee, "Vouchers Could Make Health Care Accessible to All Americans," *The Chicago Tribune*, 4 September 1991, sec. 1; Daniel E. Lee, "A Better Proposal: National Voucher System Could Make Health Care Accessible to All U.S. Citizens," *The Peoria Journal-Star*, 17 November 1991, sec. A; and Daniel E. Lee, "A Practical Health-Care Plan," *The Journal of Commerce*, 5 April 1995.

4. Congressional Budget Office, *The Economic and Budget Outlook* (August 1995), 83.

5. "An Overview of Health Care Delivery and Financing in

Germany, Japan, France, Canada, and Great Britain," *CNA Group Perspectives* (1991), 1-6.

6. See, e.g., Donald W. Light, "The Practice and Ethics of Risk-rated Health Insurance," *JAMA* 267 (1992): 2503-08.

Chapter 11: Social Security: Will the Promise Be Kept?

1. "Social Security Bill Is Signed: Gives Pensions to Aged, Jobless," *The New York Times*, 15 August 1935.

2. *Ibid.*

3. *NBC Nightly News*, 9 September 1994.

4. "Roosevelt's Statement: Text of His Declaration on Singing of New Social Security Bill," *The New York Times*, 12 August 1939.

5. "Social Security Bill Voted: Will Benefit 30,000,000," *The New York Times*, 10 August 1935.

6. "Social Security Tax Cut $905,000,000; Social Aid Widened," *The New York Times*, 6 August 1939.

7. Editorial, "The New Social Security," *The New York Times*, 14 August 1939.

8. Based on data included in "From New Deal to Raw Deal" by Michael J. Mandel, *Business Week*, 5 April 1993, 68-69.

9. *Ibid.*

10. *The Dispatch and The Rock Island Argus*, 19 October 1994. The author of the article to which the irate reader was responding was the author of this volume.

11. *Historical Statistics of the United States*, 1:349.

12. *1995 Annual Report of the Board of Trustees of the Federal Old-Age and Survivors Insurance and Disability Insurance Trust Funds*, 182.

13. *Historical Statistics of the United States*, 1:347, and *1995 OASDI Board of Trustees Report*, 159.

14. *Ibid.*, 20. The beneficiaries include those who receive disability insurance as well as those who receive retirement benefits.

15. *Ibid.*; *Statistical Abstract of the United States: 1993*, 588-89.

16. For an optimistic view of the potential for productivity gains financing programs for older Americans, see Christopher Farrell *et al.*, "The Economics of Aging: Why the Growing Number of Elderly Won't Bankrupt America," *Business Week*, 12 September 1994, 60-68.

17. *1995 OASDI Board of Trustees Report*, 12-13.

18. *Ibid.* See also *1992 Annual Report of the Board of Trustees of the Federal Old-Age and Survivors Insurance and Disability Insurance Trust Funds*, 13, the *1993 Annual Report of the Board of Trustees of the Federal Old-Age and Survivors Insurance and Disability Insurance Trust Funds*, 14, and the *1994 Annual Report of the Board of Trustees of the Federal Old-Age and Survivors Insurance and Disability Insurance Trust Funds*, 11-12.

19. *1995 OASDI Board of Trustees Report*, 26. *The 1992 OASDI Board of Trustees Report* stated that if the intermediate economic and demographic assumptions they made proved accurate, the combined OASI and DI trust funds would be exhausted in the year 2036--six years later than the 1995 report suggests.

20. *1994 OASDI Board of Trustees Report*, 8-9.

21. *Ibid.*, 24.

22. Peterson, *Facing Up*, 109-10.

23. *1995 OASDI Board of Trustees Report*, 171.

24. *Ibid.*

25. John Sabelhaus, "Deficits and Other Intergenerational Transfers: Restoring the Missing Link," *Challenge* 37 (January-February, 1994): 49. Sabelhaus, a senior research associate at the Urban Institute in Washington, D.C., suggests linking benefit levels to the earning power of younger generations. He argues that "the fraction of young people's earnings going to older people every year should be fixed at a reasonable and sustainable level." He would leave it to older people to decide how the money should be distributed. According to his calculations, the portion of young people's earnings going to older people via generational transfer programs such as Social Security has increased from 6 percent in 1960 to 14 percent in 1992. He suggests that "we need to agree on a percentage near the middle of that range and stick to it." Though he stops short of explicitly saying so, reducing the intergenerational transfer rate to 10 percent of the earnings of younger people would necessitate a reduction of nearly 30 percent in benefit levels for older people--a Draconian reduction by most measures.

26. *1995 OASDI Board of Trustees Report*, 184.

27. In 1987, The Robert Wood Johnson Foundation provided three-year grants to six programs to experiment with "service credit banking," a form of swapping of volunteer hours. For a summary of the programs, see Teresa A. Coughlin and Mark R. Meiners, "Service

Credit Banking: Issues in Program Development," *Journal of Aging & Social Policy* 2 (1990): 25-41. See also Marvin Katz, "Saving Time for a Rainy Day," *AARP Bulletin*, December 1992, 2.

28. "Bill Summary: The Kerrey-Simpson Proposal," *Congressional Digest* 74 (October 1995): 234-35.

29. Robert Kerrey, "Should Congress Pass Legislation to Partially Privatize the Social Security System? Pro," *Congressional Digest* 74 (October 1995): 240.

30. Robert J. Myers, "Should Congress Pass Legislation to Partially Privatize the Social Security System? Con," *Congressional Digest* 74 (October 1995): 253.

31. *Ibid.*, 253-255.

32. Concord Coalition, *The Zero Deficit Plan*, 34.

33. "Bill Summary: The Kerrey-Simpson Proposal," 235.

34. "Privatizing Social Security--Related Issues: Means Testing, Outside Earnings, Retirement Age, and Earnings Base," *Congresional Digest* 74 (October 1995): 233.

35. *1995 OASDI Board of Trustees Report*, 68. Actual past earnings are adjusted for inflation to bring them up to the approximate equivalent value at the time of retirement.

36. *Ibid.*, 45

37. Anne Willette, "Panel: Invest Social Security Taxes in Stocks," *USA Today*, 19 February 1996.

38. *1995 OASDI Board of Trustees Report*, 168. The intermediate projections for the year 2030 place income at 13.08 percent of taxable payroll and benefit costs at 17.26 percent of taxable payroll. Benefits would need to be reduced by 24.2 percent to bring them down to 13.08 percent of taxable payroll.

Chapter 12: From Conflict to Community

1. Robert J. Samuelson, "Great Expectations," *Newsweek*, 8 January 1996, 27. Samuelson's article is an excerpt from his book *The Good Life and Its Discontents: The American Dream in the Age of Entitlement 1945-1995* (New York: Times Books, 1995).

2. John F. Kennedy, "Inaugural Address," in Commager, ed., *Documents of American History*, 2:688-89.

3. Some of the themes in this section and in subsequent sections in this chapter are developed in greater detail in Lee, *Hope Is Where*

We Least Expect to Find It, 3-7, 37-38, 40-41 and 75-76.

4. *The Oxford English Dictionary*, 2nd ed. (Oxford: Clarendon Press, 1989), 3:42. In the 1881 Revised Version of the Bible and in subsequent versions based on this translation, *agápē* has been uniformly translated as "love." Thus, for example, the RSV translation of I Corinthians 13.13 makes reference to "faith, hope, love," rather than, as in some older translations, "faith, hope, charity."

5. *An Intermediate Greek-English Lexicon* (Oxford: At the Clarendon Press, 1961), 4, 248. I am indebted to my colleague, Thomas R. Banks, professor of classics at Augustana College, for elucidating the historical usage *agápē* among ancient Greeks.

6. Included in *The Lutheran Book of Worship* (Minneapolis: Augsburg Publishing House, 1978), 48.

7. William Wordsworth, "The Excursion," Book IX, in *The Complete Poetical Works of William Wordsworth* (Boston: Houghton Mifflin Company, 1904), 518.

8. For additional information, contact David Howard, Administrator, Clearview Nursing Home, 199 Home Road, Juneau, WI 53039.

9. For additional information about the Academy of Senior Professionals at Eckerd College (ASPEC), contact Joan Samuel-Burke, ASPEC, Eckerd College, 4200 54th Avenue South, St. Petersburg, FL 33711.

10. For additional information about Illinois READS, contact the Illinois Department on Aging, 421 East Capitol Avenue, #100, Springfield, Illinois 62701-1789.

11. For additional information about CASTLE, contact Generations Together and the University Center for Social and Urban Research, University of Pittsburgh, 121 University Place, Suite 2200, Pittsburgh, PA 15260-5907.

12. For additional information about Umoja-Unity Across Generations, see *ibid*.

13. For additional information about Project EASE (Exploring Aging through Shared Experiences,) contact the Cornell University Resource Center, 7 Cornell Business & Technology Park, Ithaca, NY 14850.

14. The bibliography was developed by Carol Silverman Gottlieb. For additional information, contact Grandfriends, Skokie School District 73.5, 8300 St. Louis, Skokie, IL 60076.

15. Sally Newman, "Designing, Implementing and Maintaining

Intergenerational Programs," a workshop sponsored by Illinois READS and the Illinois Department on Aging held at Triton College, River Grove, Illinois, September 13, 1995.

16. Quoted in brochure on Project EASE.

17. Robert J. Samuelson, "How Our American Dream Unraveled," *Newsweek*, 2 March 1992, 32.

Index